The Extended Case Method

The Extended Case Method

Four Countries, Four Decades,
Four Great Transformations,
and One Theoretical Tradition

Michael Burawoy

UNIVERSITY OF CALIFORNIA PRESS

Berkeley   *Los Angeles*   *London*

Chapters 2, 3, and 4 are slightly revised versions of articles that first appeared in *Sociological Theory* 16, no. 1 (1998), *The American Sociological Review* 68, no. 5 (2003), and *Theory and Society* 18 (1989).

University of California Press, one of the most distinguished university presses in the United States, enriches lives around the world by advancing scholarship in the humanities, social sciences, and natural sciences. Its activities are supported by the UC Press Foundation and by philanthropic contributions from individuals and institutions. For more information, visit www.ucpress.edu.

University of California Press
Berkeley and Los Angeles, California

University of California Press, Ltd.
London, England

Library of Congress Cataloging-in-Publication Data

Burawoy, Michael.
    The extended case method : four countries, four decades, four great transformations, and one theoretical tradition / Michael Burawoy.
        p.   cm.
    Includes bibliographical references and index.
    ISBN 978-0-520-25900-3 (cloth : alk. paper)
    ISBN 978-0-520-25901-0 (pbk. : alk. paper)
    1. Comparative economics.   2. Capitalism.   3. Marxism.
    4. Working class.   I. Title.
HB90.B87   2009
330.1—dc22   2008034393

Manufactured in the United States of America

18   17   16   15   14   13   12   11   10   09
10   9   8   7   6   5   4   3   2   1

This book is printed on Cascades Enviro 100, a 100% post consumer waste, recycled, de-inked fiber. FSC recycled certified and processed chlorine free. It is acid free, Ecologo certified, and manufactured by BioGas energy.

For the students with whom, from whom, and against whom I learned the secrets of participant observation

CONTENTS

TABLES

Bringing Theory to the Field

This book arose from the badgering of Loïc Wacquant, who insisted that it was time to collect these essays, new and old, and throw down the gauntlet to the Chicago School. While I'm grateful for all his encouragement, forcing me to rethink once again what I have been doing for forty years, I could not follow his proposal to inaugurate a Berkeley school of ethnography. I doubt there could ever be a such a school, since Berkeley's distinction lies in the diversity of its approaches to everything, and to ethnography in particular. Our ethnographies run the gamut from Marxism to feminism and postcolonialism, from positivism to reflexive sociology, from symbolic interaction to comparative history. As ethnographers all we have in common is a commitment to studying others in their space and time. From the beginning the ethos of Berkeley sociology has always been antischool.

To deny the existence of a Berkeley school is not to say that my vision of ethnography appeared as an immaculate conception or was cultivated in heroic ethnographic isolation. To the contrary, the essays that follow have been forged in Berkeley since the mid-1980s: in debates with my colleagues, in courses on participant observation and methodology, in dissertation seminars that have generated a stream of ethnographically based books. Before Berkeley I learned my trade from Jaap van Velsen in the Zambian tributary of the Manchester School of social anthropology, and beyond Berkeley I absorbed much from my collaborations with János Lukács in Hungary, and Pavel Krotov and Tatyana Lytkina in Russia. Inevitably, my most supportive critic has been Erik Wright, an outsider to the cult of ethnography, always quick to point out nonsense in my writing—although sometimes nonsense has virtues that he won't acknowledge.

There is a second reason why my writings cannot be tied to a Berkeley school. Not only is there a rich diversity of traditions within Berkeley but the approach adopted here—the extended case method—is found in other departments around the world, and in other disciplines, most notably anthropology and geography. Within sociology, insisting on an ethnography that forges micro-macro connections through the reconstruction of social theory is not as heretical as it once was. Yet it does continue to face resistance from a naive empiricism that regards ethnography as special because it gets at the world as it "really is," that assumes social theory grows tabula rasa out of that reality, and therefore only by ridding ourselves of biases and prejudices can we coax the field into disclosing its truth. This naive empiricism is often combined with an equally naive positivism: to grasp reality we can and must stand outside the world we study. This presumes a social world divided into two spheres: one sphere occupied by the producers of objective knowledge, separated from a second sphere inhabited by the subjects of knowledge.

In this view ethnographers must not disturb the worlds they study, but instead they must aspire to be the proverbial fly on the wall.

The approach of this book is very different. It is based on the following six postulates.

· We cannot see social reality without theory, just as we cannot see the physical world without our eyes. Everyone carries and uses social theory, cognitive maps of the world we inhabit, although not everyone is a social theorist, that is, someone who specializes in the production of such maps. Thus social theory ranges all the way from practical to tacit knowledge (knowledge we take for granted in conducting our lives) to abstract formalisms that look more like mathematical theorems than maps of the world.

· No impenetrable wall separates the worlds we study from our laboratories of science. To the contrary, we are inherently part of the world we study. What differentiates social scientists from the people they study is the theory they carry that allows them to see the world differently and, I would say, more deeply. I call the theory that we self-consciously develop analytical theory or social science, whereas the people we study possess an unreflective, usually tacit, theory that I call folk theory or common sense. Social scientists are not suspended in an ether of analytical theory; they too have their own folk theory. When it comes to their own lives, even their lives as sociologists, they all too easily suspend the insights they apply to others. Sad to say, we can be as unreflective and myopic about our everyday worlds as anyone else.

· Analytical theory or science reveals the broader context of our actions, but it also shows how the context creates the illusion of its own absence, of an everyday world that is autonomous and self-contained. We may blame ourselves for unemployment, whereas its sources are markets and governments—external forces that not only produce unemployment but also mystify that production. In revealing the connections between micro and macro we are developing what C. Wright Mills called the sociological imagination. That is our vocation.

· The university is not a neutral terrain but a field of competing theoretical perspectives and methodological approaches, research programs, if you will, that offer different insights into the way micro and macro are connected. These divergent approaches form nodal points in a hierarchical field of power, refracting the impact of forces beyond its boundaries.

· Analytical theory enables us to see and thus comprehend the world, but that does not imply automatic confirmation. To the contrary, the world has an obduracy of its own, continually challenging the causal claims and predictions we make as social scientists on the basis of our theories. That is how we develop science, not by being right but by being wrong and obsessing about it.

· Analytical theory is not necessarily incomprehensible to lay people. Social science and common sense are not insulated and incommensurable. In other words, it is possible, but not always easy, to forge a passage from common sense to social science, and it is possible that one can elaborate a good sense within the common sense. Indeed, that is the task of the public ethnographer.

These postulates have their roots in four decades of participant observation, in the factories and mines of four countries

(Zambia, the United States, Hungary, and Russia), resulting in studies of the microprocesses of four great transformations (decolonization, the transition to organized capitalism, the Soviet transition to socialism, and the transition from socialism to capitalism). You may well ask how a single ethnographer, working in a single factory, can illuminate a great transformation. Although definitive of the sociological imagination, the task may seem absurd to many a conventional ethnographer.

The answer lies with the extended case method, defined by its four extensions: the extension of observer into the lives of participants under study, the extension of observations over time and space; the extension from microprocesses to macroforces; and, finally and most important, the extension of theory. Each extension involves a dialogue: between participant and observer, between successive events in the field, between micro and macro, and between successive reconstructions of theory. These dialogues orbit around each other, each in the gravitational field of the others. To make sense of these dialogues the different studies described in this book make different simplifying assumptions.

In the first chapter I describe the genesis of the extended case method. In effect I apply the extended case method to my own participation in the academy and in the field—participations that are in dialogue with each other. In the second chapter I develop a more formal framework for the extended case method by reference to my study of race and class in postcolonial Zambia (1968–72). I end by developing two models of science: positive and reflexive, each autonomous but necessary for the other. The third chapter develops the idea of a reflexive science through the idea of the revisit. If my Zambia study was based on an extension back into history, an archeological dig, here I dwell on revisits to earlier ethnographies of the same place. The chapter sets out from a comparison of my own ethnography of a Chicago factory with one of the same factory conducted thirty years earlier. From there I examine other types of focused revisits but end by elevating the "revisit" as a trope for all ethnography.

The fourth chapter extends the ethnographic approach to comparative history, and it also extends the number of cases from two to three. It contrasts the analyses of revolutions found in the writings of Trotsky and Skocpol. It underlines the difference between the reflexive science of a participant observer and the positivist science of the comparative sociologist. In participating in the revolution that he studies, and in reconstructing the Marxist theory of socialist transition, Trotsky offers one prototype of the extended case method. The fifth chapter extends beyond three cases. It turns to the transition "back" from socialism to capitalism. It analyzes a series of successive factory, and then community, ethnographies that I carried out in Hungary and Russia between 1982 and 2002. It shows how each study built on preceding ones, wrestling first with a comparison of Hungary's state socialism and the organized capitalism of the United States and then with the Soviet transition from state socialism to market capitalism.

If the opening chapter is a self-analysis of my own trajectory, the concluding chapter focuses on my intellectual engagement with the four great transformations of the twentieth century. Here I try to assess the strengths and weaknesses of the extended case method, steering a course between romanticization of my subjects and reification of the external world. I ask what light my ethnographies have shed on these great transformations, what the latter have in common, how they are connected to each other, and what the implications are for the twenty-first century.

I have been accused of creating disasters wherever I go. After I left Zambia, the price of copper plummeted and Zambian society with it. After I left Allied Corporation, it went bankrupt along with the rest of south Chicago's industry. The area became an industrial wasteland. After I left Hungary, the Lenin Steel Works, and Hungarian industry more generally, disintegrated in the face of market forces, quickly catching up with south Chicago. I was in Russia for only seven months before the edifice of the Soviet Union crashed down on the heads of its workers. I plead innocent. I was not to blame. Correlation is not causality. All these sites became victim of what I call third-wave marketization, which began in the middle 1970s, a tsunami that continues to devastate our planet. Ethnography offers an especially potent insight into the catastrophic collapse of so many communities, while extending the extended case method to global ethnography helps us discern common patterns around the world and the forces that create them.

I may not have been the cause of disaster capitalism, but that is not to say my ethnography was not without its effects. Indeed, one might think that ethnography's direct engagement with participants lends itself to public engagement. But this is far from necessarily being the case. While Trotsky's analysis definitely fits the category of public ethnography and so did my study of Zambianization, this was not true of the Chicago factory study or the studies in Hungary and Russia, which were more clearly aimed at an academic audience. Even these intently professional studies, however, by linking microprocesses to macroforces, provide the foundation for a public sociology that turns private problems into public issues. Ethnography may not necessarily be public sociology, but by engaging with suffering and domination, hierarchy and inequality, ethnography calls attention to our accountability to a world beyond and thereby inevitably raises the specter of public sociology. This is the topic of my epilogue.

Inevitably, the ethnographer's debts are enormous since our work is inherently collaborative. To recognize the anonymous actors of our field in a ritualistic sentence or two is an inadequate acknowledgment of our responsibilities to publics, both the ones upon whom we depend in the process of research and the ones to which we are more distantly connected. As for my academic colleagues, I have acknowledged their contributions to the individual essays at the end of each chapter. I am grateful to Harvey Molotch, Mitch Duneier, and Diane Wolf for their support for this project as a whole and to Art Stinchcombe and Diane Vaughan for their comments on the chapters that are new to this book. Most important, Naomi Schneider has been a font of support for ethnography, mine and others, since she arrived at the University of California Press twenty-five years ago. She has been a potent force behind the continuing ascendancy of the extended case method.

Introduction

From Manchester to Berkeley
by Way of Chicago

On a hot and muggy September day in 1972, I was dragging my suitcases across the South Side of the Windy City in search of the University of Chicago. I'd just finished my master's in social anthropology at the University of Zambia and decided to take my chances in the United States. I had somehow sneaked in under the Chicago admissions wire, ready to pour my life savings into the first year of graduate school. Chicago had offered me no fellowship, no job. In fact, the sociology department clearly didn't want me. I was seeking out the Committee for the Comparative Study of New Nations, which had pioneered the much-calumniated development theory circulating in Africa, ideas associated with such figures at Clifford Geertz, Aristide Zolberg, Edward Shils, Lloyd Fallers, Lloyd Rudolph, and Susanne Rudolph. The Committee on New Nations had disbanded before I arrived.

After Zambia, Chicago sociology looked decidedly provincial. I had arrived in the Zambian capital, Lusaka, in 1968, four years into independence. At that time Zambia had all the vitality and optimism of a new nation. By 1970, when I enrolled for a master's degree, the University of Zambia was already populated with its first cohorts of undergraduates, an incipient elite from different backgrounds, instinctively oppositional and idealistic. They would annually take to the streets in protest against various governments, including their own, for betraying social justice, especially in dealings with apartheid South Africa. Among the faculty many in the social sciences were old hands from Africa and other developing countries, deeply engaged with the challenges facing Zambia, often working together in stimulating interdisciplinary seminars. Indeed, Africa as a whole was awash with exciting debates about socialism and transformation. These were inspiring times for social science.

TORMENTED IN ZAMBIA, REBELLING IN CHICAGO

In Zambia I had three extraordinary teachers who introduced me to the world of sociology. The first, with whom I developed the closest and longest relationship, was Jaap van Velsen—a vigorous and domineering Dutch anthropologist nurtured in the Manchester School under Max Gluckman. Jaap was a lawyer by training before he became a no-nonsense materialist social anthropologist. His *Politics of Kinship* (1964) was a study of the manipulation of kinship norms among the Lakeside Tonga of Malawi. Anticipating Pierre Bourdieu's now-celebrated theory of practice, Jaap would apply his "poststructuralism" to any institution, from the family to the law court to the United Nations (see Van Velsen 1960, 1964, 1967). He was especially interested in systems of labor migration in southern Africa. His methods and ideas, often delivered in passionate and booming off-the-cuff lectures, are deeply etched in my sociological habitus.

My second teacher was Jack Simons, an activist-intellectual within the South African Communist Party. He had been expelled from South Africa but was still very engaged with the African National Congress in exile. He would later, already in his sixties, leave for the military camps to teach Marxism to freedom fighters. With his wife, Ray Simons, the legendary South African union leader, he had just completed the now-classic history of South Africa, *Class and Colour in South Africa* (1969). Revered by the students he left behind in Cape Town, he was a fearsome presence in any context. Finally, there was Raja Jayaraman, just arrived from India, having recently completed his dissertation on caste and class on Sri Lankan tea plantations, a dissertation completed under M. N. Srinivas, the guiding father of Indian social anthropology. Raja was also of Marxist inspiration. He was definitely the gentlest of the three, but he too could develop a combative streak in the presence of his senior colleagues. They were an intimidating troika. Each week they struck gloom and terror into my soul as they openly competed to shred my essays to pieces. After this battering I was ready for any punitive pedagogy Chicago would hand out.

If Chicago faculty also prided themselves on bullying students, they could not match the intellectual virtues of my Zambian teachers. I was not prepared for the boring conventionality of Chicago sociology and the quiescent conservatism of its politics, with such notable exceptions as Richard Taub. To be sure, Chicago had had its excitement, its student revolt centered in sociology. But this had been snuffed out by 1972 when I arrived, leaving the sociology department a bastion of professionalism. With interest in other countries in remission, I turned my attention from the sociology of development to the much-vaunted Chicago School of urban ethnography. But here too I was disarmed by insularity. Its practitioners were still treating their field sites as Malinowski had treated the Trobriand Islanders, cut off from the world and from history. It seemed as if the very point of ethnography was an obsessive presentism, an abstraction from history, a repression of the past.

It was a confinement in time but also in space. I was dismayed to discover how ethnographers imprisoned neighborhoods in their physical environment—tracks, building, schools, parks, and so on. How different, indeed, from their own founders, from, for example, Thomas and Znaniecki, whose *The Polish Peasant in Europe and America* (1918–20) was an early classic of the Chicago School that traversed continents and centuries in its interpretation of letters exchanged between communities in Chicago and Poland. Even Louis Wirth's *The Ghetto* (1928) had taken history seriously. What had become of that original global and historical imagination? Indeed, what had become of ethnography, reduced to a minor moment in Chicago sociology, now inundated with network analysis and rational choice theory?

So I became a missionary for the "extended case method"—the Manchester School of ethnography, which was developed in the towns and villages of central and southern Africa and situated field sites in the wider society and its history. Social anthropologists trained in Manchester were dispatched to the colonies to do their fieldwork. I was taking the method in the other direction, from Africa to Chicago.[1] My friends laughed at me when I passionately explained how, in his original essay, Max Gluckman had sketched the social structure of South Africa by describing the opening of a bridge in Zululand (Gluckman [1940 and 1942] 1958). Equal skepticism greeted my own "extended case study"—a three-and-a-half-year study (1968–72) of the processes of racial succession in the Zambian copper industry in which I traced those processes back into colonial history and out into the postcolonial class structure (see chapter 1). I was beyond comprehension and certainly beyond the pale. There was, however, one exception. Bill Wilson had just joined the faculty and generously devoted time to this wayward, iconoclastic student. Indeed, he became quite interested in my argument about the class basis of racial orders, an argument I was then applying to South Africa.

The Marxism that had become second nature to me in Zambia was refined by the brilliant teaching of Adam Przeworski, also just arrived in Chicago but in the Political Science Department. For my dissertation I settled on the question of work organization and class consciousness, deciding to explore this through participant observation in a local factory— a Marxist resurrection of the old Chicago School studies of industrial work, long since forgotten by sociology. Little did I anticipate that this would be more than a resurrection but a serendipitous revisit to the same plant that the great Chicago ethnographer Donald Roy had studied thirty years earlier (1952a, 1952b, 1953, 1954). What was originally intended to be a devastating critique of plant sociology—bounded by the factory walls and confined to the present—turned into a historical analysis that used Roy's study as a baseline. My historical analysis sought to reconstruct Marxism by showing how the factory too was a site of politics where consent to capitalism was organized. The comparison with Roy's study allowed me to argue that this "hegemonic regime" of production politics was a feature of advanced capitalism, very different from the more despotic production politics of early competitive capitalism (see chapter 2).

PARIAH IN BERKELEY, ESCAPE TO MADISON

I survived Chicago under the protective umbrellas held out by Bill Wilson and Adam Przeworski and the comradeship of other graduate students. Through a series of rather fortuitous events and unintended consequences I landed the dream job at Berkeley (Burawoy 2005). I arrived there in 1976, fresh out of graduate school. As far as Berkeley's graduate students—many of whom had actively promoted my candidacy and were largely responsible for my getting the job—were concerned, my appeal lay with my Marxist credentials. Among the major sociology departments of the time, Berkeley's had been known for its radicalism, yet none of the faculty was teaching the newfangled Marxism. Indeed, when I arrived, students were organizing their own courses and running seminars on such topics as Marxism, feminism, and the political economy of South Africa. To arrive in this fissiparous department and to face lofty student expectations proved rather daunting.

Among other things, students could not comprehend my obsession with ethnography. Surely, they remonstrated, a Marxist cannot also be an ethnographer? Marxism deals with large-scale historical transformation, while ethnography confines itself to microprocesses, and never the two shall meet. Of course, that was a statement about Berkeley ethnography at the time, itself deeply influenced by the Chicago tradition imported in the 1950s with Herbert Blumer, Tamotsu Shibutani, and Erving Goffman. While Dorothy Smith and Arlene Kaplan Daniels had subsequently given it a feminist twist, and my new colleagues David Matza, Troy Duster, and Arlie Hochschild undoubtedly gave it a critical edge, its lineage was unmistakably Chicagoan.

From some quarters it was skepticism, but from other quarters it was outright hostility that greeted me. When it came to tenure colleagues appointed to evaluate my fitness to join their inner circle had problems that ran the gamut from bad teaching and ideological bias to weak scholarship. It appeared to me and, fortunately, many others, to be a poorly formulated and thinly veiled attack on Marxism, which had proved too popular with graduate students. Sure enough, the substantive focus of their critique lay with the flaws in my methodology. The claims I made in *Manufacturing Consent* (1979) about the nature of advanced capitalism, they averred, were speculative and unscientific, driven by a theoretical tradition that belonged to the previous century.

When it was all too clear that I would never survive at Berkeley, I gratefully accepted a position at Madison, Wisconsin, where faculty, especially the demographers, were far more open to novel ways of studying the empirical world. They didn't care about my Marxism so long as I was empirical, and that I surely was. At that time, with the exception of a language analyst, I was the only ethnographer in the department.

But here's the twist. If Berkeley graduate students thought that a Marxist ethnographer was an (oxy)moron, at Madison they took the opposite view. Students had never seen an ethnographer before; they knew me only as a Marxist. Since I did something called ethnography, that must be *the* Marxist method. My arrival was greeted with relief, especially by those "class analysis" students who were resistant to Erik Wright's analytical and quantitative approaches. For them the joining of Marxism and ethnography appeared to be a perfect and seamless marriage. This volume aims to demonstrate that Marxism and ethnography can indeed be partners, but they are by no means necessarily or unproblematically so. Too often Marxism is trapped in the clouds, just as ethnography can be glued to the ground.

That graduate students at these two departments had such opposing views of ethnography thirty years ago only underlines how participant observation had become ghettoized within the discipline. It had not always been that way. The separation can be traced to the postwar battle for the soul of sociology: Harvard's grandiose structural functionalism challenged the supremacy of the Chicago School, which reacted with antitheoretical microempiricism, brilliantly mislabeled as grounded theory. Yes, one might say that theory had been grounded, in the sense of stalled, stranded, cramped, and limited, having ditched the major theoretical traditions of our discipline. Today, we may say, with the exception of a few diminishing holdouts, ethnography has been reintegrated into diverse bodies of social theory to the benefit of both ethnography and theory.

Reflexive ethnography merely cements and spells out this assimilation by transcending conventional oppositions: participant and observer, micro and macro, history and sociology, theoretical tradition and empirical research. We transcend these oppositions not by dissolving their difference but by bringing them into dialogue. First, we do not strive to separate observer from participant, subject from object, but recognize their antagonistic coexistence. No matter how we approach our research, we are always simultaneously participant and observer, because inescapably we live in the world we study. The technique of participant observation simply makes us acutely aware of this existential and ethical conundrum. But without theory to ground us we would lose our way.

Second, there can be no microprocesses without macroforces, nor macroforces without microprocesses. The question is how we deal with their relationship. It requires that we recognize how theoretically embedded we are when we enter the field. Rather than seek to repress this as bias, we turn it into a resource for constructing the linkage of micro and macro. Third, history and sociology do not occupy watertight compartments; we are living history as we do research. Conceived of as a succession of revisits, participant observation is itself inherently historical—how we see ourselves today is inherently shaped by how we were yesterday. Once again theory helps us tie together past and present. Finally, theory lies like a stagnant pool if it is divorced from its lifeblood, empirical research, which, paradoxically, also threatens its very existence. The vitality of a theoretical tradition depends upon continually being put to the test and then meeting it with ingenious strategies of survival.

Where positivist science denies and represses these antinomies, reflexive social science centers them, making them the object of reflection, not in the abstract but by situating them in the context of their production. We are a participant and observer in the way we study others but also in the way we understand our own practice as social scientists. This is not a hindrance but an indispensable support for social research. The extended case method tries to follow these principles of reflexive science.

IN THE FIELD WITH THE EXTENDED
CASE METHOD

I was correct: my prospects for staying in Berkeley were poor. The department was locked in an internecine struggle over my tenure, but beyond the department, away from its microworld, Berkeley faculty were more open to the way I did research. Indeed, the further from the department, the more positive the evaluation, and as my case climbed through the university hierarchy, so the reception became warmer, until, in a final grand reversal, the all-powerful budget committee granted me tenure. Surely this was a case of macro damning the micro, although the outcome was never predetermined, as it was the product of academic warfare.

I returned to Berkeley from Madison in 1983 to take up unfinished tasks, to resume my defense of the extended case method, in effect connecting two opposed traditions within the department— the detailed analysis of microprocesses and the sweeping accounts of macrostructures. Analyses of local production of science, delinquency and deviance, emotional labor, and schooling stood opposed to studies of legal systems, the organization of communism, the history of managerial ideology, social revolution, industrial revolution, the social bases of liberal democracy, the changing character of the welfare state, and so forth. Although I didn't see myself as a bridge—indeed, I was irredeemably identified with one faction of the department—at first subconsciously and then ever more consciously I took it upon myself to sew together these two visions of sociology: on the one hand by elaborating a method that would move from heaven to earth through studying the microfoundations of macroprocesses and, on the other, by elaborating a method that would move from earth to heaven through studying the macrofoundations of microprocesses.

I had to excavate and bring to the surface the tacit skills I had learned in Zambia under the guidance of my teacher Jaap Van Velsen. What was it that I did when I practiced the so-called extended case method? I needed to understand its theory of practice, its methodological assumptions, and even its philosophical foundations. I became more reflective in the way I conducted research. *Manufacturing Consent* made claims about the way industrial work was organized in capitalism and the class consciousness of its workers. To make the argument more convincing it was incumbent on me to show how things were different in noncapitalist societies. But what noncapitalist societies could I study?

On August 14, 1980, the Polish working class erupted in a way no working class had ever done before. Moreover, it was collective action organized against state socialism and perhaps, so I thought, on behalf of a democratic socialism. My attention was riveted by what came to be known as Solidarity's self-limiting revolution, and I resolved to make my way into the Polish proletariat. As so often happens with academics, my bags were not even packed when events passed me by. On December 13, 1981, sixteen months after it had begun, the movement was suppressed by a military coup. The gates to Poland slammed shut before this ethnographer could reach them.

I did the next best thing. by accepting the invitation of Iván Szelényi to visit Hungary. Why had Hungary escaped such a working-class revolt? After all, in 1956 it was the Hungarian and not the Polish working class that staged the most dramatic confrontation and self-organization against the party-state. One might have expected the Solidarity movement to have taken shape in Hungary, not Poland. So from 1983 to 1989 I migrated from factory to factory in search of an answer, trying to understand the specifically socialist character of Hungarian work organization, work regulation, and working-class consciousness. My sorties into the hidden abode of socialist production pursued a two-layered comparison: why Poland and not Hungary had been the scene of working-class mobilization in 1980 and why a working-class revolt had occurred in state socialism rather than advanced capitalism (here the comparison was between Hungary and the United States). How could the divergent class experiences in the United States and in Hungary be attributed to the very different political economies in which workers were embedded (see chapter 4)?

In this case my comparative studies allowed me to explore the macrofoundations of microprocesses. That is, I started with social processes on the shop floor and extended out to the macroforces shaping them. If south Chicago and now Hungary offered me the opportunity to study the macrofoundations of a microsociology, what about microfoundations of a macrosociology? Here I became a participant observer within the field of sociology, within the production of knowledge. Curious as to how the dedicated scholarship of Theda Skocpol had produced such a wooden theory of revolution, while Leon Trotsky's deep involvement in the Russian Revolution generated such a compelling account, I compared their methodologies. I contrasted Skocpol's clearly enunciated science at a distance with Trotsky's science of engagement (see chapter 3). In this way I tried to understand how Trotsky became such an astute critic of the Russian Revolution, how his reflective participant observation had enabled him to grasp the social processes that underlay its inevitability as well as its dénouement. Compared with Skocpol's positivist science, which presupposed that all revolutions happen (and turn out) in the same way, Trotsky's reflexive science differentiated the French, German, and Russian revolutions. Each had its distinctive dynamics and outcomes. But Trotsky's theory did not spring tabula rasa from the data but from wrestling with and refashioning Marxist theory. The pessimism of Skocpol and the optimism of Trotsky derived not so much from the obduracy or malleability of the world as from the way each engaged and interpreted it.

Here lies the secret of the extended case method—theory is not discovered but revised, not induced but improved, not deconstructed but reconstructed. The aim of theory is not to be boringly right but brilliantly wrong. In short, theory exists to be extended in the face of external anomalies and internal contradictions. We don't start with data, we start with theory. Without theory we are blind—we cannot see the world. Theory is the necessary lens that we bring to our relationship to the world and thereby to make sense of its infinite manifold. Everyone necessarily possesses theory—understanding how the world works, linking cause and effect—but some specialize in its production. The practice of social science is becoming aware that theory is its precondition.

Those who would have us strip ourselves of theory before we enter the field are deceiving themselves. In their supposed purity they become the unconscious victims of the bias they seek to avoid. Far better to become conscious of our theoretical baggage, turning it to our advantage rather than letting it drag us down into the marshlands of empiricism. And, of course, last but not least, theory makes it possible for us to extend from the micro to the macro, to identify the forces at work in confining and reproducing micro social processes.

BACK IN BERKELEY WITH THE EXTENDED CASE METHOD

While I became more conscious of the methodological principles guiding my research even as I did the research, I discovered those principles not from gazing at my navel—although there was quite a bit of that—but through interacting with others, particularly in teaching. Teaching is research through other means. Teaching is not about filling empty vessels with useful knowledge; it is a dialogue of self-realization, both teacher and taught. Teaching is a form of participant observation—a process of learning what it means to be a sociologist.

On returning to Berkeley I began teaching the required introductory methodology course for first-year graduate students but only after I had taken a reading course under the supervision of the then–graduate student Tom Long. Under his guidance I steeped myself in philosophy of science and then set about organizing the methodology course around a single question: Is sociology a science? In the first half of the semester we interrogated the different meanings of science, ranging from the crudest inductivism to Feyerabend's anarchism, culminating with the methodology of scientific research programs, and in the second half we examined hermeneutic alternatives to and critiques of sociology as science, many of which harbored misguided criticisms of science. We ended up with Habermas's ecumenical account of knowledge and human interests, combining positivist, interpretive, and critical approaches. In teaching this course I convinced myself of the centrality of theory to all social research.

The inspiration behind and motivation for these explorations in the philosophy of science and antiscience lay with the participant observation seminars I had continued to run, seminars that generated many profound and unanswered questions about our quest for knowledge. The seminar works as follows: Students arrive with their half-baked projects, and I tell them that in three days they have to give me a short proposal that describes why they want to study the particular site they have chosen, how they are going to study it, and, most important, what they expect to find. Their expectations are bound to be wrong, I tell them, and so immediately this sets up a puzzle—why did they think X and yet find Y, with what theory are they working that is so clearly wrong? I tell them that their proposal is the first draft of the final paper, and the semester will entail revising it many times to accommodate at least some of the surprises (anomalies) that the field will throw up. They begin with a theory—even if they are not aware of it—and they will never leave theory. Theory guides their research from day to day, suggesting hypotheses to be investigated and anomalies to be tackled.

In this version of ethnography we don't deliver our minds from preconceptions but clarify and problematize them; we don't accumulate data day after day only finally to code it and thereby infer theory at the end, as though no one else had thought of these matters before, but we continually engage theory with data, and theory with other theories. Theory is the condensation of accumulated knowledge that joins sociologists to one another; it is what makes us a community of scientists. We are theory bound.

A course like this runs itself. I may dominate the conversation for the first week or two, but then I'm slowly marginalized as students quickly learn how to engage each other's work. My ignorance of their sites becomes a pedagogical virtue. Students, hitherto shy and retiring, flower as they develop the confidence that comes with a monopoly of knowledge about their sites. Students may be responsible for their own project, but they participate in everyone else's project. I work with students one on one in my office and by e-mail, going through their notes and their analysis. Tell me, I ask them, why should I care about your site, your findings, how does this add to some body of sociological knowledge, some sociological theory of how the world works? What theory that you consider important is challenged by your observations, and how then can you improve it?

I taught this course for fifteen years—sometimes it degenerated, disintegrated, but other times it fused into a collective spirit that transcended its participants. On one such occasion I suggested we continue meeting for a second semester, and so we did. It was a particularly convivial group. They liked cooking (and I liked eating), so as we consumed sumptuous meals we planned the rewriting of the papers they had produced the previous semester. In some instances this involved further research. Slowly but surely, often painfully, the papers took shape until we had the manuscript that became *Ethnography Unbound* (Burawoy, Burton, et al. 1991). For me this was the place and time to formulate the principles of the extended case method that we had followed, to write out the knowledge accumulated in teaching and doing participant observation. As a book it did unexpectedly well in disseminating an alternative approach to participant observation.

The principles are quite simple. The first principle is the extension of the observer into the community being studied. The observer joins the participants in the rhythm of their life, in their space and their time. The observer may remain an observer (nonparticipant observation) or be an active member (participant observation). The observer may declare her intentions—overt participant observation—or remain incognito—covert participant observation. The second principle is the extension of observations over time and space. There is no way to predetermine how long the observer is in the field, but it has to be long enough to discern the social processes that give integrity to the site. Here we look for signifying events and dramas, rituals of reproduction as well struggles and contradictions. The third principle is the extension from the microprocesses to macroforces, looking at the way the latter shape and indeed are shaped by the former. We have to be careful not to reify those forces that are themselves the product of social processes—even if those social processes are invisible to the participant observer. The fourth principle is the extension of theory that is the ultimate goal and foundation of the extended case method. We start with theory that guides our interaction with others and permits us to identify relevant forces beyond our site. In the process its inadequacies become apparent in the anomalies and contradictions we seek to rectify. Whether theory is lay or academic, it turns the site into a case that gives meaning to the site beyond its own particularity.

A decade after I began *Ethnography Unbound,* I found myself grounded as department chair and supervising a bunch of brilliant but obstreperous students conducting ethnographies in different parts of the world. I invited them to use their dissertation research to write a book called *Global Ethnography* (Burawoy et al. 2000). Could the extended case method be extended beyond the locality, the region, and even the nation to the globe? They couldn't resist the challenge. During the first semester we read some of the great theories of globalization—the most exciting seminar I've been part of at Berkeley. But we concluded that none of the theories was adequate to the task of global ethnography. Most were floating in the sky, unable to grasp the diversity of studies we embraced: welfare workers in Hungary, shipyard workers in San Francisco, homeless recyclers in San Francisco, women's movements in northern Brazil, nurses from Kerala, software engineers in Ireland, breast cancer movements in the San Francisco Bay Area, union organizing in Pittsburgh, village wastelands in Hungary. While each study could be read on its own, and while we mapped out three approaches to globalization—supranational forces, transnational connections, and postnational consciousness—there really was no worthwhile global theory to reconstruct. So we were left, like the feminists before us, to build up something de novo from the ground.

While *Ethnography Unbound* and *Global Ethnography* were openly collective projects both in process and in product, they are but the tip of the collaborative iceberg that shaped my reflexive ethnography. For nearly thirty years I have held a dissertation seminar that met weekly or biweekly. It has been the forge for many dissertations and books. In these seminars, in the dark chamber of my abode, we learned together, sometimes quite tortuously, what we were up to. The essays that follow were first presented in these seminars, and therefore it is to their participants that I dedicate this book.

ONE

The Extended Case Method

Race and Class in Postcolonial Africa

Methodology can only bring us reflective understanding of the
means which have *demonstrated* their value in practice by raising
them to the level of explicit consciousness; it is no more the precondition of fruitful intellectual work than the knowledge of anatomy
is the precondition of "correct" walking.

> Max Weber, *The Methodology of the Social Sciences*

True, anatomical knowledge is not usually a precondition for
"correct" walking. But when the ground beneath our feet is always
shaking, we need a crutch. As social scientists we are thrown off
balance by our presence in the world we study, by absorption in the
society we observe, by dwelling alongside those we make "other."
Beyond our individual involvement is the broader ethnographic
predicament—producing theories, concepts, and facts that desta-
bilize the world we seek to comprehend. So we desperately need
methodology to keep us erect, while we navigate a terrain that
moves and shifts even as we attempt to traverse it.

Like other handicaps, the ethnographic condition can be dealt with in one of two ways: containing it or turning it to our advantage. In the first strategy we minimize our predicament by limiting our involvement in the world we study, insulating ourselves from our subjects, observing them from the outside, interrogating them through intermediaries. We keep our feet on the ground by adhering to a set of data-collecting procedures that assure our distance. This is the positive approach. It is best exemplified by survey research in which every effort is made to suspend our participation in the world we study. We try to avoid affecting the situation we study and attempt to standardize the collection of data, bracket external conditions, and make sure our sample is representative.

In the alternative strategy we thematize our participation in the world we study. We keep ourselves steady by rooting ourselves in theory, which guides our dialogue with participants. Michael Polanyi (1958) elaborates this idea in detail, rejecting a positivist objectivity based on "sense data" in favor of a commitment to the "rationality" of theory—cognitive maps through which we apprehend the world. This "dwelling in" theory is at the basis of what I call the reflexive model of science—a model of science that embraces not detachment but engagement as the road to knowledge. Premised upon our own participation in the world we study, reflexive science deploys multiple dialogues to reach explanations of empirical phenomena. Reflexive science starts out from dialogue, virtual or real, between observer and participants, then embeds such dialogue within a second dialogue between local processes and extralocal forces that in turn can be comprehended only through a third, expanding dialogue of theory with itself. Objectivity is not measured by procedures that assure an accurate mapping of the world but by the growth of knowledge, that is, the imaginative and parsimonious reconstruction of theory to accommodate anomalies (see Kuhn 1962; Popper 1963; and Lakatos 1978).

The extended case method applies reflexive science to ethnography in order to extract the general from the unique, to move from the "micro" to the "macro," to connect the present to the past in anticipation of the future, all by building on preexisting theory. In my own use of the extended case method I have drawn on my experiences as a research officer in the Zambian copper industry to elaborate Fanon's theory of postcolonialism. I tried to expose the roots of consent to American capitalism by applying Gramsci's theory of hegemony to my experiences as a machine operator in a South Chicago factory. I have explored the nature of work organization and class formation under socialism by combining Szelényi's theory of class structure and Kornai's theory of the shortage economy. This was based on laboring in Hungarian factories—champagne, auto manufacturing, and steel. Subsequently, I worked my way outward from a small furniture factory in northern Russia in order to develop theories of the transition from socialism to capitalism. Here I drew on Marxist notions of merchant and finance capital. How can I justify these extravagant leaps across space and time, from the singular to the general, from the mundane to the grand historical themes of the late twentieth century? That is the question that motivates this chapter.

Although it is more usual for ethnographic studies to confine themselves to claims within the dimensions of the everyday worlds they examine, I am not alone in "extending out" from the field. Indeed, this was one of the hallmarks of the Manchester School of social anthropology, which first coined the phrase "extended case method."[1] Instead of collecting data from informants about what "natives ought to do," Manchester anthropologists began to fill their diaries with accounts of what "natives" actually were doing, with accounts of real events, struggles, and dramas that took place over space and time. They brought out discrepancies between normative prescriptions and everyday practices—discrepancies they traced to internal contradictions but also to the intrusion of colonialism. Manchester anthropology began to restore African communities to their broader, world historical context.

Not just in Africa but in the United States too there is a rich but inchoate tradition of scholarship in the implicit style of the extended case method. Community ethnographies have not always stopped at the tracks but incorporated the wider contexts of racism and labor markets as well as urban political regimes.[2] Workplace ethnographies, traditionally confined to "plant sociology," have also taken into account such external factors as race and ethnicity, citizenship, markets, and local politics (see Lamphere et al. 1993; Thomas 1985; Smith 1990; and Blum 1991). Participant observation studies of social movements locate them in their political and economic context (see Fantasia 1988; Johnston 1994; and Ray 1998). Ethnographies of the school have always sought to explain how education is shaped by and at the same influences wider patterns of social inequality (see Willis 1977 and MacLeod 1987). Family ethnographies have found it impossible to ignore influences beyond the household, upholding Dorothy Smith's feminist injunction to locate lived experience within its extralocal determinations.[3]

The rudiments of the extended case method abound in these examples and elsewhere. What I propose, therefore, is to bring "reflective understanding" to the extended case method by raising it to the "level of explicit consciousness." But, contra Weber, this is not simply a clarificatory exercise. It has real repercussions for the way we conduct social science. Indeed, it leads to an alternative model of social science and thus to alternative explanatory and interpretive practices—something social scientists are reluctant to countenance. We prefer to debate appropriate techniques or even tolerate the rejection of science altogether rather than face the possibility of two coexisting models of science, which would wreak havoc with our methodological prescriptions. Still, I hope to demonstrate that reflexive science has its payoff, enabling the exploration of broad historical patterns and macrostructures without relinquishing either ethnography or science.

By ethnography I mean writing about the world from the standpoint of participant observation; by science I mean falsifiable and generalizable explanations of empirical phenomena. In developing my argument it will be necessary to distinguish (a) research method (here survey research and the extended case method), which is the deployment of (b) techniques of empirical investigation (here interviewing and participant observation) to best approximate (c) a scientific model (positive or reflexive) that lays out the presuppositions and principles for producing science. In elaborating the different dimensions of the extended case method, I seek to present it as a science, albeit a reflexive science, to improve its execution by recognizing its limitations and to draw out broader implications for the way we study the world.

In order to illustrate and explicate the extended case method, I return to a study conducted between 1968 and 1972 in the then-newly independent African country of Zambia. Of all my studies I have chosen this one because it most effectively illustrates both the virtues and the limits of the extended case method. First, the virtues: The extended case method is able to dig beneath the political binaries of colonizer and colonized, white and black, metropolis and periphery, capital and labor to discover multiple processes, interests, and identities. At the same time the postcolonial context provides fertile ground for recondensing these proliferating differences around local, national, and global links. Second, the limits: The extended case method comes up against the very forces it displays. As the renascent field of "colonial" studies makes clear, the colonies were not simply the site of exotica but of experiments in new tactics of power, subsequently reimported to the metropolis (see, for example, Stoler 1995 and Mitchell 1988). Domination took on especially raw and exaggerated forms, transparently implicating sociologists, and especially anthropologists, coloring their vision in unexplicated ways (Clifford and Marcus 1986; Asad 1973). Colonial and postcolonial regimes of power throw into relief limits inherent to the extended case method.

Accordingly, this chapter is constructed as follows: I begin with a narrative of my study of the Zambian copper industry, highlighting the social embeddedness of reflexive research (Burawoy 1972a, 1972b, 1974). I then show how my study violated each of the four principles of positive science. If there were only this model of science, I would have to abandon either the extended case method or science. However, the extended case method is not alone in violating positive principles. I show that survey research, the quintessentially positive method, transgresses its own principles because of inescapable context effects stemming from the indissoluble connection between interviewer and respondent, and from the embeddedness of the interview in a wider field of social relations. We can either live with the gap between positive principles and practice, all the while trying to close it, or formulate an alternative model of science that takes context as its point of departure, that thematizes our presence in the world we study. That alternative is the "reflexive" model of science that, when applied to the technique of participant observation, gives rise to the extended case method.

In saving both science and the extended case method, however, I do not eliminate the gap between them. Making context and dialogue the basis of an alternative science unavoidably brings into prominence power effects that divide the extended case method from the principles of reflexive science. Postmodernism has done much to highlight these power effects but, rather than make do with an inadequate science, it rejects science altogether. I find myself working on the borders of postmodernism, without ever overstepping the boundaries. If we choose to remain on the side of science, we have to live with its self-determined limitations, whether they be the context effects of positive science or the power effects of reflexive science. Given that the world is neither without context nor without power, both sciences are flawed. But we do have a choice. So I finally ask when, where, and why we deploy each of the two models of science and their corresponding methods.

THE ETHNOGRAPHIC CONDITION EMBRACED

Reflexive science sets out from a dialogue between us and them, between social scientists and the people we study. It does not spring from an Archimedean point outside space and time; it does not create knowledge or theory tabula rasa. It starts out from a stock of academic theory on the one side and existent folk theory or indigenous narratives on the other. Both sides begin their interaction from real locations.

My own study of the Zambian copper mines began from publicly debated dilemmas of the legacies of colonialism. I traveled to the Copperbelt in 1968 in search of the policies and strategies of transnational corporations toward the postcolonial regime. The two mining companies, Anglo American Corporation and Roan Selection Trust, had their roots in the colonial order of Northern Rhodesia, a British protectorate until 1964. How were these companies responding to Zambian independence, whose stated objective was to reappropriate control of the nation's economy? This was not a trivial question since the copper industry employed about fifty thousand people, 90 percent African and 10 percent expatriate. At the time of independence the mines provided 90 percent of foreign exchange and 50 to 70 percent of government revenue. As far as Whitehall (and later the Federation of Rhodesia and Nyasaland) had been concerned, Northern Rhodesia's reason for existence was its copper. Road and rail transportation, land and agriculture, taxation and trade, labor and education, nationality and race were all designed to maximize the export of copper. Zambia was the archetypal enclave economy, with copper mining its organizing principle.

It was easier to study how mineworkers were faring than to disclose the mysterious corporate practices of Anglo American Corporation and Roan Selection Trust. Mine was not a study that could be accomplished by combing through documents because, as I was to learn, they revealed so little. Interviews, conducted from the outside, were no more useful since managers were protected by layers of public relations officials. Instead I took advantage of my recently won mathematics degree and my contact at Anglo's headquarters to land myself a job in the Personnel Research Unit of the Copper Industry Service Bureau. Located in Kitwe, at the heart of the mining region, this unit was the center of industrial relations, both policy and practice.

Once there my attention turned to the more specific question of labor force localization, or what was called African advancement but since independence had come to be called Zambianization. Colonial rule left Zambia's four million people with barely one hundred university graduates and just more than twelve hundred Africans with secondary school certificates. So the country remained heavily dependent on white managers and experts. Historically, the mining industry had been organized according to the color bar principle, that is, no black person should exercise authority over any white person. A major aim of the anticolonial movement was to eradicate all such traces of white supremacy. How had things changed in the postcolonial period? I began with the figures put out by the new government's Zambianization Committee, which painted a rosy picture of achievement. Four years after independence fewer expatriates and more Zambians held "expatriate" (white) positions. What lay behind this portrait of deracialization?

If comprehension of managerial strategies was largely barred to outsiders, any serious study of Zambianization was totally off limits. Racial succession in what had been an apartheid order was simply too explosive a question to openly investigate. Yet it hung like a heavy cloud over all aspects of industrial relations. I could not have been better placed to observe the different forces at work. Not only was I sitting in the mining industry's data-gathering center but I became an active contributor to the industry's new job-evaluation scheme, which aimed to integrate black and white pay scales. As part of my job I learned the stakes in negotiations among management, unions, and government.

So much for the perspective from the top. How did Zambianization look from inside and from the bottom? Here I had to be more surreptitious. I organized a survey of the working and living conditions of African miners, unrelated to Zambianization. But as interviewers I chose young Zambian personnel officers who, I had reason to believe, were at the storm's eye of Zambianization. We would meet every week in the nominally desegregated Rokana Club to discuss the progress of the survey but also Zambianization. Still, this was not enough. I worked in the Personnel Research Unit for one and a half years and continued the research for another two years while I was a master's student at the University of Zambia. There I recruited undergraduates to join me in studying postcolonial work organization, underground and on surface. At least officially, that was our goal; we were also exploring Zambianization from below, from the standpoint of the vast majority of unskilled and semi-skilled workers. How did they feel about the Zambianization of supervisors and lower-level managers?

Our extended observations showed that white management used two types of organizational maneuvers to meet government Zambianization targets as well as management's own interest in maintaining the color bar. The first strategy was blanket Zambianization. In the days of colonialism the personnel manager was king, reigning over his African suppliants and to a lesser extent over whites, too. The personnel department was lord of the company town, of life in the mine and the "compound."[4] An obvious target, the department was entirely and rapidly Zambianized but at the same time shunted aside and stripped of its powers, especially over expatriate employees. They were placed under the guardianship of the newly created "staff development adviser"—one of the white former personnel managers.

The second strategy was shadow Zambianization. During the three and a half years of our research the position of mine captain, that is, the highest level of underground supervision, was Zambianized. A number of old white captains were promoted into the newly created post of assistant underground manager and took with them many of their old powers and responsibilities. Any Zambian successor had to operate in the shadow of his predecessor. He became a buffer between his subordinates and the "real" mine captain, now removed to a comfortable office on the surface.

These maneuvers to maintain the color bar had several organizationally dysfunctional consequences. First, the organization became increasingly top heavy as the layers of management thickened. Second, conflict increased between workers and their new Zambian supervisors, who were less effective, even if less abusive, than their predecessors. Maintaining the color bar through Zambianization was a recipe for organizational rupture, conflict, and inefficiency.

If blanket and shadow Zambianization undermined the organization, why did it continue? What were the forces behind the retention of the color bar? How could a nationalist black government ignore the continuity of the racial order, as it effectively did in its Zambianization report? I sought the answer in the broader constellation of interests. First, while the government embraced the rhetoric of Zambianization, African trade unions, representing the unskilled and semiskilled miners, were more interested in higher wages and better working conditions than in the upward mobility of supervisors. Second, Zambian successors, caught between black subordinates and white bosses, were a lightning rod for racial and class tensions. They were organizationally weaker than white management, which retained a virtual monopoly of knowledge and experience.

Third, corporate executives in the industry had long fought to raise the color bar and replace white with black since this reduced labor costs. If the executives faced organized resistance from white staff before, now they were threatened with exodus. Fourth, the Zambian government regarded the mining industry as a sacred cow, the source of revenue for its nation-building projects. It did not dare jeopardize profits from copper. Moreover, it was content to let expatriates run the industry because, although they had economic power, they did not pose a political threat. They were on limited three-year contracts that could be terminated at will. Zambian managers, as a powerful faction of the dominant class, could pose many more problems for a Zambian government. This balance of forces meant that, despite independence, the overall class and racial patterns in the mines did not change substantially.

From the microworlds of Zambianization I "extended out" to the class forces maintaining not only the old racial order but underdevelopment in general. That is to say, obstacles to development arose not only from dependence on copper in a world economy controlled by advanced capitalist nations but also from the reproduction of the class relations inherited from colonialism. An emergent African "national bourgeoisie" had class interests in a racial order that inhibited economic transformation. Thus my study had reconstructed and reconfigured indigenous narratives into a class analysis of postcolonialism, which, as I will show, fed back into society in unanticipated ways. First, I want to translate this research into the language and terms of the extended case method and the science it represents.

POSITIVE SCIENCE REVISITED

What is positive science? For August Comte sociology was to replace metaphysics and uncover empirical laws of society. It was the last discipline to enter the kingdom of science, but once admitted it would rule over the unruly, producing order and progress out of chaos. Thus positivism is at once science and ideology. Today sociology has, for the most part, dropped its pretensions to a ruling ideology, and we can call this stripped-down version of positivism simply positive science. The premise that distinguishes positive from reflexive science is that there is an "external" world that can be construed as separate from and incommensurable with those who study it. Alvin Gouldner (1970) once called this premise methodological dualism—social scientists are exempt from the theories they develop about others. Positive science calls for the distancing of observer from the object of study, a disposition of detachment. The purpose of positive science is to produce the most accurate mapping of the workings of this external world, to mirror the world (Rorty 1979).

Constituting the observer as outsider requires an effort of estrangement, facilitated by procedural objectivity. In his exemplary discussion of "analytic fieldwork," Jack Katz (1983) lays out the "4R's," what I refer to as the four prescriptive tenets of positive science. First, sociologists must avoid affecting and thus distorting the worlds they study. This is the injunction against reactivity.

Second, the external world is an infinite manifold, so we need criteria for selecting data. This is the principle of reliability. Third, the code of selection should be formulated unambiguously so that any other social scientist studying the same phenomena could produce the same results. This is the principle of replicability. Fourth, we must guarantee that the slice of the world we examine is typical of the whole. This is the principle of representativeness.

Katz accepts these principles as definitive of social science. He tries to show how participant observation can live up to the positivist ambition, namely, the 4R's, if it follows "analytic induction," or what he prefers to call analytic research. However, in the process he radically destabilizes his methodological principles, embracing rather than proscribing reactivity, dissolving the boundary between fact and fiction, and summoning readers to replicate findings from their own experiences. Still, unperturbed, he holds on to the 4R's. I take the opposite tack, forsaking positive science for reflexive science, which is more appropriate to the extended case method. I justify invoking and elaborating this alternative by first showing how the extended case method violates the 4R's and then how even survey research fails to live up to those same positive principles. My intention here is not to reject positive science but to show how positive science rejects the extended case method and in particular my study of Zambianization.

Positive Science Violated

The extended case method makes no pretense to positive science but, to the contrary, deliberately violates the 4R's. My Zambianization research broke the injunction against reactivity. I was anything but a nonintervening observer. I entered the Personnel Research Unit just as it was undertaking a mammoth job-evaluation exercise to categorize the complex industrywide occupational structure with a view to bringing white and black pay structures into a single hierarchy. It was critical that the job hierarchy already established within each racial group be maintained. In order to give the impression of fairness, integrating the two pay scales was based on a joint team of "experts" from union and management, which "evaluated" each job according to a pregiven set of characteristics, experience, education, dexterity, effort, and so forth. An English consulting company, brought in to attempt to match the evaluation of jobs with the preexisting hierarchy, failed abysmally. With my mathematical training I was able to turn the task into a simple problem of linear programming and thereby helped to reproduce the very racial order that became the focus of my research in *The Colour of Class on the Copper Mines* (1972a).

Reliability was also violated. Having a fixed coda or prism through which to observe and extract information makes one unresponsive to the flux of everyday life. Living in the time and space of those one studies makes it difficult to fit the world into a predefined template. One begins with one set of questions and ends with very different ones. Thus I entered the mining industry in search of some company policy guiding relations with the Zambian government. It was only by working for the company executives that I realized that there was no such policy. Nor was it rational, as I subsequently realized, to follow a predetermined strategy in situations of great uncertainty—political uncertainty (frequent government crises, changes in ministerial personnel, or surprise moves such as the nationalization of the mines); economic uncertainty (especially the volatile world price of copper); and technical uncertainty (unexpected problems of excavation, mine disasters). In such a turbulent environment managers need to be flexible, not hamstrung by detailed plans. As I discovered, those policies that did exist were constructed in posthoc fashion, by "experts" like myself, to justify decisions already made. Had I not been a participant in these processes, I would still be looking for that elusive company policy or, more likely, would have concocted a policy from company rationalizations. In short, with the extended case method dialogue between participant and observer provides an ever-changing sieve for collecting data. This is not to deny that we come to the field with presuppositions, questions, and frameworks but that they are more like prisms than templates and they are emergent rather than fixed.

By the same token, replicability was also problematic. The data I gathered was very much contingent on who I was—a white male recently graduated from a British university with a degree in mathematics, a newcomer to colonialism, and an idealist to boot. Every one of these characteristics shaped my entry and performance in social situations and how people spoke to me of racial issues. More than that, anyone who subsequently replicated my study of Zambianization would come up with very different observations. History is not a laboratory experiment that can be replicated again and again under the same conditions. There is something unique about the ethnographic encounter. It certainly would have been interesting for someone else to repeat the study, either simultaneously or subsequently, not as a replication but as an extension of my own study.[5]

And so, finally, we come to the inevitable question of representativeness that dominates the positivist critique of ethnography. How representative were my observations of the process of Zambianization within my two cases? How representative were my case studies of all the case studies at the one mine I studied, let alone of the six other mines or indeed of industries beyond? How could I draw any conclusions beyond my two unique cases? And if I could not generalize, why did I bother to devote three and a half years to the study?

These are valid criticisms from the standpoint of positive science, and if this were the only model of science, I would indeed have wasted my time. However, there is a second approach to science, a reflexive approach that also seeks generalizable and falsifiable explanations. This alternative does not appear magically but, true to its own principles, arises from a critical engagement with positive science. But first I must show that no method, not even the best survey research, can live up to positive principles, for the principles of reflexive science spring from this irrevocable gap between positive science and its practice.

Positive Science Delimited

Survey research is avowedly positive in its method. It tries to live up to the 4R's by delivering the 4S's. In order to overcome the problem of reactivity, the interview is constructed as a uniform, neutral stimulus that elicits varied responses. The respondent is supposed to react to the question and the question alone, stripped of the medium in which it is posed. To confront the problem of reliability and achieve a consistent set of criteria for the selection of data, the interview is standardized; identical questions are asked in identical ways of each respondent. For replicability not only has the question to be a stimulus, "isolated" from the interview, but the external conditions must be controlled, that is, stabilized or deemed irrelevant. Finally, for representativeness the respondents must be a carefully selected sample of the broader targeted population.

Despite their best efforts survey researchers have always and inevitably fallen short of their positive goals. The interview is a social context, embedded in other contexts, all of which lend meaning to and are independent of the question itself. There are four types of context effects. The well-documented interview effects create the problem of reactivity, in which interviewer characteristics (for example, race or gender) or the interview schedule itself (for example, order or form of questions) significantly affects responses (see Hyman et al. 1954; Converse and Schuman 1974; and Schuman and Presser 1981). There are also respondent effects in which the meaning of questions has an irreducible ambiguity, dependent on the different worlds from which the respondents come. Standardizing the questions cannot eliminate respondent effects (see Cicourel 1967, and Forsyth and Lessler 1991). Field effects simply recognize that interviews cannot be isolated from the political, social, and economics contexts within which they take place. Responses to interviews conducted at different points in time or in different places will be shaped by such extraneous conditions. Replication is thwarted by external factors we do not control. We cannot even disentangle their unmediated impact from their mediated impact on the respondent during the interview itself.[6] Finally, situation effects threaten the principle of representativeness. Insofar as meaning, attitudes, and even knowledge do not reside with individuals but are constituted in social situations, we should be sampling from a population of social situations and not a population of individuals.[7] But we have no idea how to determine the population of relevant social situations, let alone how to draw a sample.

There is nothing new here—serious survey researchers spend their lives trying to minimize and/or control for context effects, assuming them to be noise that can be investigated if not expurgated. If early research into survey research simply revealed interview effects, more recent work has begun to theorize those effects (Suchman and Jordan 1990; Schaeffer 1991; and Tanur 1992). The interview is viewed as a distorted conversation in which one of the interlocutors is absent (the researcher), in which the conversation follows a predetermined trajectory with prescribed responses, and in which dialogue is precluded.[8] Unable to establish common ground with the respondent, the interviewer cannot avoid misunderstandings and mistakes. One response, therefore, is to move toward a more "narrative" interview. Instead of foisting the standardized interview on respondents, the interviewer allows respondents to tell their own story, to offer their own narrative (Mishler 1986). The interviewer proceeds through dialogue, reducing distortion but incurring reactivity and violating reliability, replicability, and often representativeness.

In other words, no one denies the importance of context effects. Survey researchers look upon them as a challenge—they must be measured, reduced, and controlled. However, if one takes the view that context is not noise that disguises reality but reality itself, then improving survey research is tackling the wrong problem with the wrong tools. Thus many regard the ineluctability of context effects as a demonstration of the irremediable flaws of positive science, justifying abandoning science altogether in favor of an interpretive approach to the social world. We can find influential representatives of this "hermeneutic" school across the disciplines: philosophers such as Hans Gadamer (1975) and Richard Rorty (1979) reduce social science to dialogue and conversation; anthropologists such as Clifford Geertz (1973, 1983) regard the art of ethnography as thick description or the excavation of local knowledge; sociologists such as Zygmunt Bauman (1987) argue that intellectuals should abandon their legislative pretensions for an interpretive role, mediating between communities; feminists such as Donna Haraway call for networks of "situated knowledges" (1991, chap. 9).

This is not the approach I propose to follow here. Faced with the ineluctable gap between positive principles and research practice, I neither abandon science altogether nor resign myself to refining practice in order to approach unachievable positive principles. Instead I propose an alternative model of science, a reflexive science, that takes context as a point of departure but not a point of conclusion.

REFLEXIVE SCIENCE DEFINED

Reflexivity in the social sciences is frequently regarded as the enemy of science. Long ago Peter Winch (1958) argued that individual reflexivity, that is, the self-monitoring of behavior, leads to an irrevocable uncertainty in human action, making scientific prediction impossible. All social science can do is reveal the discursive and nondiscursive worlds of the people it studies. Similar views have become common in anthropology wherever the "linguistic" or "interpretive" turn has taken hold. In its extreme form we are so bound by our own preconceptions that we can do little more than gaze into our biographies. Within sociology reflexivity has been put to more positive use. Alvin Gouldner (1970) turned sociology onto itself to discover the "domain assumptions" of reigning paradigms in "Western" sociology, arguing that they were increasingly out of sync with the world they claimed to mirror. More recently, Pierre Bourdieu (1977; 1990; Bourdieu and Wacquant 1992) invites us to a reflexive sociology that explicitly seeks to deepen the scientific foundations of sociology. Recognizing our own place within the disciplinary field enables us to objectify our relation to those we study, which will make us better scientists.

I take a slightly different approach. Rather than arguing that there is one model of science that is best carried out with reflexive awareness, I propose a methodological duality, the coexistence and interdependence of two models of science—positive and reflexive.[9] Where positive science proposes to insulate subject from object, reflexive science elevates dialogue as its defining principle and intersubjectivity between participant and observer as its premise. It enjoins what positive science separates: participant and observer, knowledge and social situation, situation and its field of location, folk theory and academic theory. The principles of this reflexive science can be derived from the context effects that pose as impediments to positive science.

Intervention

The first context that I discussed was the interview itself, which is not simply a stimulus to reveal the true state of the interviewee but an intervention into her life. The interview extracts her from her own space and time and subjects her to the space and time of the interviewer. In the view of reflexive science intervention is not only an unavoidable part of social research but a virtue to be exploited. It is by mutual reaction that we discover the properties of the social order. Interventions create perturbations that are not noise to be expurgated but music to be appreciated, transmitting the hidden secrets of the participant's world. Institutions reveal much about themselves when under stress or in crisis, when they face the unexpected as well as the routine. Instead of the prohibition against reactivity, which can never be realized, reflexive science prescribes and takes advantage of intervention.

Process

The second context is the multiple meanings attached to the interviewer's "stimulus," which undermines the reliability of research. One can standardize the question but not the respondent's interpretation of the question. Respondents come to the interview with multiple experiences derived from different situations that they are then asked to collapse into a single data point. Even asking someone's race or gender can turn out to be complicated, requiring that the respondent reduce a diverse array of experiences to a single item on a check list. There is a double reduction: first aggregation and then the condensation of experience.

Reflexive science commands the observer to unpack those situational experiences by moving with the participants through their space and time. The move may be virtual, as in historical interpretation; real, as in participant observation; or some combination of the two, as in the clinical interview. But there is another complication. Not only does each situational experience produce its own "situational knowledge," but that knowledge may be discursive or nondiscursive. If the discursive dimension of social interaction, what we may call narrative, can be reached through interview, the nondiscursive, that is, the unexplicated, unacknowledged, or tacit knowledge, sometimes referred to as practical consciousness, which underlies all social interaction, calls for more. It may be discovered through "analysis," for example, or through participation, "doing" things with and to those who are being studied (Garfinkel 1967).

The task of reflexive science does not stop with situational comprehension, with the recovery of situational knowledge. First, there are always multiple knowledges, reflecting the position of different actors within a social situation. Reflexive science would be impossibly cumbersome if its goal were the display of multiple narratives, multiple voices. But worse still, situational knowledge is knowledge located in a specific space and time. Neither space nor time can be frozen, and so situational knowledges are in continual flux. Therefore, like any other science, reflexive science has to perform some reduction. In this instance the reduction is an aggregation—the aggregation of situational knowledge into social process. Just as survey research aggregates data points from a large number of cases into statistical distributions from which causal inferences can be made, reflexive science collects multiple readings of a single case and aggregates them into social processes. The move from situation to process is accomplished differently in different reflexive methods, but it is always reliant on existing theory. Later in this chapter I will discuss how it works with the extended case method.

Structuration

The third context is the external field within which the interview occurs. The field cannot be held constant, so the purpose of replication is thwarted. It is not simply that social scientists shape the world they study in idiosyncratic and therefore nonreplicable ways but that the external field has its own autonomous dynamic. This wider field of relations cannot be bracketed or suspended, yet it is also beyond the purview of participant observation. We therefore look upon the external field as the conditions of existence of the locale within which research occurs. Accordingly, we move beyond social processes to delineate the social forces that impress themselves on the ethnographic locale. These social forces are the effects of other social processes that for the most part lie outside the realm of investigation. Viewed as external to the observer, these social forces can be studied with positive methods that become the handmaidens of reflexive science.[10]

Reflexive science insists, therefore, on studying the everyday world from the standpoint of its structuration, that is, by regarding it as simultaneously shaped by and shaping an external field of forces.[11] This force field may have systemic features of its own, operating with its own principles of coordination and contradiction, and its own dynamics, as it imposes itself on multiple locales.

Reconstruction

The fourth context effect relates to the second, the priority of the social situation over the individual, which problematizes sampling on the basis of individuals. If representation is not feasible, is there any other way of producing generality? Instead of inferring generality directly from data, we can move from one generality to another, that is, to a more inclusive generality. We begin with our favorite theory but seek not confirmations but refutations that inspire us to deepen that theory. Instead of discovering grounded theory, we elaborate existing theory.[12] We do not worry about the uniqueness of our case since we are not as interested in its representativeness as its contribution to reconstructing theory.[13] Our theoretical point of departure can range from the folk theory of participants to any abstract law. We require only that the scientist consider it worth developing.

But what distinguishes a "progressive" from a "degenerate" reconstruction? Following Karl Popper (1963, chap. 10) and Imre Lakatos (1978), we seek reconstructions that leave core postulates intact, that do as well as the preexisting theory upon which they are built, and that absorb anomalies with parsimony, offering novel angles of vision. Finally, reconstructions should lead to surprising predictions, some of which are corroborated. These are heavy demands that are rarely realized but ones that should guide progressive reconstruction of theory.

Dialogue is the unifying principle of reflexive science, which is dialogical in each of its four dimensions. It calls for intervention of the observer in the life of the participant; it demands an analysis of interaction within social situations; it uncovers local processes in a relationship of mutual determination with external social forces; and it regards theory as emerging not only in dialogue between participant and observer but also among observers now viewed as participants in a scientific community. Theories do not spring tabula rasa from the data but are carried forward through intellectual debate and division. They then reenter the wider world of participants, there to be adopted, refuted, and extended in intended and unintended ways, circulating back into science.[14] Science offers no final truth, no certainties, but exists in a state of continual revision.

THE EXTENDED CASE METHOD

Reflexive science is to the extended case method what positive science is to survey research—the relation of a model to method, legitimating principle to situated practice. Just as we codified survey research so we must now do the same for the extended case method. In this section I return to my Zambianization study to illustrate the extended case method, pointing to ways in which it might have benefited from greater methodological self-consciousness. In the section that follows the one on Zambianization, I will use my case study in the opposite way, to cast light on inherent limitations of reflexive science.

Extending the Observer to the Participant

In the positive view participant observation brings insight through proximity but at the cost of distortion. The reflexive perspective embraces participation as intervention precisely because it distorts and disturbs. A social order reveals itself in the way it responds to pressure. Even the most passive observer produces ripples worthy of examination, while the activist who seeks to transform the world can learn much from its obduracy.[15]

The most seismic interventions are often entry into and departure from the field. Any group will often put up a great deal of formal and informal resistance to being studied at close quarters—resistance that discloses much about the core values and interests of its members as well as its capacity to ward off danger. Leaving the field is also an intervention since it is then that participants often declare well-kept secrets or pose revealing questions that they had never dared ask the ethnographer before. But the biggest bombshell often comes when outsiders return their findings to the participants. Few people like to be partialized, reduced to reified forces or in any other way made an object of sociological research. Furthermore, most communities are riven by conflicts so that it is impossible to navigate them to everyone's satisfaction, no matter how careful the observer. However painful, ethnographers always learn a great deal from their final intervention.

When I had completed my study of Zambianization, I decided to seek permission for publication from the top executives of Anglo American who had first employed me and then sponsored the research that I had conducted on the mines. They had no idea that I had been studying Zambianization for three years. When I showed them my report, they were shocked and dismayed that I had dared to broach such a sensitive issue. After reading the manuscript, they bluntly refused to allow publication on the ground that it was politically explosive. I countered that the report was based on their own data. They finally threw me a token concession. Since the mines had just been nationalized, the publication decision was no longer theirs but a government responsibility. I took my manuscript to the person in the Ministry of Mines who was responsible for Zambianization. He was an expatriate, new to the job but not to the mines, who saw the report as a way of making his mark by challenging the practices of the mining companies. Based as it was on careful, detailed, inside research, he considered it a powerful weapon to advance Zambianization. "Because it criticizes the government, the trade unions, the Zambian successor, the expatriates and the corporations; because it criticizes everyone, it must be objective," he said.

The monograph was duly published under the title *The Colour of Class on the Copper Mines* by the Institute for African Studies at the University of Zambia. It received a lot of publicity. Its class analysis was hostile to the mining companies as well as to the government and expatriates. Yet corporate managers in Lusaka used it to discipline mine management on the Copperbelt. The stamp of academic certification made it an effective weapon in the hands of the mining companies—a happy marriage of science and power.

No claims to impartiality can release us either from the dilemmas of being part of the world we study or from the unintended consequences of what we write. What we write circulates into the world we seek to comprehend and from there sprays dirt in our face. As I suggest in the next section, this response represents both a confirmation and a challenge to the theory expounded in *The Colour of Class on the Copper Mines*.

Extending Observations over Space and Time

Such dramatic culminations of research happen in miniature every day. Ethnographers join participants for extended periods of time as well as in different places. Each day one enters the field, prepared to test the hypotheses generated from the previous day's intervention. Fieldwork is a sequence of experiments that continue until one's theory is in sync with the world one studies. It is a process of successive approximation that can, of course, go awry. Wild perturbations between observations and expectations signify poor understanding, while occasional shocks force one into a healthy rethinking of emergent theorizing. At this level theorizing is compiling situational knowledge into an account of social process. How does this work?

Situations involve relations of copresence, providing the conditions for practices that reproduce relations. The archetype of this conceptualization of social situations is the Marxian treatment of production. As workers transform nature into useful things, so they simultaneously produce their own means of existence (necessary labor) and the basis of profit (surplus labor), that is, they reproduce the worker on one side and the capitalist on the other. But this process continues: laborers return the next day, because they have no alternative source of survival. They are therefore subject to the power of capital, or what I have called the political regime of production, which regulates the division of labor, the mobility between positions in the division of labor, rewards, and so on. The point is simple: Production becomes reproduction only under a particular structure of power. We can compile situational knowledge into an account of social process because regimes of power structure situations into processes.

This can be applied to my case study. Zambianization takes place under the erosion of "colonial despotism" toward a less punitive production regime but one still based on the color bar. Working with the vocabulary of Anthony Giddens and William Sewell, one can say that, within this political regime, resources (money, skill, education, prestige, etc.) are distributed along racial lines supported by schemas (norms, beliefs, theories, etc.)

of racial supremacy.[16] The Zambianization process is set in motion when a Zambian is promoted to replace an expatriate. The expatriate seeks to preserve his job (a resource) and looks upon the new incumbent as inferior (schema). Management intervenes to open a new job for the expatriate, who takes with him some of his old authority and responsibility, leaving his successor with few resources. The successor's subordinates, seeing him as a diminished version of his predecessor, withdraw their support and confidence. Unable or unwilling to seek support from his white boss, the new Zambian supervisor resorts to more authoritarian rule, which confirms his subordinates' worst suspicions. In their view the new Zambian successor is worse than his white predecessor—he is trying to re-create the despotism of the past. Subordinates further withdraw cooperation, and the cycle continues until a new equilibrium of force and consent are reached. The regime of power, that is, the color bar, is reproduced.

Three issues are noteworthy. A social situation becomes a social process because social action presupposes and reproduces its regime of power. By participating in terms of the color bar, the color bar is reproduced. Next, in the struggles around the regime of power, history and macrostructures are invoked as resources and schema *within* the social situation. The Zambian successor complains that whites continue to rule the roost, that independence has brought no change. Zambian workers see their new black boss as re-creating the despotic past or imposing a new tribal supremacy. Finally, interventions from outside the social situation have consequences structured by the regime of power. Management may create positions for displaced expatriates as "aids" to the Zambian successor, but the effect is to weaken him. Management may recruit high school graduates to improve the quality of personnel managers, but the effect is to exacerbate conflict between old-timers and young Turks.

The reproduction of the color bar causes hierarchical social relations to change: relations between black and white become more distance and indirect, while relations between black and black become more tense and conflictual. Reproduction of the regime of power is assured from the inside through the deployment of resources and schemas. It is also reproduced from the outside, beyond the realm of participant observation, but this requires the analysis of social forces.

Extending out from Process to Force

I could have closed my study of Zambianization with a demonstration of the general law of the color bar: however the organization changes, authority always flows from white to black. I could have given the law even more power by drawing on evidence from the very different context of the United States, where gender and racial lines also have an uncanny way of reproducing themselves.[17] This would be the strategy of inductive generalization, namely, to seek out common patterns among diverse cases, so that context can be discounted. This might be called the segregative or horizontal approach, in which cases are aggregated as though they were independent atoms. The extended case method, on the other hand, deploys a different comparative strategy, tracing the source of small differences to external forces. This might be called the integrative or vertical approach. Here the purpose of the comparison is to causally connect the cases. Instead of reducing cases to instances of a general law, we make each case work through its connection to other cases.

The Colour of Class on the Copper Mines offered two such connected comparisons. The dominant one was a comparison of Zambianization after independence with African advancement under colonial rule. The second, much less developed, compared the bottom-up Zambianization of the mines with the top-down Zambianization of government. In order to understand why the color bar remained on the Copperbelt despite democratization and the formal dissolution of racism, I dug back into history. Under colonial rule the mining companies had persistently tried to "advance Africans" into positions hitherto monopolized by whites. What little was accomplished took place through job fragmentation and deskilling of white jobs. African trade unions were always ambivalent about this view of African advancement since the majority of their members were more interested in wage increases and improved working conditions. The colonial regime was pressured by the mining companies and the colonial office in London to support gradual African advancement, as much as a safety valve for frustrated aspirations as for profit. The white settler community was an influential counterweight that opposed any upward mobility for Africans. For the most part the colonial state tried to keep out of the fray, entering only as adjudicator when the machinery of industrial relations broke down.

The successor Zambian government, no longer tied to London, became even more beholden to the mining companies as a major source of revenue. While white managers lost their formal political power, their leverage remained since the mines depended upon their expertise. For its part the Zambian political elite retained expatriates in the commanding heights of the copper industry because it did not want to depend on an indigenous, potentially rival, economic elite. Still, the postcolonial government had to respond to nationalist clamor that Zambians run their own country. It did so, not by a more vigorous pursuit of Zambianization but by nationalizing the mines, which left internal organization untouched. Zambianization from above in the capital propelled Zambianization from below on the Copperbelt.

Far from being independent, the two cases inversely determine each other. The roots of color bar persistence on the Copperbelt lie in its erosion within government. This is the principle of structuration—locating social processes at the site of research in a relation of mutual determination within a field of social forces. But can we go further and ask whether these extralocal forces exhibit a processual character of their own? Do they have a certain "systematicity" that tends to reproduce itself? Once more we can only proceed to such questions with the aid of theory, in this case, Marxist theory. *The Colour of Class on the Copper Mines* partook in a debate about the capitalist state, arguing that the postcolonial state preserved the overall class structure not because it was an instrument of capital but because it was institutionally autonomous from but dependent upon capital. Here was an emergent understanding of the structuring of class forces—a tendency for them to be reproduced domestically on the basis of a national regime of power.

I could have extended the principle of structuration by regarding the arrangement of state and classes within Zambia as a structured process nested in an external constellation of international forces. Instead I stopped at the national level and looked upon international forces not as constraints but as resources mobilized by the ruling elite to legitimate its domination. The new African elite focused on forces beyond national control— terms of trade, price of copper, Western experts, transnational corporations—in order to obscure the class character of post- colonialism. The African governing class deployed neocolonial- ism in its own version of the extended case method, denying its own class power by claiming impotence before external forces. This perspective of the new elites found its representative within academic discourse as underdevelopment theory, popularized by Paul Baran and then Gundar Frank. Later it would be chal- lenged by comparative studies that focused on the capacity of the state to engineer "dependent development" within a chang- ing world economy. The debate continues today with the emphatic rejection of the entire "developmentalist" project as destructive of underdeveloped countries (Escobar 1995; Ferguson 1990). However, my interest at the time lay in con- fronting neocolonialism and underdevelopment theory with class analysis, which confined both the local and the extralocal to national boundaries. Looking back now, I underestimated the importance of international forces. Zambia's dependence on a single commodity, copper, whose price has continued to fall on world markets, brought it under the spell of the International Monetary Fund and its structural adjustment programs. Twenty-five years after nationalizing the copper mines, the Zambian government was trying to sell them off to reprivatize them. The government brought back expatriate managers to make the mines more attractive to foreign investors. The Zambian economy is being recolonized at the behest of its own African government.

Extending Theory

The first three "extensions"—intervention, process, and structuration—all call for existing theory. But our stance toward theory itself is kamikaze. In our fieldwork we do not look for confirmations but for theory's refutations. We need first the courage of our convictions, then the courage to challenge our convictions, and finally the imagination to sustain our courage with theoretical reconstruction. If these reconstructions come at too great a cost, we may have to abandon our theory altogether and start afresh with a new, interesting theory for which our case is once more an anomaly.

I was not methodologically self-conscious about theory extension in *The Colour of Class,* but the strategy pervaded the monograph. The very concept of succession was drawn from Alvin Gouldner's (1954) case study of the organizational reverberations of a managerial succession.[18] But where his was a "natural succession," Zambianization was a case of "forced succession," imposed from above and resisted from below. The Zambian successor had to contend with suspicion from his subordinates and resistance to or indifference from his supervisor, as well as his own doubts about his abilities.

Theorization of social process was extended to theorization of the broader social forces. First, I deconstructed the government's Zambianization report. Hidden behind its data lay the real processes of forced succession under the color bar principle. Contrary to the implications of the report, expatriates were as firmly in control of the industry as ever. On the other hand, I drew back from the neocolonial thesis that blamed Zambia's continued backwardness on a conspiracy of international forces.

Again, the point was not that the claims were wrong—obviously, Zambia was held in the vise of multinationals and international trade—but rather that their partiality obscured the class interests of the new ruling elite.

I was more forthright in rejecting theories that attributed underdevelopment to the cultural backwardness of Zambian workers or, as was more common, to their anomic and undisciplined industrial behavior. Robert Bates (1971), for example, claimed that the postindependence Zambian government had failed to discipline the mineworkers. However, careful examination of his and other data on productivity, absenteeism, turnover, disciplinary cases, and strikes provides no basis for his claims. He simply adopted management's and government's class ideology of the "lazy Zambian worker," blaming workers for the inefficiencies and conflicts whose sources lay elsewhere, such as in the continuing color bar (Burawoy 1972b).

Frantz Fanon's theory of the "postcolonial revolution" guided my analysis (Fanon [1952] 1968a, [1961] 1968b). Although I was not explicit in my reconstruction, as I would be now, I sought to extend his theory to Zambia, a colony without a peasant-based national liberation struggle. My analysis of the multinationals, mineworkers, Zambian managers, and expatriates paralleled his dissection of the class interests of the national bourgeoisie, intellectuals, and the peasantry. I turned the government's claims of worker indiscipline, indolence, and anomie against the new ruling elite itself, whose extravagance and self-indulgence emanated from rapid upward mobility. As to the mineworkers themselves, they were the prototype of Fanon's labor aristocracy. They pursued their narrow economic interests, showed little concern for the color bar, and saw nationalization of the mines as a government ruse to impose harsher discipline. *The Colour of Class on the Copper Mines* did more than recast Fanon's class categories; it set the class map in motion by connecting the macroforces, propelling the movement from African advancement to Zambianization, to the microprocesses of succession.

Theory is essential to each dimension of the extended case method. It guides interventions, it constitutes situated knowledges into social processes, and it locates those social processes in their wider context of determination. Moreover, theory is not something stored up in the academy but itself becomes an intervention into the world it seeks to comprehend. Indeed, *The Colour of Class on the Copper Mines* became its own self-refuting prophecy. My man in the ministry, then the media, and finally the mining companies all set out to change the world I had described. They sought to overturn the new governing elite's interest in reproducing the color bar on the Copperbelt.

This refutation, like any other, is not cause for theoretical dejection but an opportunity for theoretical expansion. The forces revealed in my publication efforts corroborated the view of the mining companies as flexibly adapting to government initiatives. Yet they also showed that the government did not always turn a blind eye to the continuation of the color bar, that the interests of the postcolonial state were not as homogeneous as I presented them, and that social forces are themselves the contingent outcome of social processes. In the positive mode social science stands back and observes the world it studies, whereas in the reflexive mode social theory intervenes in the world it seeks to grasp, destabilizing its own analysis.

THE EFFECTS OF POWER

In defending reflexive science and the extended case method, I am not laying claim to any panacea. Just as there is an insurmountable hiatus between survey research and the positive model it seeks to emulate, so a similar hiatus separates the extended case method and the principles of reflexive science. Whereas in the positive model hiatus is the result of context effects, in the reflexive model it is the result of the effects of power. Intervention, process, structuration, and reconstruction are threatened by domination, silencing, objectification, and normalization. However, the self-limitations of reflexive principles resulting from the ubiquity of power are no more reason to abandon the extended case method than context effects are reason to abandon survey research. The goal is to examine those limitations in order to take them into account and perhaps even reduce them.

Domination

The intervening social scientist cannot avoid domination, both dominating and being dominated. Entry is often a prolonged and surreptitious power struggle between the intrusive outsider and the resisting insider.[19] As I hunted through the mining companies' records and participated in high-level negotiations, I deceived them as to my true purpose. To penetrate the shields of the powerful, the social scientist has to be lucky and/or devious; the powerless are more vulnerable. But even they have their defenses. Thus, in making my way to the other side of the color bar, I had to use the pretext of a survey to make contact with Zambian personnel officers and enlist the help of Zambian students to discover the views of unskilled and semiskilled workers. But this introduced another layer of power within the research team—my whiteness, with all its resources, and their blackness. The students worked underground, in the smelter, and laying railroad tracks, while I conducted interviews with the managers. There was no doubt that I was the bwana, and they worked to rule, delivering field notes but holding back their views. I was replicating the color bar within the research team.

Nor do domination and resistance miraculously evaporate on entering the field. The intervening social scientist faces two interrelated moments of domination, first as participant and second as observer. As participants in sites invested with hierarchies, competing ideologies, and struggles over resources, we are trapped in networks of power. On whomever's side we are, managers or workers, white or black, men or women, we are automatically implicated in relations of domination. As observers, no matter how we like to deceive ourselves, we are on "our own side," as Alvin Gouldner (1973) would say. We are in the field for ulterior reasons. Our mission may be noble—broadening social movements, promoting social justice, challenging the horizons of everyday life—but there is no escaping the elementary divergence between intellectuals, no matter how organic, and the interests of their declared constituency. In short, relations of domination may not be as blatant as they were in the raw racial and class order of the Zambian Copperbelt, but they are nevertheless always there to render our knowledge partial.

Silencing

This brings up the second face of power—silencing. Ruling ideology presents the interests of the dominant class as the interests of all. The nationalist rhetoric of the Zambianization report concealed diverse class and racial interests. How does one disclose this underlying configuration of interests? As participant observers in various workplaces in and away from the mines, we registered the discordant voices of workers, expatriates, and Zambian successors. This is the meat and potatoes of fieldwork. As I compiled our extended observations made in different situations into a social process—the process of Zambianization understood as forced succession—so these voices were reduced to, congealed into, interests. I was able to disclose the specific and conflictual interests that stood behind the rhetoric of nationalism. But this new crystallization of interests inevitably excluded, marginalized, and distorted other voices.

Thus, if I had been truer to the earlier Fanon of *Black Skin, White Masks* rather than the later *The Wretched of the Earth,* I might have explored the formation of colonial subjectivities, especially the Zambian successor, who is the prototype of Fanon's "colonial Negro," caught up in a white world that rejects him as a racial inferior. If my own color had not prevented it, I could have examined the way the colonial and postcolonial regimes induce pathologies that incapacitate the successor and thereby reproduce the Manichean world of white and black, turning African against African. Since silencing is inevitable, we must be on the lookout for repressed or new voices to dislodge and challenge our artificially frozen configurations and be ready to reframe our theories to include new voices but without dissolving into a babble.

Objectification

In the extended case method the second extension—from voices in social situations to interests in social processes—is followed by a third extension, from interests in social processes to the forces of social structure. Structuration involves locating social processes in the context of their external determination. Thus Zambianization followed the color bar, despite being antithetical to nationalist ideology, because of the balance of external forces, which appear all-determining. Objectification, that is, hypostatizing social forces as external and natural, is an inherent danger of this approach. There are simply limits to the temporal and spatial reach of participant observation, beyond which we substitute forces for processes.

Objectification is more than a methodological device, however; it also reflects the very real power exercised by political, economic, and cultural systems over lifeworlds (Habermas 1987). But their power should not be exaggerated. Forces are always the hypostatized effects of concealed processes, that is, each system depends upon the shifting processes of its own internal lifeworld. Also, lifeworlds—both those we observe directly and those we reduce to forces—are themselves traversed by power, generating needs that escape into the social sphere. Around such discursive need formation congeal social movements that can dislodge systemic forces (Fraser 1989). Finally, systemic forces contain their own contradictions, which burst forth unexpectedly, as when my man in the ministry encouraged a public attack on the mining industry's conduct of Zambianization. Even as we embrace objectification, we should be always prepared for subterranean processes to erupt and break up the field of forces.

Normalization

Finally, reconstructing theory is itself a coercive process of double fitting. On the one side, complex situations are tailored to fit a theory. The field site is reduced to a case, albeit one that is anomalous vis-à-vis theory. On the other side, theory is then tailored to the case, recomposed to digest the anomaly. This mutual fashioning creates an apparatus for reducing the world to categories that can be investigated, sites that can be evaluated, people that can be controlled.[20]

In order to assimilate Zambianization to a form of managerial succession, I expanded Gouldner's theory by introducing the distinction between natural and forced succession. Usual attrition leads to "natural" succession, but Zambianization was a forced succession. In normalizing what was in effect a transfer of control, I played straight into the hands of the mining companies. Racial succession gave them the conceptual arsenal to discipline their own managers. In his review of my book Ben Magubane picked up on this normalizing effect of "succession," which overlooked the "intense but silent class struggle of decolonization," the fact that Zambia was being held to ransom by expatriates (1974: 598).

Magubane overlooked the other side of my analysis, the application of Fanon's theory of decolonization to the Zambian case, the extension beyond the microdynamics of Zambianization to the class forces upholding the color bar. But here too normalization was at work. It was astonishing to see how a refashioning of Fanon's theory of postcolonialism could be harnessed politically by the very forces it condemned. Yet one should not be entirely surprised, given Marxism's history as a tool of despotism.

Some formal features of Fanon's analysis of colonialism, however, do lend themselves to adoption by multinational capital. He presumes, for example, the destruction of precolonial cultures and thus the fragility of "local" or subjugated knowledges (Lazarus 1993). I too gave scant attention to cultural contestation that drew sustenance from beneath colonial regimes of power, modes of resistance discovered and celebrated by subaltern and postcolonial studies. Challenging or tempering normalization would have required embedding the analysis in perspectives from below, taking subaltern categories more seriously, and, in short, working more closely with those whose interests the study purported to serve.[21]

These four power effects only add grist to the mill of postmodern critics. If context effects demonstrate the impossibility of science, power effects show how dangerous and self-defeating it is. But abandoning science altogether leaves power unaffected and the hegemony of positive science untouched. Postmodernism's dismissal of all science ignores the pivotal distinction between positive and reflexive models.[22] A self-critical positive science concentrates on context effects but thereby obscures the functioning of power. Constructing "detachment" and "distance" depends upon unproblematized relations of power. A self-critical reflexive science, on the other hand, takes context for granted but displays the effects of power so that they can be better understood and contained. The limits of reflexive science lay the basis for a critical theory of society, by displaying the limits of human freedom.

THE IMPLICATIONS OF TWO MODELS
OF SCIENCE

Methodological thinking can bring more than Weber claims, more than reflective understanding of already proven practice. In codifying positive science, we subject it to immanent critique, highlighting the gap between principles and practice. This directs our attention not only to the possibilities of improving positive methods but also to formulating an alternative conception of science. Table 1 summarizes my argument, describing the two models of science and corresponding methods, and in each case points to the gap between model and method. There is a circularity in the models: Each takes as its own basis the limits of the other. Positive science is limited by context, which supplies the foundation of reflexive science, while reflexive science is limited by power, the hidden premise of positive science. Knowing the liabilities of each model-method, we can work toward their containment. If we accept this framework, then we have to confront a new set of questions and implications.

Technique, Method, and Model

What is the relationship between techniques of data gathering and model-methods? Does the technique of participant observation, that is, the study of others in their space and time, have to follow the extended case method and reflexive science? Does the technique of the interview, that is, the study of others in the

Table 1. *The Gap between Principles and Practice of Science*

	Positive Science			Reflexive Science	
Positive Principles	*Survey Research Method*	*Context Effects*	*Reflexive Principles*	*Extended Case Method*	*Power Effects*
Reactivity	Stimulus/response	Interview	Intervention	Extending observer to participant	Domination
Reliability	Standardization	Respondent	Process	Extending observations over time and space	Silencing
Replicability	Stabilization of conditions	Field	Structuration	Extension from process to forces	Objectification
Representativeness	Sample to population	Situation	Reconstruction	Extension of theory	Normalization

Table 2. *Four Methods of Social Science*

| | Models of Science | |
Techniques of Research	*Positive*	*Reflexive*
Interview	Survey research	Clinical research
Participant observation	Grounded theory	Extended case method

interviewee's space and time, have to follow survey research and a positive model of science? In each case the answer is obviously no. The techniques of participant observation and interviewing can be conducted according to either reflexive or positive methods, as presented in table 2.

Participant observation, conducted according to positive principles, becomes grounded theory, which brackets involvement as bias and concentrates on deriving decontextualized generalizations from systematic analysis of data (see Glaser and Strauss 1967; Strauss 1987; Becker 1958; Becker et al. 1961; and Gans 1968). Here theory is the result and not the precondition of research. Social scientists are outsiders, and ethnographers are outsiders within, strangers whose objectivity is vouchsafed by distance. Nonparticipant observation is preferred to participant observation. In other words, reactivity is proscribed. To achieve reliability ethnographers gather and analyze their data in a systematic fashion. Coding and recoding field notes into emergent categories provide the prism for further observation. Replication enters as a call for clarity in how categories are derived from data and is less concerned with the replicability of data collection. It creates pressures to suspend context so as to make cases comparable. Finally, to establish the representativeness of their results, ethnographers should maximize variation within the field through constant comparison, searching for extreme cases in what is called theoretical sampling.[23]

Just as participant observation can follow positive principles, interviews can follow the precepts of reflexive science, in what I call the clinical method. The psychoanalytic variant is a prototype, especially when the analyst is seen as reflexive anthropologist (Chodorow 1999). The relation between analyst and analysand is dialogic and interventionist. Each reconstitutes the other. The analyst tries to recover and work through situationally specific experiences using dream analysis and free association. Process is the leitmotif of psychoanalysis. The element of structuration, that is, locating psychological processes in their wider social context, may not always be present. But here Fanon is an exemplar. His brilliant essays on colonialism, which derive from clinical work in Algeria, demonstrate the interdependence of psychic processes and economic, political, social, and cultural contexts. Finally, the analyst works with an existing body of theory that is continually evolving through attention to concrete cases. Theory is reconstructed.[24] The clinical interview not only instantiates the principles of reflexive science but thematizes its limitations—domination of analyst over analysand, silencing of the past, objectification of personality structures, while the theory itself is heavy on normalizing.

Extending to Historical Research

Can this binary view of science be extended to techniques other than interviewing and participant observation? What does it mean to extend reflexive science to historical research? I deal with this question in chapter 3, where I compare the approaches of Theda Skocpol and Leon Trotsky with the study of classical revolutions. Both are concerned with a comparison of successful and failed revolutions. Beyond that their approaches are diametrically opposed—the one following positive principles and the other reflexive principles. Where Skocpol situates herself outside history to discover the necessary conditions of revolution, Trotsky stands at the center of history to reconstruct Marx's theory of revolution. Where Skocpol standardizes revolutions in order to discover the universal factors that make for their success, Trotsky makes every revolution distinct in revealing its defining social processes. Where Skocpol develops a single explanation of revolution that spans three centuries as though historical time were of no importance, Trotsky shows how the movement of world history—combined and uneven development of capitalism on a world scale—sets off different processes for each revolution. In the one case detachment, factor analysis, decontextualization, and induction; in the other case intervention, process, structuration, and reconstruction. Once more we have two models of science and two methods.

I chose Skocpol and Trotsky to highlight the contrast between positive and reflexive methods. But one need go no further than Max Weber's analysis of the origins of capitalism for an illustration of the extended case method. In asking what it means to be a scientist in a disenchanted, rationalized world and then asking where that world came from, he is placing himself within history. Virtual participation gives him the psychological processes linking Calvinist predestination to the spirit of capitalism, which he then locates within a broad array of historical forces, including the rise of a legal order, systematic accounting, and wage labor. Throughout he is engaging with and building upon materialist theories of the origins of capitalism. Of course, historians are usually less self-conscious in their methodological precepts, and their work cannot be so easily divided into one or other model of science. The purpose here, however, is to open up the imagination to different ways of doing social science rather than abandoning science altogether when the 4R's seem out of reach.

Industrial and Craft Modes of Science

Having established two models of science, we must now ask what the criteria are for each model that distinguish between "good" and "bad" science—science well executed and science badly executed. The regulatory principles of positive science—reactivity, reliability, replicability, and representativeness—define a procedural objectivity, a process of gathering knowledge. We can call it an industrial mode in which process guarantees the product. Conception is separated from execution, and engineers define each task in the division of labor so as to assure the quality of the final product. In the corresponding view of science, theory is separated from research practice so that the latter can be carried out according to predefined procedures. The prototype of the industrial mode is survey research where different tasks are parceled out in a detailed division of labor—the researcher, the designer, the interviewer, the respondent—ordered by a bureaucratic structure. The interviewer and the respondent are subordinated to the schedule, constructed by the researcher. The purpose is to obtain an accurate mapping of the world by delineating the procedures for gathering knowledge.

The regulatory principles of reflexive science—intervention, process, structuration, and reconstruction—rely on an embedded objectivity, "dwelling-in" theory. Here we have a craft mode of knowledge production in which the product governs the process. The goal of research is not directed at establishing a definitive "truth" about an external world but at the continual improvement of existing theory. Theory and research are inextricable. The extended case method is thus a form of craft production of knowledge wherein the conceiver of research is simultaneously the executor. The individual participant observer carries out all the tasks of the research process in collaboration with his subjects. The research process is not arbitrary, but it cannot be reduced to a set of uniform procedures. The weight of evaluation lies with the product, whether reconstruction pushes theory forward or merely makes it more complex, whether reconstruction leads to more parsimonious theories with greater empirical content, whether reconstruction leads to the discovery of new and surprising facts.

To put it another way, following Weber we can distinguish an objectivity based on formal rationality—what I have called procedural objectivity—from one based on substantive rationality—or what I have called embedded objectivity. We can even go so far as to say that underlying our two models of science are two different theories of action—instrumental action on the one side and communicative action on the other.

The coexistence of two models of science with their own regulative principles—their own notions of what is a good and bad science, that is, their own notions of objectivity—has profound consequences for evaluating any given piece of research. It means that we should be careful not to level positive criticisms at reflexive methods or reflexive criticisms at positive methods. It is as inappropriate to demand that the extended case method follow the 4R's as it is to impose intervention, process, structuration, and reconstruction on survey research. One cannot dismiss the extended case method because the practitioner alters the world she studies, because her data are idiosyncratic, because she extends out from the local to the extralocal, or because she only has a single case. The extended case method simply dances to another tune. Listen to the tune before evaluating the dance.

A Tale of Two Handmaidens

The coexistence of two models of science has important repercussions for the way we think of methodology. Because, conventionally, there is only one model of science, and it, moreover, usually remains invisible, method and technique are rolled into one.[25] In this monocratic scheme methodological thinking concentrates on the relative virtues of techniques. Some (for example, Sieber 1973) are ecumenical and argue that one chooses the technique or combination of techniques appropriate for the problem being investigated. Others claim that some techniques are superior to others. Thus, in the heyday of the Chicago School, participant observation of the detached, male, professional sociologist reigned over social surveys, sullied by their association with muckraking women reformers (see Bulmer 1984; Fitzpatrick 1990; Deegan 1988; and Gordon 1992). Only later, as quantitative sociology asserted itself, did survey research come to be regarded as more objective and scientific than methods based on participant observation. In the struggle for disciplinary hegemony each technique tried to demonstrate its own superiority by calling attention to the biases of the other. The elaboration of a binary view of science, however, turns the debate away from techniques and toward the explication of methods, tied to alternative models of science.

With only one model of science, techniques may vie for a place in the sun. With two models of science, any given method may be accompanied by a second method as its subordinate complement. Survey research suffers from context effects that can best be studied and minimized with reflexive methods. To minimize interview, respondent, field, and situation effects, survey researchers use clinical or extended case methods. Reflexive methods become the handmaiden of positive methods.[26] Can positive methods also be the handmaidens of reflexive science? Here too the answer would seem to be affirmative. The extended case method embeds social processes in the wider array of social forces. The latter are constituted as external to the observer and therefore can be studied with positive methods. Max Weber, after all, depended on the empirical generalizations he developed in *Economy and Society* in order to undertake the extended case analysis of the rise of capitalism in *The Protestant Ethic and the Spirit of Capitalism.* In extending out from the processes of Zambianization, I made use of surveys that portrayed miners as a social force bent on protecting their privileged status as an aristocracy of labor. Just as reflexive methods can serve survey research, so positive methods can serve the extended case method.

Impediments to Science: From Context to Power

It might be argued that the choice between positive and reflexive methods turns on the problem being studied—positive methods are more appropriate to the study of enduring systemic properties, while reflexive methods are better attuned to studying everyday social interaction; positive methods are better deployed for the objective world and reflexive methods for the subjective world. Such an instrumental view of method misses deep differences between the two conceptions of science that orient us to the world we study—to stand aside or to intervene, to seek detachment or to enter into dialogue. Usually, it is not the problem that determines the method but the method that shapes the problem. Our commitment to one or the other model of science, it turns out, endures across the problems we choose to investigate.

We should ask, then, whether there are broad factors predisposing one to adopt one or the other model of science. Can we turn the extended case method on itself and locate each model historically? As I have shown, the challenge for positive methods is to minimize or control for context. Survey research becomes the less problematic the more interviews are stimuli unaffected by the character of the interviewer, the more respondents interpret questions in identical ways, the more external conditions remain fixed, and the more situations do not produce different knowledges. Survey research most closely approximates positive goals when the specifics of situations and localities are destroyed. It works best in a reified world that homogenizes all experience, when—to use Jürgen Habermas's vocabulary—the system colonizes the lifeworld (Habermas 1984, 1987). Positive science realizes itself when we are powerless to resist wider systems of economy and polity. Some analyses of the information society, postmodernity, and space-time distanciation do indeed suggest that we are moving toward a contextless world made for the social survey.

Reflexive science, on the other hand, takes context and situation as its points of departure. It thrives on context and seeks to reduce the effects of power—domination, silencing, objectification, and normalization. Reflexive science realizes itself with the elimination of power effects, with the emancipation of the lifeworld. Even as that utopian point may be receding, the extended case method measures the distance to be traveled. In highlighting the ethnographic worlds of the local, it challenges the postulated omnipotence of the global, whether it be international capital, neoliberal politics, space of flows, or mass culture. Reflexive science valorizes context, challenges reification, and thereby establishes the limits of positive methods.

TWO

The Ethnographic Revisit

Capitalism in Transition and Other Histories

Tacking back and forth through forty years of fieldwork, Clifford Geertz (1995) describes how changes in the two towns he studied, Pare in Indonesia and Sefrou in Morocco, cannot be separated from their nation-states—the one beleaguered by a succession of political contestations and the other the product of dissolving structures. These two states, in turn, cannot be separated from competing and transmogrifying world hegemonies that entangle anthropologists as well as their subjects. Just as Geertz's field sites have been reconfigured, so has the discipline of anthropology. After decades of expansion, starting in the 1950s, many more anthropologists now are swarming the globe. They come not only from Western centers but also from former colonies. Anthropologists are ever more skeptical of positive science and embrace the interpretive turn, itself pioneered by Geertz, that gives pride of place to culture as narrative and text. "When everything changes, from the small and immediate to the vast and abstract—the object of study, the world immediately around it, the student, the world immediately around him, and the wider world around them both—there seems to be no place to stand so as to locate just what has altered and how" (Geertz 1995: 2). This is the challenge of the ethnographic revisit: to disentangle movements of the external world from the researcher's own shifting involvement with that same world, all the while recognizing that the two are not independent.

With their detailed ethnographic revisits to classic sites, earlier anthropologists tended toward realism, focusing on the dynamic properties of the world they studied, whereas more recently they have increasingly veered in a constructivist direction in which the ethnographer becomes the central figure in interpreting change. They have found it hard to steer a balanced course. On the other hand, sociologist-ethnographers, grounded theorists in particular, have simply ducked the challenge altogether. Too often they remain trapped in the contemporary, riveted to and contained in their sites, from where they bracket questions of historical change, social process, wider contexts, and theoretical traditions, as well as their own relation to the people they study. While sociology in general has taken a historical turn—whether as a deprovincializing aid to social theory or as an analytical comparative history with its own mission, whether as historical demography or longitudinal survey research—ethnography has been slow to emancipate itself from the eternal present. My purpose here is to encourage and consolidate what historical interest there exists within sociology-as-ethnography, transporting it from its unconscious past into a historicized world by elaborating the notion of ethnography-as-revisit. This, in turn, lays the foundations for a reflexive ethnography.[1]

Let me define my terms. An ethnographic revisit occurs when an ethnographer undertakes participant observation, that is, studying others in their space and time, with a view to comparing his or her site with the same one studied at an earlier point in time, whether by this ethnographer or someone else. This is to be distinguished from an ethnographic reanalysis, which involves the interrogation of an already existing ethnography without any further fieldwork. Both Richard Colignon's (1996) critical reexamination and reinterpretation of Selznick's *TVA and the Grass Roots* (1949) and Franke and Kaul's (1978) reexamination of the Hawthorne studies are examples of reanalyses. A revisit must also be distinguished from an ethnographic update, which brings an earlier study up to the present but does not reengage it. August de Belmont Hollingshead's (1975) empirical account of changes in Elmtown is an update because it does not seriously engage with the original study. Herbert Gans updates *The Urban Villagers* (1982), not so much by adding new field data as by addressing new literatures on class and poverty. These are not hard and fast distinctions, but they nonetheless guide my choice of the ethnographic revisits I examine in this chapter.

There is one final but fundamental distinction—that between revisit and replication. Ethnographers perennially face the criticism that their research is not transpersonally replicable—that one ethnographer will view the field differently from another.[2] To strive for replicability is to strip ourselves of our prejudices, biases, theories, and so on before entering the field and to minimize the impact of our presence once we are in the field. Rather than dive into the pool fully clothed, we stand naked on the side. With the revisit we believe the contrary: There is no way of seeing clearly without a theoretical lens, just as there is no passive, neutral position. The revisit demands that we be self-conscious and deliberate about the theories we use and that we capitalize on the effects of our interventions. There is also, however, a second meaning of *replication* that concerns not controlling conditions of research but testing the robustness of findings. We replicate a study in order to show that the findings hold across the widest variety of cases, that—to use one of Hughes's (1958) examples—the need to deal with dirty work applies as much to physicians as janitors. Replication means searching for similarity across difference. When we revisit, however, our purpose is not to seek constancy across two encounters but to understand and explain variation, in particular to comprehend difference over time.

In short, the ethnographic revisit champions what replication strives in vain to repress. Where replication is concerned with minimizing intervention to control research conditions and with maximizing the diversity of cases to secure the constancy of findings, the purpose of the revisit is exactly the opposite: to focus on the inescapable dilemmas of participating in the world we study, on the necessity of bringing theory to the field, all with a view to developing explanations of historical change. As I will show, to place the revisit rather than replication at the center of ethnography is to reenvision ethnography's connection to social science and to the world it seeks to comprehend.

WHAT SOCIOLOGY CAN LEARN
FROM ANTHROPOLOGY

Anthropologists routinely revisit their own sites and those of others, or reanalyze canonical works, while sociologist-ethnographers seldom revisit their own sites, let alone those of their forebears.

Even reanalyses are rare. Why should the two disciplines differ so dramatically? It is worth considering a number of mundane hypotheses, if only to dispel disciplinary stereotypes. The first hypothesis, as to why anthropologists are so fond of revisits, is that fieldwork has long been a tradition in their discipline, and they have accumulated, therefore, a vast stock of classic studies to revisit. Ethnography is so new to sociology that there are few worthy classic studies to revisit. This hypothesis doesn't stand up to scrutiny, though, as sociologists have been doing systematic fieldwork almost as long as anthropologists. Franz Boas began his first fieldwork among the Kwakiutl in 1886, only a little more than a decade before Du Bois worked on *The Philadelphia Negro* (1899). Bronislaw Malinowski first set out for the Trobriand Islands in 1915, and at the same time W. I. Thomas and Florian Znaniecki were collecting data for their *The Polish Peasant in Europe and America* (1918–20).

A second hypothesis might turn the analytic eye to the present. Anthropologists, having conquered the world, can now only revisit old sites (or study themselves). As in the case of archeologists, there are only so many sites to excavate. Sociologists, on the other hand, have so many unexplored sites to cultivate, even in their own backyards, that they have no need to retread the old. This second hypothesis doesn't work either, especially now that anthropologists have spread into advanced capitalism where they compete with sociologists (see, for example, Susser and Patterson 2001). Moreover, sociologists are always returning to the same places to do their ethnographies, but rarely, it would seem, to revisit. That is, generations of sociologists have studied Chicago, but never, or almost never, have they systematically compared their fieldwork with that of a predecessor.

This brings me to a third, rather bleak, hypothesis: that the early ethnographies in sociology were so poorly done, so ad hoc, that they are not worth revisiting. I hope to disabuse the reader of this idea by the time I have finished. Sociologists have been quite capable of superbly detailed ethnography, just as anthropologists can be guilty of sloppy fieldwork. Moreover, flawed fieldwork does not discourage revisits, but, as I will show, it often stimulates them.

A fourth hypothesis is that the worlds studied by the early sociologist-ethnographers have changed so dramatically that the sites are unrecognizable, whereas anthropological sites are more enduring. This too does not make sense. Sharon Hutchinson's (1996) Nuerland has been invaded, colonized, and beset by civil war since Evans-Pritchard was there in the 1930s, but that did not stop her from using Evans-Pritchard as a baseline to understand the impact of decolonization, war, Christianity, and transnational capital. Similarly, Elizabeth Colson (1971) followed the Gwembe Tonga after they had been displaced by flooding from the Kariba Dam. Sociological sites, on the other hand, are not all demolished. To be sure, urban renewal overtook Herbert Gans's (1982) West End, but William Foot Whyte's (1943) North End is still recognizable despite the changes it has sustained. The drama of change and the dissolution of old sites do become factors in revisits, but this does not distinguish the anthropologist from the ethnographer-sociologist.

If the distinction is not in the nature of the site being studied, then perhaps it lies with the observer—the anthropologist's romance with the past or the sociologist's attachment to the present. One does not have to resort to such an essentialist and unlikely psychology. One might simply argue that anthropologists invest so much in their research site—learning the language, the practices, rituals, and so on—that they are drawn back to their own sites rather than driven to excavate new ones. But this fifth hypothesis doesn't explain the anthropologist's relish for studying other people's sites, revisiting other people's studies.

Perhaps the answer lies with the disciplinary projects of anthropology and sociology. So my sixth hypothesis is that anthropologists have been trained to study the "other" as exotic (or they came to anthropology with this in mind), and they are therefore more reflexive—more likely to ask who they are and where they came from. Sociologists, because they study the familiar (i.e., their own society), are less reflexive, less likely to think about themselves and their traditions. But here too the difference is not clear—sociologists have a trained capacity to exoticize a different world, even if they are next-door neighbors. Indeed, some would say that was their craft—making the normal abnormal and then making it normal again.

Still, in turning to the discipline for an explanation, I think one may be getting nearer to the mark. Ethnography in U.S. sociology has followed a twisted road. It began as the dominant approach in the field when the Chicago School prevailed, but with the spread of sociology and the expansion of the university, it succumbed to the twin forces of survey research and structural functionalism—what Mills called abstracted empiricism and grand theory (1959). His point, of course, was that sociology had lost touch with social reality. Even before he wrote his polemic, the Chicago School had taken up this challenge, reconstituting itself under the influence of Everett Hughes, but also of Anselm Strauss, into what Fine (1995) has called the Second Chicago School, creating an alternative to theoreticism and empiricism.

To deductive grand theory these sociologists counterposed grounded theory, discovered in the empirical data. To survey research they counterposed field research based on in situ observation of the microsocial. Here we find the great studies of Goffman, Becker, Gusfield, Gans, Davis, Freidson, and others. They reclaimed ethnography for science, an inductive science of close observation, codified in Glaser and Strauss's *The Discovery of Grounded Theory* (1967) and reaching its apotheosis in Becker's craft manual, *Tricks of the Trade* (1998).

Forced to carve out its own "scientific" niche, participant observation turned inward. To put their best positivist foot forward, participant observers (1) pretended to be neutral insiders and thus silenced the ways fieldworkers are irrevocably implicated in the world they study, (2) repressed preexisting theory as a dangerous contamination, (3) sometimes even eclipsed processual change in the search for singular descriptions of micrositurations, and (4) suspended as unknowable the historical and macrocontext of the microanalysis.[3] In studying ethnographic revisits I will provide correctives along all four dimensions—thematizing the observer as participant, reconstruction of theory, internal processes, and external forces—thereby establishing the four principles of the extended case method and reflexive ethnography (see chapter 1, and Burawoy, Burton, et al. 1991; Burawoy, Blum, et al. 2000).

My criticism of sociologist-ethnographers should not be misunderstood. There is much to be studied and gleaned from the present. The long tradition of community studies, dominated by the Chicago School, has made enormous contributions to our understanding of urban life. The symbolic interactionists and the ethnomethodologists have deployed participant observation to great advantage, sustaining this marginal technique in face of the ascendancy of quantitative research. As an embattled minority participant observers insulated themselves both from changes in the discipline and from changes in the world. Today, when historical sociology is mainstream, when grand theory is no longer so imperial, when survey research is itself increasingly concerned with longitudinal analysis, when globalization is the topic of the day, participant observation should come out from its protected corner to embrace history, context, and theory.[4] In this project sociologists have much to learn from anthropologists, from both their insights and their oversights. Anthropologists offer an inspiration but also a warning.

Within anthropology the trajectory of ethnography has been very different. Its canonical texts were ethnographic. Just as sociology returns again and again to Marx, Weber, and Durkheim, so anthropology returned to Boas, Mead, Malinowski, Evans-Pritchard, Radcliffe-Brown, and the rest—and will continue to do so as long as they define the anthropological tradition. When the very possibility of ethnography was threatened by anticolonial revolts, anthropology reverberated in shock. Acknowledging how dependent they were on forces they no longer controlled, anthropologists willy-nilly became exceedingly conscious of the world beyond their field site. They revisited (and reanalyzed) the innocent studies that were their canon and that, so often, had been conducted under the protective guardianship of colonialism—conditions that remained silent in the original studies. The isolation of the village, of the tribe, was a conjuring act that depended on the coercive presence of a colonial administration (Asad 1973). Simultaneous with this heightened historical consciousness came a questioning of the anthropological theories that emerged from these hitherto unstated conditions and a questioning of the way their texts already contained within them particular relations of colonial domination (Clifford and Marcus 1986). Thus history, theory, and context came to be deeply impressed upon the anthropologist's sensibility (Comaroff and Comaroff 1991, 1992; Mintz 1985; Vincent 1990; E. Wolf 1982).

While the anthropologist was thrown into a turbulent world order, the sociologist-ethnographer retreated into secure enclaves in both the discipline and the community. The sociologists threw up false boundaries around their sites to ward off accusations that they did not practice science, while the anthropologists forsook science as they opened the floodgates of world history. Once the former colonial subject was released from anthropological confinement and allowed to traverse the world, the trope of revisit became as natural to the practice of anthropology as it was to the movements of its subjects. The revisit is so taken for granted by the anthropologist that perhaps it takes a sociologist to exhume the significance and variety of revisits.

In the remainder of this chapter I design a framework to critically appropriate the classic revisits of anthropology and to bring sociology-as-ethnography out of its dark ages.

DISSECTING THE FOCUSED REVISIT: *MANUFACTURING CONSENT*[5]

Revisits come in different types. However, the most comprehensive is the focused revisit, which entails an intensive comparison of one's own fieldwork with an earlier ethnography of the same site, usually conducted by someone else. Like the focused interview

(Merton, Fiske, and Kendall 1956), the focused revisit takes as its point of departure an already investigated situation, but one that takes on very different meanings because of changes in historical context and the interests and perspectives of the revisitor.

The scheme of focused revisits that I develop here derives from my own serendipitous revisit to a factory studied by Donald Roy, one of the great ethnographers of the Chicago School. Roy studied Geer Company in 1944–45, and I studied that same factory thirty years later, in 1974–75, after it had become the engine division of Allied Corporation (Roy 1952a, 1952b, 1953, 1954; Burawoy 1979). Like Roy, I was employed as a machine operator. For both of us it was a source of income as well as our dissertation fieldwork. As I grew accustomed to the workplace, I was reminded of other piecework machine shops, not least Roy's classic accounts of output restriction.[6] There were the machine operators on piece rates, working at their radial drills, speed drills, mills, and lathes, while the auxiliary workers (inspectors, set-up men, crib attendants, dispatchers, truck drivers) were on hourly rates. I observed the same piecework game of "making out" (making the piece rate), and the same patterns of output restriction, namely, goldbricking (slowing down when piece rates were too difficult) or "quota restriction" (not busting rates when they were easy). In turning to Roy's dissertation (1952b) I discovered a series of remarkable coincidences that left me in no doubt that I had miraculously landed in his factory thirty years later. What made it even more exceptional was the rare quality of Roy's 546-page dissertation. If I had planned to do a revisit, I could not have chosen a better predecessor than Roy—the exhaustive detail, the brilliant use of events, his familiarity with industrial work, his rich portraits of shop-floor games.[7]

In fact, Roy's findings were so compelling that I was at a loss to know what more I could contribute. For all the talk of science, I knew that to replicate Roy's study would not earn me a doctoral degree, let alone a job. As Robert Merton confirmed long ago, in academia the real reward comes not from replication but from originality.[8] My first instinct was reactive—to denounce Roy as a myopic Chicago participant observer, interested in promoting human relations on the shop floor, who did not understand the workings of capitalism or the way state and market impressed themselves on shop-floor relations. But if external context was so important in shaping the shop floor, then one would expect changes in the state and the market to produce experiences in 1974 that were different from those of 1944. But everything seemed to be the same. Or was it?

I painstakingly examined Roy's dissertation and discovered, indeed, a series of small but significant changes in the factory. First, the old authoritarian relation between management and worker had dissipated. This change was marked by the disappearance of the "time and study men," who would clock operators' jobs when their backs were turned, in pursuit of piece rates that could be tightened. Second, if vertical tension had relaxed, horizontal conflicts had intensified. Instead of the collusion between operators and auxiliary workers that Roy described, I observed hostility and antagonism. Truck drivers, inspectors, and crib attendants were the bane of my life. As Roy and I reported our experiences, they were different, but what to make of those differences? I now consider four hypothetical explanations for our different experiences, although at the time of my study I considered only the fourth.

Observer as Participant

My first hypothesis is that Roy's experiences at Geer and mine at Allied differed because we had a different relationship to the people we studied. After all, Roy was not new to blue-collar work like I was; he was a veteran of many industries. He was accepted by his coworkers whereas I—an Englishman and a student to boot—could never be. Perhaps his blue-collar pride flared up more easily at managerial edicts; perhaps he could more effectively obtain the respect and thus the cooperation of auxiliary workers? Our divergent biographies therefore might explain our different experiences, but so might our location in the workplace. I was a miscellaneous machine operator who could roam the shop floor with ease, while Roy was stuck to his radial drill. No wonder, one might conclude, he, more than I, experienced management as authoritarian. Finally, a third set of factors might have intervened—our embodiment as racialized or gendered subjects. Although many have criticized *Manufacturing Consent* for not giving weight to race and gender, it is not obvious that either was important for explaining the discrepancies between Roy's experiences and mine, as we were both white and male. Still, in my time whiteness might have signified something very different because, unlike Roy, I was working alongside African Americans. This racial moment may have disrupted lateral relations with other workers and bound me closer to white management.

I argue that none of these factors—not biography, location, or environment—could explain the difference in our experience of work because both of us observed every other operator on the shop floor going through the same shared and common experience, regardless of their biography, location, or race. Work was organized as a collective game, and all workers evaluated others as well as themselves in terms of "making out." We all played the same game and experienced its victories and defeats in the same way—at least that was what both Roy and I gleaned from all the emotional talk around us.

Reconstructing Theory

If it was not the different relations we had to those we studied that shaped our different experiences of work, perhaps it was the theory we each brought to the factory. Undoubtedly, we came to the shop floor with different theories. Roy was a dissident within the human relations school. He argued against the findings of the Western Electric Studies, that restriction of output was the product of workers' failing to understand the rules of economic rationality. To the contrary, Roy argued, workers understood economic rationality much better than management, which was always putting obstacles in the way of their "making out"—obstacles that operators cleverly circumvented in order to meet managerial expectations without compromising their own economic interests. If rates were impossible to make, workers would signal this by slowing down. If piece rates were easy, workers would be sure not to draw attention to that ease by rate busting, lest it lead to rate cutting. Not workers but management, it turned out, was being irrational by introducing counterproductive rules that impeded the free flow of work.

Like Roy, I was a dissident but within the Marxist tradition. I tried to demonstrate that the workplace was not the locus for the crystallization of class consciousness hostile to capitalism but was an arena for manufacturing consent. I showed how the political and ideological apparatuses of the state, so fondly theorized by Gramsci, Poulantzas, Miliband, Habermas, Althusser, and others, found their counterpart within production. On the shop floor I found the organization of class compromise and the constitution of the individual as an industrial citizen. Borrowing from Gramsci, I called this the hegemonic organization of production, or the hegemonic regime of production.

If our theories were so different, could they explain the different experiences that Roy and I had in the workplace? Certainly different theories have different empirical foci, select different data. But at least in this case theoretical differences cannot explain why I experienced more lateral conflict and Roy more vertical conflict, why he battled with time-and-study men, whereas in my time they were nowhere to be found. If theory alone were the explanation for our different accounts, then Allied Corporation would look the same as Geer Company if examined through the same theoretical lens. When I focus my theory of hegemony on Geer Company, however, I discover a more despotic workplace than Allied, one that favors coercion over consent, with fewer institutions constituting workers as individuals or binding their interests to the company. Equally, were Roy to have trained his human relations lens on Allied, he would have perceived a more participatory management culture. Whereas Geer treated workers as "yardbirds," Allied's management expanded worker rights and extended more human respect and in exchange obtained more worker cooperation. Differences remained, therefore, even as we each take our own theory to the workplace of the other.

I am not saying that theories can never explain discrepancies in observations made by two researchers, but in this case work was so tightly structured and collectively organized that our lived experiences were largely impervious to the influence of consciousness brought to the shop floor from without, including our own sociological theories.

Internal Processes

So far I have considered only constructivist explanations for the difference in our experiences—that is, explanations that focus on the relations that Roy and I had to our coworkers (whether due to biography, location, or embodiment) or explanations that focus on the theories we used to make sense of what we saw. I now turn to the realist explanations for the differences we observed—that is, explanations that consider how our accounts reflect attributes of the world being studied (rather than products of our theoretical or practical engagement with the site). Like constructivist explanations, realist explanations are also of two types: the first attributes divergence to internal processes and the second to external forces.

Is it possible to explain the shift from despotic to hegemonic regimes of production by reference to processes within the factory? Roy did observe internal processes of a cyclical character (1952b). Rules would be imposed from above to restrict informal bargaining and collusion, but over time workers would stretch and circumvent the rules until another avalanche of managerial decrees descended from on high. Could such cyclical change explain a secular change over thirty years? It is conceivable that the shift from despotism to hegemony was an artifact of our different placement in the cycle between patterns of bureaucratic imposition and indulgence. But this explanation does not work, because I too observed a similar oscillation between intensified rules and their relaxation during my year on the shop floor. So this rules out the possibility that Roy and I were simply at different points in the cycle. Besides, the shift over thirty years cannot be reduced to the application or nonapplication of rules but also involved the introduction of completely new sets of rules regarding the bidding on jobs, grievance machinery, collective bargaining, and so on. Annual cyclical change could not explain the overall shift in the thirty years. Therefore we must turn to external factors to explain the secular shift to a hegemonic regime.

External Forces

The shift from despotism at Geer Company to hegemony at Allied Corporation is compatible with a shift reported in the industrial relations literature. The system of internal labor markets (both in terms of bidding on jobs and the system of layoffs through bumping), as well as the elaboration of grievance machinery and collective bargaining, became common features in the organized sectors of U.S. industry after World War II. These changes were consolidated by the "pattern bargaining" between trade unions and leading corporations within the major industrial sectors. I drew on the literature that documented the more corporatist industrial relations to explain what had happened on the shop floor since Roy's fieldwork. While the overall transformation of the system of state-regulated industrial relations was one factor governing the move from despotism to hegemony, the absorption of the independent Geer Company into the multinational Allied Corporation was the second factor. Allied's engine division had a guaranteed market and was thereby protected from competition—the very pressure that stimulated despotism. Here, then, were my twin explanations for the shift from despotism to hegemony: Geer Company's move from the competitive sector to the monopoly sector, and the transformation of industrial relations at the national level. Both forces originated from beyond the plant itself.

What do I mean by *external forces?* I use the term *external forces,* rather than, say, *external context,* to underline the way the environment is experienced as powers emanating from beyond the field site, shaping the site yet existing largely outside the control of the site. These forces are not fixed but are in flux. They appear and disappear in ways that are often incomprehensible and unpredictable to the participants. External context, by contrast, is a more passive, static, and inertial concept that misses the dynamism of the social order.

This brings up another question: From among the myriad potential external forces at work, how does one identify those that are most important? They cannot be determined from the perspective of participant observation alone but, in addition, require the adoption of a theoretical framework for their delimitation and conceptualization. But theory is necessary not just to grasp the forces operative beyond the site but also to conceptualize the very distinction between internal and external, local and extralocal. For example, Marxist theory directs one first to the firm and its labor process (the local or internal) and then to an environment (the extralocal or external) comprised of markets and states. The internal and the external are combined within a more general theory of the development of capitalism. In sum,

Table 3. *Potential Explanations for the Divergence between Roy's Original Ethnography and Burawoy's Revisit*

Explanations	Internal	External
Constructivist	Observer as participant	Reconstructing Theory
	(a) Biography (work experience)	(a) Human relations (Roy)
		(b) Marxism (Burawoy)
	(b) Location (in production)	
	(c) Embodiment (language, race, age)	
Realist	Internal Processes	External Forces
	Cyclical imposition and relaxation of rules	(a) Absorption of factory into monopoly sector
		(b) Secular national shift in industrial relations

theory is a sine qua non of both types of realist explanation for change between successive ethnographies of the same site.

Table 3 assembles the four hypothetical explanations for the discrepancy between Roy's dissertation and my account of the Geer/Allied shop floor. Along one dimension I distinguish between constructivist and realist explanations—the former focusing on changes in knowledge of the object (whether the result of different relations to the field or alternative theory), and the latter focusing on changes in the object of knowledge (whether these changes are the result of internal processes or external forces). The second dimension refers to the distinction between internal and external explanations of change—between relations constituted in the field and theories imported from outside, or between internal processes and external forces.

Critique and Autocritique

In claiming external forces as the explanation for the discrepancy in our accounts, I am not saying that the other three dimensions are unimportant. Far from it. The impact of those external forces—the changing state and market context of the company—could have been observed only through participant observation, could have been detected only with the aid of some theoretical framework, and could have had their actual effects only through the mediation of social processes within the workplace. My approach here, however, is very different from the Chicago School's, exemplified by Roy's (1980) review of *Manufacturing Consent.* Roy was curiously uninterested in explaining changes and continuities in the organization of work or in placing our labor processes in their respective economic and political contexts or in evaluating how our respective theoretical frameworks shed different light on what had happened during those thirty years. For Roy our two studies merely showed that there are different ways to "skin a worker." He evinced no interest in the factors that might explain why "skinning" took one form earlier and another form later.[9]

If there are limitations to Roy's Chicago method, there are also limitations to my use of the Manchester method.[10] Even though I still believe that external forces offer the most accurate explanation for the discrepancies between our accounts, in hindsight the way I conceptualized markets and states was deeply problematic.[11] I was guilty of reifying external forces as natural and eternal, overlooking that they are themselves the product of unfolding social processes. Here I was indeed shortsighted. Markets and states do change. Indeed, soon after I left Allied in

1974 the hegemonic regime came under assault from the global-ization of markets (which in fact led to the disintegration of Allied) and the Reagan state's offensive against trade unions. In forging class compromise and individualizing workers, the hege-monic regime made those very same workers vulnerable to such offensives from without. If I had been *more* attentive to Marxist theory, I would have recognized that states and markets change. More than that, I would have noticed that the hegemonic regime had sowed the seeds of its own destruction by disempowering the workers whose consent it organized. The hegemonic regime that I saw as the culmination of industrial relations in advanced capi-talism was actually on the verge of disappearing.

The problem was not with the choice of external forces as the explanation of change from Geer to Allied but my failure to take sufficiently seriously the other three elements in table 3. I should have deployed theoretical reconstruction to recognize internal processes (elsewhere within the economy or state) that might have produced those external forces. Furthermore, had I problematized my own embodied participation at Allied, I might have appreciated the peculiarities of manufacturing that were being replaced by ascendant varieties of newly gendered and racialized labor processes. The lesson here is that revisits demand that ethnographers consider all four elements set out in table 3.

From Elements to Types of Focused Revisits

The four elements in table 3 define reflexive ethnography, that is, an approach to participant observation that recognizes that we are part of the world we study. Reflexive ethnography presumes

Table 4. *Typology and Examples of Classic (Focused) Revisits*

Explanations	Internal	External
Constructivist	Type 1: Refutation	Type 2: Reconstruction
	(a) Freeman (1983) revisits Mead (1928)	(a) Weiner (1976) revisits Malinowski (1922)
	(b) Boelen (1992) revisits Whyte (1943)	(b) Lewis (1951) revisits Redfield (1930)
Realist	Type 3: Empiricism	Type 4: Structuralism
	(a) Lynd and Lynd (1937) revisit Lynd and Lynd (1929)	(a) Hutchinson (1996) revisits Evans-Pritchard (1940)
	(b) Caplow et al. (1982) revisit Lynd and Lynd (1929)	(b) Moore and Vaughan (1994) revisit Richards (1939)

an "external" real world, but it is one that we can know only through our constructed relation to it. There is no transcendence of this dilemma—realist and constructivist approaches provide each other's corrective.[12] Following Bourdieu, I believe that interrogating one's relation to the world one studies is not an obstacle but a necessary condition for understanding and explanation.[13] In particular, as ethnographers we enter only part of the world we study. That is, we face human limitations on what we can examine through participant observation, which makes the distinction between internal and external inescapable. Once again, by cross-classifying these two dimensions, we get four ways of explaining the discrepancy between an original study and its revisit. It so happens that actual focused revisits tend to emphasize one or another of these four explanations, giving rise to the four types shown in table 4.

Not only do focused revisits tend to fall into one of four types but each type assumes a quite distinctive modal character.

Type 1 revisits focus on the relations between observer and participant, and they tend to be refutational. That is to say, the successor uses the revisit to refute the claims of the predecessor, for example, Derek Freeman's (1983) denunciation of Margaret Mead's *Coming of Age in Samoa* (1928) and Marianne Boelen's (1992) vilification of William Foot Whyte's *Street Corner Society* (1943).

Type 2 revisits focus on theoretical differences, and they tend to be reconstructive. That is to say, the successor uses the revisit to reconstruct the theory of the predecessor, for example, Annette Weiner's (1976) feminist reconstruction of Bronislaw Malinowski's *Argonauts of the Western Pacific* (1922) and Oscar Lewis's (1951) historicist reconstruction of the Robert Redfield's *Tepoztlan: A Mexican Village* (1930).

Type 3 revisits focus on internal processes, and they tend to be empiricist. That is, the successor tends to describe rather than explain changes over time. Such is Robert Lynd and Helen Lynd's (1937) revisit to their own first study, *Middletown: A Study in Modern American Culture* (1929) and the subsequent revisit to Middletown by Theodore Caplow and his colleagues (Caplow and Bahr 1979; Caplow and Chadwick 1979; Caplow et al. 1982; Bahr, Caplow, and Chadwick 1983).

Type 4 revisits focus on external forces, and they tend to be structuralist. That is, they rely on a configuration of external forces to explain the discrepancy between the two studies. Here my two main examples are Sharon Hutchinson's (1996) revisit to Evans-Pritchard's *The Nuer* (1940) and Henrietta Moore and Megan Vaughan's (1994) revisit to Audrey Richards's *Land, Labour and Diet in Northern Rhodesia* (1939).

FOCUSED REVISITS OF A CONSTRUCTIVIST KIND

The distinguishing assumption of the constructivist revisit is that the site being studied at two points in time does not itself change, but rather it is the different relation of the ethnographer to the site (type 1) or the different theory that the ethnographer brings to the site (type 2) that accounts for the discrepancy in observations. Our knowledge of the site but not the site itself changes, in the first instance through refutation and in the second instance through reconstruction. We call these revisits constructivist because they depend upon the involvement or perspective of the ethnographer, that is, upon his or her agency.

Type 1: Refutation

Perhaps the most famous case of refutation is Derek Freeman's (1983) revisit to Margaret Mead's (1928) study of Samoan female adolescents. In her iconic *Coming of Age in Samoa* Mead claimed that Samoans had an easy, placid transition to adulthood, marked by a relaxed and free sexuality, so different from the anxious, tension-filled, guilt-ridden, and rebellious adolescence found in the United States. Based on multiple sources—accounts of missionaries and explorers, archives, and his own fieldwork in 1940, 1965, 1968, and 1981—Freeman claimed Samoans were a proud, vindictive, punitive, and competitive people. Far from easygoing, they were defiant individuals; far from placid, they were often more bellicose; far from their celebrated sexual liberation, Samoans prized virginity—among them, adultery excited rage, and rape was common. Samoan adolescents, Freeman claimed, were as delinquent as those in the West.

How could Mead have been so wrong? Freeman had a long list of indictments. Mead knew little about Samoa before she arrived; she never mastered the language; she focused narrowly on adolescents without studying the wider society; her fieldwork was short, lasting only three months out of the nine months she spent on Samoa; she lived with expatriates rather than with her informants; she relied on self-reporting of the teenage girls, who later declared that they were just teasing her. Mead was naive, inexperienced, unprepared, and finally hoaxed.[14] Worse still, and here we see how theory enters the picture, Freeman accused Mead of dogmatic defense of the cultural research program of her supervisor, Franz Boas. By showing that the trauma of adolescence was not universal, Mead was lending support to the importance of culture as opposed to biology. But the evidence, said Freeman, did not sustain her claims.

This attack on a foundational classic of cultural anthropology reverberated through the discipline.[15] Social and cultural anthropologists regrouped largely in defense of Mead. While recognizing potential flaws in her fieldwork, and tendentious interpretations of her own field notes, they turned the spotlight back on Freeman. Refutation inspired refutation. Critics found his citations of sources opportunistic, they wondered how he (a middle-aged white man) and his wife might have been more successful in discovering the sex lives of female adolescents than the twenty-three-year-old Mead. They accused him of relying on informants who had their own axe to grind, making him appear either more gullible than Mead or simply cynical. They complained that he said little about his own relations to the people he studied, except that he knew the language better than Mead. They were skeptical of his claim that being made an honorary chief meant that Samoans trusted him more than Mead. His critics considered him to have been gripped by a pathological refutational frenzy that lasted from his first fieldwork until he died in 2001.

Freeman brought further vituperation upon himself by refusing to offer an alternative theory of adolescence, biological or other, that would explain the data that he had mobilized against Mead. He followed Karl Popper, to whom he dedicated his 1983 book, but only halfway. Popper (1963) insisted that refutations be accompanied by bold conjectures, but that would have required Freeman to move to a type 2 revisit—theory reconstruction. Other anthropologists have come up with such reconstructions, partial resolutions of the controversy. Thus Bradd Shore (1983) argued that Samoan character was ambiguous, displaying Mead-type features in some situations and Freeman-like features in others. He proposed a richer theory of Samoan ethos than did either Mead or Freeman.

Others have tried to resolve the contradiction in a realist manner, proposing that Mead and Freeman were studying different Samoans. In refuting Mead, Freeman was forced to homogenize all Samoa. He did not distinguish the Samoa colonized by the Dutch from the Samoa colonized by the United States. Data collected from anywhere in Samoa between 1830 and 1987 were grist for his refutational mill. Yet even Mead herself recognized major changes that overtook Samoa during this period and suggested that the period of her fieldwork was especially harmonious. Weiner (1983) argued that Samoan character varied with the influence of missions. In the area studied by Freeman, competition among several denominations led Samoans to be more defiant than in Mead's Manu'a, where there was only a single mission. Such real differences between the communities, Weiner claimed, went a long way to reconciling the divergent accounts. We are here moving in the direction of realist revisits.

In short, Freeman's obsessive focus on refutation, based on the distorting relations of ethnographer to the field, occluded both the reconstruction of theory and historical change as strategies to reconcile predecessor and successor studies. The same narrow refutational focus can be found in Marianne Boelen's (1992) revisit to William Foot Whyte's *Street Corner Society* (1943). Based on a series of short visits to Cornerville in the 1970s and 1980s, Boelen accused Whyte of all manner of sins—from not knowing Italian, ignoring family, not understanding Italian village life, and poor ethics to defending flawed Chicago School theories of gangs. Unlike Mead, who died five years before Freeman's book was published, Whyte was still alive to rebut Boelen's accusations (Orlandella 1992; Whyte 1992). In Whyte's account his Italian was better than the gang members', he did not consider the family or the Italian village as immediately relevant to street corner society, his ethical stances were clear and beyond reproach, and, finally, his theory of the slum, far from embracing Chicago's disorganization theories, was their refutation. Like Freeman, Boelen was fixated on refutation without proffering her own theory or considering the possibility of historical change between the time of Whyte's study and her own observations.

Boelen's critique of sociology's iconic ethnography barely rippled the disciplinary waters, in part because ethnography is more marginal in sociology than in anthropology and in part because the critique was poorly executed. Even if Boelen had approached her revisit with Freeman's seriousness, she would have had to confront a sociological establishment mobilized to defend its archetypal ethnography. As a graduate student, and female to boot, she would have been at a severe disadvantage. As Freeman discovered, it is always an uphill task to refute an entrenched study that has become a pillar of the discipline and, in Mead's case, a monument to America's cultural self-understanding. One might say that Freeman had to develop a pathological commitment to refutation if he were to make any headway. In the business of refutation the balance of power usually favors the predecessor, especially if he or she is alive to undermine or discredit the refuting successor.[16] The evidence brought to bear in the refutation must be either especially compelling or resonant with alternative or emergent disciplinary powers. Rather than cutting giants down to size or trampling them to the ground, it is often easier to stand on their shoulders, which is the strategy of the next set of revisits—the reconstruction of theory.

Type 2: Reconstruction

We have seen how some refutational revisitors, not content to highlight the distorting effects of poorly conducted fieldwork, also claimed that their predecessors imported arbitrary theory at the behest of an influential teacher or as a devotee of a favored school of thought. In these examples the revisitors failed, however, to put up their own alternative theory. They pursued the destruction of theory but not its reconstruction. It is reconstruction that distinguishes type 2 revisits.

One cannot be surprised that feminist theory is at the forefront of theoretical reconstruction of the classic ethnographies. There have been feminist reanalyses of canonical works, such as Gough's (1971) famous reconstruction of Evans-Pritchard's (1940) work on the Nuer. The classic feminist focused revisit, however, is Annette Weiner's (1976) revisit to Bronislaw Malinowski's study of the Trobriand Islanders (1922). Malinowski did his fieldwork between 1915 and 1918, and Weiner did hers in a neighboring village in 1971 and 1972. Although by no means the first to revisit this sacred site, Weiner's study is a dramatic reconstruction from the perspective of Trobriand women. Where Malinowski focused on the rituals and ceremonies around the exchange of yams, Weiner dwelt on "mortuary ceremonies," conducted by women after the death of a kinsman, when the kin of the diseased exchange bundles of specially prepared banana leaves and skirts (also made out of banana leaves). While men work in the yam gardens, women labor over their bundles. These two objects of exchange represent different spheres of power: control of the intergenerational transfer of property in the case of men and control of ancestral identity in the case of women. Thus the rituals of death similarly divide into two types: those concerned with reestablishing intergenerational linkages through the distribution of property and those concerned with repairing one's "dala" identity, or ancestry, by distributing bundles of banana leaves. Women monopolize a power domain of their own, immortality in cosmic time, while they share control of the material world with men in historical time.

Weiner committed herself to repositioning women in Trobriand society and, by extension, in all societies. Theretofore anthropologists had reduced gender to kinship or had seen women as powerless objects, exchanged by men (Levi-Strauss 1969). In taking the perspective of these supposed objects (i.e., in subjectifying their experiences), Weiner showed them to wield significant power, institutionalized in material practices and elaborate rituals. Her revisit therefore served to reconstruct a classic study by offering a more complete, deeper understanding of the power relations between men and women. While Weiner may have been inspired to develop her reinterpretation by virtue of being a woman and living with women, these were not sufficient conditions for her gender analysis; we know this from the women anthropologists who preceded her. The turn to her particular understanding of gender was shaped by feminism. Rather than impugn Malinowski's fieldwork as limited by his focus on men and a myriad of other foibles that could be gleaned from his diaries, she attended to its theoretical limitations.

At the same time Weiner's study is curiously ahistorical in that she made no attempt to consider what changes might have taken place in the fifty-five years that had elapsed between her study and Malinowski's. Determining change might have been difficult for Weiner, as Malinowski had paid so little attention to mortuary rituals. It would have required her to first reconstruct Malinowski's account of the Trobriand Islanders as they were in 1915—a daunting task, but one that, as I will show, some type 4 revisits have attempted.

Still, in some type 2 revisits, in particular, Oscar Lewis's (1951) classic revisit to Robert Redfield's (1930) Tepoztlan, the successor reconstructs the theory of history used by the predecessor. Redfield studied Tepoztlan in 1926, and Lewis studied the village seventeen years later, in 1943, ostensibly to discover what had changed. But he became much less interested in studying the change in Tepoztlan than in taking Redfield to task for his portrait of an integrated, homogeneous, isolated, and smoothly functioning village, glossing over "violence, disruption, cruelty, disease, suffering and maladjustment" (Lewis 1951: 428–29). Lewis stressed the individualism of the villagers, their political schisms, their lack of cooperation, the struggles between the landed and landless, and conflicts among villages in the area. Instead of upholding Redfield's isolation of Tepoztlan, Lewis situated the village in a web of wider political and economic forces and traced features of Tepoztlan to the Mexican Revolution.

How did Lewis explain the differences between his account and Redfield's? First, he ruled out historical change during the seventeen years as sufficient to explain their discrepant portraits of Tepoztlan. Rather, Lewis criticized Redfield's folk-urban continuum—the theory that historical change can be measured as movement from folk to urban forms. While Lewis did grant some validity to Redfield's theory—communities do become more secular and individualized over time—he held the folk-urban continuum responsible for Redfield's sentimental portrait of Tepoztlan. Lewis's criticisms were multiple: The idea of a folk-urban continuum creates a false separation of town and country and an illusory isolation of the village; it overlooks the internal dynamics and diversity of villages; and, most important, it ignores the impact of broader historical changes. Also, Redfield substitutes position on a continuum from rural to urban for the study of real historical change. Thus in the final analysis Lewis attributed Redfield's romanticization of Tepoztlan to his myopic theory of history.[17]

For Lewis to stop here would leave his revisit as type 1, but he advances to Type 2 by providing his own broadly Marxist theory of social change. He situated Tepoztlan within an array of historically specific external influences, such as new roads and improved transportation, commerce, land reform, new technology, and the expansion of schooling. Like Weiner, Lewis did not use Redfield's study as a baseline to assess social change. Lewis thought that Redfield's ethnography was based on a misguided theory of history, which he, Lewis, replaced with his own context-dependent understanding of history.

The story does not end here. In *The Little Community* (1960: 132–48) Redfield subsequently offered a reanalysis of Lewis's focused revisit. He agreed with Lewis: historical change cannot explain the discrepancy between their two portraits of Tepoztlan. But Redfield denied the relevance of the folk-urban continuum because he hadn't even developed the theory at the time he wrote *Tepoztlan*. Instead he attributed their differences to the question each posed: "The hidden question behind my book is, 'What do these people enjoy?' The hidden question behind Dr. Lewis' book is, 'What do these people suffer from?'" (Redfield 1960: 136). And, Redfield continued, this is how it should be—we need multiple and complementary perspectives on the same site. Each has its own truth.[18] We are back to a type 2 reanalysis. But this misses Lewis's point—that questions derive from theories, and some theories are superior to others. Even if the folk-urban continuum did not spring fully formed from Tepoztlan, its embryo was already there in the early study, casting its spell as an inadequate synchronic theory of social change.[19]

When Lewis claimed some theories have a better grasp of social change than others, he was undoubtedly heading in a realist direction. Today we find anthropologists taking a constructivist turn, locking themselves into type 2 revisits that rule out explanatory history altogether as either impossible or dangerous. In the late 1980s James Ferguson revisited the Zambian Copperbelt, about thirty years after the famous studies of the Manchester School (Ferguson 1999). In his account of deindustrialization, retrenchment, and return migration to the rural areas—the result of plummeting copper prices, International Monetary Fund–sponsored structural adjustment, and a raging AIDS epidemic—Ferguson discredited the Mancunians' teleology of urbanization and industrialization as a mythology of development (see, for example, Gluckman 1961b). Rather than subscribing to a theory of underdevelopment and decline, however, Ferguson refused any theory of history for fear of generating a new mythology. Although there are realist moments to his ethnography, and the data he offers could be reinterpreted through a realist lens, Ferguson replaced Manchester School teleology with an antitheory that disengaged from any causal account of social change. In other words, his revisit went beyond pure refutation to theory reconstruction (type 2), but the new theory is the apotheosis of constructivism, explicitly repudiating the realist endeavor. Constructivism, brought to a head, now topples over.

FOCUSED REVISITS OF A REALIST KIND

To the simpleminded realist focused revisits are designed specifically to study historical change. We have seen, however, that revisits may never mention history or mention it only to discount it. Constructivist revisits pretend there is no change, and the differences between predecessor and successor accounts are the result of the ethnographers' participation in the field site or of the theory they bring to the site. The revisits I now consider start from the opposite assumption—that discrepant accounts are the result of changes in the world, but, as I will show, they are often modified by considering the effects of the ethnographer's participation and theory. The constructivist perspective brings a needed note of realism to the realist revisit by insisting that we cannot know the external world without having a relationship with it. In what follows, constructivism disturbs rather than dismisses, corrects rather than discounts, deepens rather than dislodges the realist revisit.

I divide realist revisits into two types: type 3 revisits, which give primary attention to internal processes, and type 4 revisits, which give more weight to external forces. This is a hard distinction to sustain, especially when the time span between studies is long. Only if the revisit is an empirical description, cataloging changes in a community's economy, social structure, culture, and so on, can a purely internal focus be sustained. I therefore call these revisits empiricist. As soon as the focus shifts to explaining social change, the ethnographer is almost inevitably driven to consider forces beyond the field site.[20] Even the most brilliant ethnographers have failed in their endeavors to reduce historical change to an internal dynamics. Thus Edmund Leach's account of the oscillation between egalitarian *gumlao* and hierarchical *gumsa* organization in Highland Burma and Fredrik Barth's account of the cyclical movement of concentration and dispersal of land-ownership among the Swat Pathans have both come under trenchant criticism for ignoring wider forces.[21] Revisits that thematize the configuration of external forces, whether economic, political, or cultural, I call structuralist revisits. But the emphasis on external forces should not come at the expense of the examination of internal processes. The mark of the best structuralist revisits is their attention to the way internal processes mediate the effect of external forces.

Sustaining the distinction between internal and external compels us to problematize it but without relinquishing it. Just as type 1 refutational revisits by themselves are unsatisfactory and require incorporation into type 2 revisits of reconstruction, so type 3 revisits that dwell on internal processes are equally unsatisfactory by themselves, requiring incorporation within type 4 revisits that thematize external forces.

Type 3: Empiricism

A compelling empiricist revisit is hard to find, but Robert Lynd and Helen Lynd's (1937) revisit to their own study of Middletown is at least a partial case. Insofar as they described Middletown's change between 1925 and 1935, they confined their attention to the community, but as soon as they ventured into explanation, they were driven to explore forces beyond the community. Without so much as recognizing it, they reconstructed the theory they had used in the first study—a reconstruction that can be traced to their own biographies and their changed relation to Middletown. In other words, their revisit, ostensibly an investigation of internal processes, bleeds in all directions into type 1 and 2 constructivist explanations as well as type 4 structuralist explanations.

The first Middletown study (Lynd and Lynd 1929), which I call Middletown I, was most unusual for its time in focusing on social change. Taking their baseline year as 1890, the Lynds reconstructed the intervening thirty-five years from diaries, newspapers, and oral histories.[22] To capture a total picture of Middletown they adopted a scheme used by the anthropologist W. H. R. Rivers that divided community life into six domains: making a living, making a home, training the young, organizing leisure, practicing religion, and engaging in community activities. The Lynds argued that the long arm of the job increasingly shaped all other domains. The expansion of industry entailed deskilling, monotonous work, unemployment, and declining chances of upward mobility. Employment lost its intrinsic rewards, and money became the arbiter of consumption. The exigencies of industrial production led to new patterns of leisure (organized around the automobile, in particular) and of homemaking (with new gadgets and fewer servants), as well as the rise of advertising (in newspapers, which expanded their circulation). The pace of change was greatest in the economy, which set the rhythm for the other domains—leisure, education, and home underwent major changes, while religion and government changed more slowly.

In all realms the Lynds discerned the profound effects of class. The previous thirty-five years had witnessed, so they claimed, a growing division between a working class that manipulated physical objects and a business class that manipulated human beings (stretching all the way from the lowest clerical workers to the highest corporate executive). They discovered a growing class divide in access to housing, schooling, welfare, and medical services; in patterns of the domestic division of labor, leisure, reading, and religious practices; and in influence over government, media, and public opinion. The business class controlled ideology, promoting progress, laissez faire, civic loyalty, and patriotism, while the working class became ever more atomized, bereft of an alternative symbolic universe.

If we should congratulate the Lynds on adopting a historical perspective, we should also be cautious in endorsing their study's content, especially after the historian Stephan Thernstrom (1964) demolished a similar retrospective history found in Warner and Low's (1947) study of Yankee City. This is all the more reason to focus on the Lynds' revisit to Middletown in 1935, *Middletown in Transition,* which I call Middletown II.

Robert Lynd returned to Middletown with a team of five graduate students but without Helen Lynd. The team set about examining the same six arenas of life that structured the first book. With the depression the dominance of the economy had become even stronger, but the Lynds were struck by continuity rather than discontinuity, in particular, by Middletowners' reassertion of old values, customs, and practices in opposition to change emanating from outside. They documented the emergence and consolidation of big business as a controlling force in the city; the expansion and then contraction of unions as big business fought to maintain the open shop in Middletown; the stranglehold of big business on government and the press; the growth and centralization of relief for the unemployed; adaptation of the family as women gained employment and men lost prestige; expansion of education; stratification of leisure patterns; and the continuity of religious practices that provided consolation and security.

So much for the Lynds' empiricist account. But there is a second register, an explanation of the changes, interwoven with the description. Capitalist competition and crises of overproduction produced the disappearance of small businesses, making the power of big business all the more visible; uncertain employment for the working class, which was living from hand to mouth; diminished opportunities for upward mobility as rungs on the economic ladder disappeared; resulting in a more transparent class system. The two-class model had to be replaced by six classes. Already one can discern a change in the Lynds' theoretical system: In Middletown I change came about internally through increases in the division of labor; in Middletown II change was produced by the dynamics of capitalism bound by an ineluctable logic of competition, overproduction, and polarization. The influence of Marxism is clear but unremarked. Market forces were absorbing Middletown into greater America; the federal government was delivering relief, supporting trade unions, and funding public works, while from distant places came radio transmissions, syndicated newspaper columns, and standardized education. Middletown was being swept up in a maelstrom beyond its control and comprehension.

The Lynds could not confine themselves to internal processes, but how conscious were they of the shift in their own theoretical perspective? Two long and strikingly anomalous chapters in Middletown II have no parallels in Middletown I. The first anomalous chapter is devoted to Family X, which dominated the local economy, government, the press, charity, trade unions, and education. Yet Family X was barely mentioned in Middletown I, although its power, even then, must have been apparent to all. The second anomalous chapter is titled the "Middletown Spirit"; it examines the ruling-class ideology and the possibilities of a counterideology based on working-class consciousness. If Middletown I was a study of culture as social relations, Middletown II became a study of culture as masking and reproducing relations of power.

Different theoretical perspectives select different empirical foci: instead of the inordinately long chapter on religion we find one on the hegemony of Family X.[23] It's not just that Middletown had changed—the Lynds, or at least Robert Lynd, had modified their theoretical framework.

But why? Did the refocused theory simply mirror changes in the world? In other words, does the world simply stamp itself onto the sociologist who faithfully reports change? That was the Lynds' position in 1925 when they described themselves as simply recording "observed phenomena" with no attempt to "prove any thesis" (1929: 4, 6). The intellectual ambience of Middletown II was entirely different. Robert Lynd started out by declaring that research without a viewpoint is impossible and that his viewpoint was at odds with that of the people he studied. In those ten intervening years Lynd had become persuaded that laissez-faire capitalism was unworkable, that planning was necessary, and that trade unions should be supported. He had begun to participate in the New Deal as a member of the National Recovery Administration's Consumers Advisory Board, and he had been influenced by what he regarded as the successes of Soviet planning (see M. Smith 1994). As we know from Robert Lynd's *Knowledge for What* (1939), he took up an ever more hostile posture toward capitalism. In ten years he had come a long way from the declared empiricism in Middletown I, and his revisit was shaped by his own transformation as much as by Middletown's, by his adoption of a theory of capitalism that thematized the power of forces beyond Middletown and patterns of domination within Middletown. In short, there's more than a whiff of type 1, 2, and 4 revisits in this ostensibly type 3 revisit to Middletown.

If the Lynds were never the empiricists they originally claimed to be, the second revisit (Middletown III), conducted between 1976 and 1978 by Theodore Caplow and his collaborators, did attempt a purely empirical description of changes within Middletown. While the researchers did spend time—serially—in Middletown, their results were largely based on the replication of two surveys that the Lynds administered in 1924—one of housewives and the other of adolescents. Leaving aside changes in the meaning of questions or the differential bias in the samples themselves, Caplow and his collaborators concluded that values had not changed much over fifty years and that the lifestyles of the working class and the business class had converged (Bahr, Caplow, and Chadwick 1983; Caplow and Bahr 1979; Caplow and Chadwick 1979). In their best-known volume, *Middletown Families,* Caplow and colleagues (1982) noted that despite changes in the economy, state, and mass media, the family maintained its integrity as a Middletown institution.

Caplow and colleagues (1982) debunked the idea that the American family was in decline, but they were not interested in explaining its persistence—how and why it persisted alongside changes in other domains. Nor were they interested in explaining the significant changes in the family that they did observe, namely, increased solidarity, smaller generation gaps, and closer marital communication. Such a task might have led them to examine the relations between family and other spheres or to investigate the impact of forces beyond the community. In choosing to focus on replicating the Lynds' Middletown I surveys, Caplow and colleagues necessarily overlooked questions of class domination at the center of Middletown II and, in particular, the power of Family X.[24] Indeed, lurking behind their empiricism was a set of choices—choices made by default but choices nonetheless: techniques of investigation that define the researcher's relation to the community, values that determine what not to study, theories to be refuted and reconstructed.[25]

Caplow and his collaborators shed further light on the distinction between replication and revisit, for their return to Middletown was indeed a replication that attempted to control the relation of observer to participant. That is, they asked the same questions under the simulated conditions of a parallel sample of the population—all for the purpose of isolating and measuring changes in beliefs, lifestyle, and so on.[26] The trouble is, of course, as in the natural sciences, one never knows to what extent responses to a survey reflect something real that can be used to test a hypothesis or to what extent they are a construction of the survey instrument (Collins 1985; Collins and Pinch 1993). The focused revisit makes no pretense to control all conditions and confronts these questions of realism and constructivism head on. There is a second sense, however, in which the replication studies of Middletown III are limited, and that is in their failure to explain what has or has not changed. That would mean reconstructing rather than refuting theories, and of course, it would entail going beyond Middletown itself. This brings us, conveniently and finally, to type 4 revisits.

Type 4: Structuralism

Parallel to the Lynds' return to Middletown is Raymond Firth's classic revisit to Tikopia, an isolated and small Polynesian island that he first studied in 1928–29 and to which he returned in 1952 (Firth 1936, 1959). Like the Lynds in their revisit to Middletown,

Firth was not about to deconstruct or reconstruct his own original study. Rather, he took it as a baseline from which to assess social change during the twenty-four years that had elapsed between the two studies. Having constructed Tikopia as an isolated and self-sustaining entity, the impulse to social change came primarily from without. Indeed, Firth arrived just after a rare hurricane—an external force if ever there was one—had devastated the island, causing widespread famine. As a counterpart to the depression that hit Middletown, the hurricane became Firth's test of the resilience of the social order, a test that for the most part was met. But Firth was more concerned to discern long-term tendencies, independent of the hurricane and the famine it provoked. He emphasized Tikopian society's selective incorporation of changes emanating from without—labor migration to other islands, the expansion of commerce and a money economy, the influx of Western commodities, the expansion of Christian missions, the intrusion of colonial rule. In the face of these irreversible forces of so-called modernization, the Tikopian social order still retained its integrity. Its lineage system attenuated but didn't disappear, gift exchange and barter held money at bay, and residence and kinship patterns were less ritualized, but the principles remained despite pressure on land, and the chiefs' power was less ceremonial but also strengthened as it became the basis of colonial rule. In short, an array of unexplicated, unexplored external forces had their effects but were mediated by the social processes of a homogeneous Tikopian society.

More recent structuralist revisits problematize Firth's assumptions. They examine the contingency of external forces as well as the deep schisms these forces induce within societies. They think more deeply about the implication of the original ethnographers'

living in the world they study and even the impact of their presence on the world that is revisited.[27] Sharon Hutchinson (1996)
and Henrietta Moore and Megan Vaughan (1994) replace Firth's
homogeneous society undergoing modernization with societies
beset by domination, contestation, and indeterminacy. These
revisits reflect the profoundly different theoretical lenses that the
ethnographers bring to their fieldwork.

Hutchinson's revisit is the most comprehensive attempt to
study what has happened to the Nuer of the southern Sudan—
those isolated, independent, cattle-minded warriors immortal-
ized by Evans-Pritchard in his classic studies of the 1930s (1940,
1951, 1956). Hutchinson did her first fieldwork in 1980–83, just
before the outbreak of the second civil war between the
"African" South and the "Arab" North. She returned to
Nuerland in 1990, while it was still in the midst of the devastating war. Hutchinson took Evans-Pritchard's accounts of the
Nuer as her baseline point of reference and asked what had
changed during sixty years of colonialism, with the succession of
a national government in Khartoum (northern Sudan), and then
two civil wars. Her questions were entirely different from those
of Evans-Pritchard. Where he was interested in the functional
unity of the Nuer community, viewing it as an isolated order,
insulated from colonialism, wars, droughts, and diseases,
Hutchinson focused on the latter. Where he looked for the peace
in the feud, the integrative effects of human animosities and
ritual slayings, she focused on discord and antagonism in order
to understand the transformation of the Nuer community.

Instead of reconstructing Evans-Pritchard's original studies,
relocating them in their world-historical context, Hutchinson
deployed the clever methodological device of comparing two

Nuer communities—one in the western Nuer territory that more closely approximated Evans-Pritchard's enclosed world and another in the eastern Nuer territory that had been more firmly integrated into wider economic, political, and cultural fields. Administered by the Sudanese People's Liberation Army (SPLA), the western community became a bastion of resistance to Islamicization from the north. Still, even there, despite being swept into war, markets, and states, the Nuer managed to maintain their cattle-based society. Exchanging cattle, especially as bridewealth, continued to cement the Nuer, but this was possible only by regulating and marginalizing the role of money. As the Nuer say, "Money does not have blood." It cannot re-create complex kin relations, precisely because it is a universal medium of exchange. Instead of commodifying cattle, the Nuer "cattle-ified" money. As in the case of bridewealth, so in the case of bloodwealth, cattle continue to be means of payment. In Nuer feuds cattle were forfeited as compensation for slaying one's enemy. When guns replaced spears or when the Nuer began killing those they did not know, they retained bloodwealth but only where it concerned the integrity of the local community.

Change may have taken place within the terms of the old order, but nonetheless it was intensely contested. As war accelerated Nuer integration into wider economic, political, and social structures, Nuer youth exploited new opportunities for mobility through education. An emergent class of educated Nuer men—bull-boys, as they were called—threatened the existing order by refusing scarring marks of initiation (scarification). Initiation lies at the heart of Nuer society, tying men to cattle wealth and women to human procreation. Thus the newly educated classes were at the center of controversy. Equally, cattle sacrifice was contested as communities became poorer, as Western medicines became more effective in the face of illness and disease, and as the spreading Christianity sought to desacralize cattle. The SPLA promoted Christianity both to unite the different southern factions in waging war against the north and as a world religion to contest Islam in an international theater. Finally, the discovery of oil and the building of the Jonglei Canal (which could ruin the southern Sudan environmentally) increased the stakes and thus the intensity of war. Indeed, southern Sudan became a maelstrom of global and local forces.

Rather than reifying and freezing external forces, Hutchinson endowed them with their own historicity, following their unexpected twists and turns but also recognizing the appearance of new forces as old ones receded. Uncertainty came not only from without but also from within Nuerland, where social processes had a profound openness—a cacophony of disputing voices opened the future to multiple possibilities. Unstable compromises were struck between money and cattle, Nuer religion and Christianity, prophets and evangelists, guns and spears, all with different and unstable outcomes in different areas. The radical indeterminacy of both external forces and internal processes had a realism of terrifying proportions.

For all its indeterminacy Hutchinson's revisit is realist to the core. She does not try to deconstruct or reconstruct Evans-Pritchard's account. The next revisit, however, does precisely that—it problematizes the original study much as Freeman did to Mead and Weiner did to Malinowski. In *Land, Labour and Diet in Northern Rhodesia* (1939), another of anthropology's African classics, Audrey Richards postulated the breakdown of Bemba society as its men migrated to the mines of southern

Africa in the 1930s. She attributed her postulated breakdown to
the slash-and-burn agriculture (*citimene* system), which could
not survive the absence of able-bodied men to cut down the trees.
Henrietta Moore and Diane Vaughan (1994) returned to the
Northern Province of Zambia (Northern Rhodesia) in the 1980s
only to discover that the *citimene* system was still alive, if not well.
Why was Richards so wrong and yet so widely believed?

Moore and Vaughan's first task was to reexamine *Land,
Labour and Diet* in the light of the data Richards herself compiled and then in the light of data gathered by subsequent
anthropologists, including themselves. Moore and Vaughan discovered that Bemba women were more resourceful than
Richards had acknowledged—they cultivated relish on their
own land and found all sorts of ways to cajole men into cutting
down trees. This was Richards's sin of omission—she overlooked the significance of female labor and its power of adaptation. Her second sin was one of commission; namely, she
endorsed the obsession of both Bemba chiefs and colonial
administrators with the *citimene* system, an obsession that
stemmed from the way the Bemba used shifting cultivation to
elude the control of their overlords, whether that control was to
extract taxes or enforce tribal obligations. So it was said by
Bemba chiefs and colonial administrators alike—*citimene* was
responsible for the decay of society. Richards not only reproduced the reigning interpretation but gave ammunition to successive administrations, which wished to stamp out *citimene*.
Land, Labour and Diet was forged in a particular configuration
of social forces and extent knowledge, and it then contributed to
their reproduction. As a particular account of Bemba history it
also became part of that history.

The conventional wisdom that Richards propagated—that Bemba society was in a state of breakdown—was deployed by colonial and postcolonial administrations to justify their attempts to transform Bemba agriculture. Even as late as the 1980s the Zambian government's agrarian reforms assumed that *citimene* was moribund. It responded to the Zambian copper industry's steep decline by encouraging miners to return "home" (i.e., to rural areas), where they were offered incentives to begin farming hybrid maize. Moore and Vaughan show how it was this return of men (not their absence) that led to impoverishment as the farmers now demanded enormous amounts of female labor, delivered at the expense of subsistence agriculture and domestic tasks. In particular, this compulsory labor caused women to wean their children prematurely, leading to higher infant mortality. It was not the cash economy, *citimene,* or male absenteeism that threatened Bemba livelihood, as Richards and conventional wisdom had it, but the regulation of female labor by male workers returning from the Copperbelt.

This is a most complex revisit. On one hand, Moore and Vaughan did to Richards precisely what the Lynds did not do to themselves and Hutchinson did not do to Evans-Pritchard—namely, to locate the original study in the social context of its production, recognizing its contribution to the history that the successor study uncovers, drawing out the link between power and knowledge. On the other hand, unlike Freeman, who also proposed ways in which Mead shaped the world she described, Moore and Vaughan did not sacrifice history. They were still able to offer an account of the transformation of Bemba agriculture from the 1930s, taking their reconstruction of Richards's classic study as their point of departure. But here is the final paradox:

Moore and Vaughan did not consider the ways that their own analysis might have been one-sided, governed by specific feminist and Foucauldian assumptions, and thereby contributed to discourses that would shape the Bemba world of future revisits. While they located Richards in the world she produced, they did not locate themselves in their own relation to the Bemba. Indeed, they write all too little about their own fieldwork, their own interaction with the Bemba. In restoring Richards to history, ironically, Moore and Vaughan placed themselves outside history.

Moore and Vaughan did not take the final step toward grounding themselves because they did not engage in any self-conscious theorizing. They had no theory to help them step outside themselves. As in the indeterminacy of outcomes in Nuerland, the openness of the future stems from a refusal of theorization, beyond orienting propositions about gender, power, and knowledge. Both these revisits contrast vividly with my own structuralist study in which I viewed the hegemonic organization of work as the "end of history" and had no conception of reversal or alternative paths. Where I froze external forces to produce a structural overdetermination, Hutchinson and Moore and Vaughan left external forces in the hands of the gods to produce a structural undetermination. My error was the opposite of theirs, but the source was the same—an ignorance of the processes behind the external forces. I did not examine the processes behind state transformation or market globalization; Hutchinson did not study the strategies of war in the Sudan or the World Bank's development schemes; Moore and Vaughan did not attempt an analysis of the declining copper industry or the Zambian state's strategies of rural development. The revisits to the Nuer and the Bemba reversed the determinism of their predecessors, whether it was the static functionalism of the one or imminent breakdown of the other. These anthropologists' aversion to explanatory theory led to an empiricism without limits, just as my failure to take Marxist theory sufficiently seriously led me to reification without possibilities. In all cases the problem was the undertheorization of external forces. We need to deploy our theories to grasp the limits of the possible and the possibilities within limits.

REVISIT AS THE ETHNOGRAPHIC TROPE

I am now in a position to extend the analysis of the focused revisit to other dimensions of ethnography. But first to recap: The focused revisit entails a focused dialogue between the studies of the successor and predecessor. From this dialogue I have elucidated four explanations for the divergence of accounts of the "same" site at two points in time. I distinguished revisits based on whether they were constructivist (i.e., focused on the advance—refutation or reconstruction—of "knowledge of the object") or whether they were realist (i.e., focused on historical change in the "object of knowledge").

In the constructivist class I distinguished type 1 from type 2 revisits. Type 1 revisits focus on a claimed distortion in the original study brought about by the relation of ethnographer to the people being studied. These revisits aim to show how misguided the first study was, thereby discrediting it without substituting an alternative interpretation. The peculiarity here is refutation without reconstruction. The type 2 revisit focuses on the theory brought to bear by the original ethnographer and replaces it with an alternative theory. In neither case is the revisit itself exploited for its insight into historical change, which is the focus of types 3 and 4. Type 3 revisits concentrate on internal processes of change. Such a confinement proves possible only in so far as there is no attempt to explain change, that is, only if we limit ourselves to describing it. Finally, type 4 revisits admit external forces into the framework of explanation. Here ignorance of those external forces—their appearance, and disappearance, and their dynamics—leads either to structural determinacy or, more usually, to historical indeterminacy, to which even the effects of the original study may contribute.

I have argued that the nine revisits discussed here tend to fall into, rather than across, the four types. This suggests that the dimensions I used to define the four types have a certain robustness with respect to the actual practice of focused revisiting. Still, the distinctions are far from watertight. Take the more imposing distinction between constructivism and realism. While constructivist revisits seem to be able to suspend historical change, that is precisely their shortcoming. On the other hand, I have shown how realist revisits continually face constructivist challenges, underlining the dilemmas of participating in a world while externalizing and objectifying it. If there is bleeding across the constructivist-realist dimension, the boundary between internal and external is a veritable river of blood. Refutation easily leads to reconstruction and empiricism to structuralism. However fluid and permeable the line between internal and external may be, the distinction itself is nonetheless necessary. First, theorizing cannot be reduced to the ethnographer's relation to the field. Theorizing cannot begin tabula rasa with every new fieldwork—it's not possible for ethnographers to strip themselves of their prejudices. Even if it were possible, researchers wouldn't get far as a scientific collectivity if they insisted always on returning to ground zero—they necessarily come to the field bearing theory. Simply put, the mutually enhancing dialogue between participant observation and theory reconstruction depends on the relatively autonomous logics of each. Second, everything cannot be a topic of study: An ethnographer must distinguish the arena of participant observation from what lies beyond that arena. The necessity of the demarcation between internal and external is therefore practical—ethnographers are part of the world they study but *only* part of it— but it is represented and justified in terms of the theories they deploy.

In short, reflexive ethnography recognizes two dilemmas: There is a world outside ourselves (realist moment), but ethnographers can know it only through their relation to it (constructivist moment); and ethnographers are part of that world (internal moment) but *only* part of it (external moment)., There is no way to transcend these dilemmas, and so reflexive ethnography must consider all four moments, even if in the final analysis it concentrates on only one or two. The practitioners of other sociological methods have no reason to gloat—the same dilemmas also apply to them; they are just less glaring and less invasive. Reflexive ethnography clarifies and anticipates the methodological challenges facing all social science. Ethnographers can say to their scientific detractors: "De te fabula narratur!" (The story applies to you).

Now that I have demonstrated the principles of reflexive ethnography at work in the focused revisit, which is still rather esoteric for sociologists, can these principles be applied to other aspects of fieldwork? Can ethnography be conceptualized more broadly through the lens of the "revisit"? In addition to the focused revisit I delineate five other types of revisit—rolling, serial, heuristic, archeological, and valedictory. Here my intent is to show how sociologists have begun to deploy these in their ethnographies, thereby gesturing to, and even embracing, history, context, and theory.

Fieldwork: The Rolling Revisit

I begin with the mundane routines of fieldwork, the elementary form of ethnography. Conventionally, fieldwork is regarded as a succession of discrete periods of observation that accumulate in field notes, later to be coded, sorted, and analyzed when all the data are in. Every visit to the field is unconnected to previous and subsequent ones, so in the final analysis visits are aggregated as though they were independent events. In the reflexive view of fieldwork, on the other hand, visits to the field are a succession of experimental trials, each intervention separated from the next one, to be sure, but each in conversation with the previous ones. In this conception fieldwork is a rolling revisit. Every entry into the field is followed not just by writing about what happened but also by an analysis in which questions are posed, hypotheses are formulated, and theory is elaborated—all to be checked out during successive visits. In this rendition field notes are a continuous dialogue between observation and theory.

In his appendix to *Street Corner Society* (1955) William Foot Whyte describes the detached process of accumulating data, writing everything down, and sorting it into folders, but he also writes of the conversation between theory and data. Thus he writes of the influence that the anthropologist Conrad

Arensberg had in encouraging Whyte's focus on social interaction among particular individuals and how that interaction reflected the social structures in which they were embedded. Arensberg provided the theoretical frame that Whyte was to elaborate so famously. Accordingly, Whyte's field notes became filled with detailed events and conversations between particular individuals. His epiphany came when he discovered the link between performance at bowling and position within the gang and later when he related mental illness (e.g., Doc's dizzy spells) to the disruption of customary roles. He carried out experiments in the field to test his theories. Thus he cured Long John of his nightmares by restoring him to his former place in the gang. Once Whyte realized what his project was about—after eighteen months in the field he was forced to write a report to renew his grant—his field notes did indeed become more like a dialogue of theory and data. It would have happened much earlier if he had subscribed to, rather than stumbled upon, the idea of the rolling revisit.

While field notes are a running dialogue between observation and theory, fieldwork is a running interaction between ethnographer and participant. It involves a self-conscious recognition of the way embodiment, location, and biography affect the ethnographer's relations to the people studied and thus how those relations influence what is observed and the data that are collected. Whyte was only too aware of the significance of his ethnicity, his large physical size, and his relative youth, as well as his upper-middle-class background and his connection to Harvard, for making and sustaining contact with the various groups in Cornerville. His relation to the community changed with his status, when, for example, his new wife came to live with him. But it also altered as his interests shifted from gangs to racketeering and politics. Throughout, he was strategic in how he positioned himself within the community, acting as secretary of the Italian Community Club, becoming part of local election campaigns (one of which led him into illegal repeat voting), and even organizing a demonstration at the mayor's office. By his own admission he began his research as a nonparticipating observer and ended as a nonobserving participant.

These, then, are constructivist moments in the field. They focus on the way knowledge of the field changes, as though the field itself remains unchanged. The assumption of a fixed site is a useful but ultimately problematical fiction. Fields have dynamics of their own that often erupt with outside interventions. Again, Whyte was far ahead of his time in focusing on the dynamics of the field itself. By studying the rise and fall of the Norton Gang, its relation to the Italian Community Club, the evolution of political campaigns, and the continuing struggles for control of gambling houses, Whyte was able to tease out the relations between individuals and social structures and among social structures themselves. Human behavior and the groups to which individuals belong could only be understood, Whyte averred, through analyzing their change through time. Largely a function of internal dynamics and life trajectories of individuals, these changes were also affected by such external events as election campaigns and police raids. Whyte's extensions to macrostructures and history were limited, but he definitely pointed to the wider world in which the gangs were embedded.

Reflexive fieldwork, in short, calls attention to realist as well as constructivist moments. It demands that the field be understood as always in flux, so that the rolling revisit records the processual dynamics of the site itself. But, more than that, the rolling revisit demands attention to disruptions of the field from outside, which shift its character and take it off in new directions. Still, remember that this field-in-flux can be grasped only through theoretical lenses and through the ethnographer's interactions with those she or he studies.

Long-term Field Research: The Serial Revisit

George Foster and colleagues have advanced the idea of long-term field research in which ethnographers, either as individuals or as a team, revisit a field site regularly over many years (they arbitrarily say more than ten) with a view to understanding historical change and continuity.[28] Their collection of cases of long-term field research ranges from Louise Lamphere's (1979) overview of the dense thicket of Navajo ethnographies to Evon Vogt's (1979) account of the Harvard Chiapas Project (1957–75).

A subspecies of this long-term research is what I call the serial revisit, in which the same ethnographer conducts separated stints of fieldwork at the same site over a number of years. This is how Elizabeth Colson (1989) describes her own multiple revisits to the Gwembe Tonga of Northern Rhodesia since her first research there in 1956. She and her colleague, Thayer Scudder, followed the resettlement of the Tonga after the completion of the Kariba Dam in 1959 and subsequently studied how the Tonga fared under the postcolonial dispensation (Scudder and Colson 1979). They noted how their relations with the Tonga shifted as their concern for the fate of the Tonga intensified but also as they and their informants aged. At the same time Colson and Scudder's theoretical framework shifted from a focus on kinship and ritual to the absorption of the Tonga into a national and regional political economy and from there to the broadest analysis of resettlement patterns and refugee problems in a global context. All four dimensions of reflexive ethnography were at work as this project evolved over three decades.

Most serial revisits within sociology are unashamedly realist. Thus between 1975 and 1989 Elijah Anderson studied uneven urban development in Philadelphia within what he called Village-Northton (Anderson 1990). With the exodus of manufacturing from the surrounding area, one side, namely, the middle-class Village, became gentrified and whiter, while the other side, lower-class Northton, became poorer and blacker. Anderson described changing patterns of social control and etiquette on the streets, the replacement of the "old heads" by the young drug dealers, changing sex codes, and spillover effects from one community to the other. Sudhir Venkatesh, whose work is more historically self-conscious, studied the Robert Taylor Homes in Chicago during a ten-year period, plotting the rise and fall of the modern ghetto (Venkatesh 2000). He tied changing modes of community control (the rise of gangs, of informal economy, and of mothers' groups) to rising unemployment and the withdrawal of state services (especially the withdrawal of police and the destruction of public housing).

Not all serial revisits exploit the temporal extension of fieldwork to study social change. Quite to the contrary, they are often used to extract what does not change. Ruth Horowitz (1983) studied youth gangs in a poor Mexican American neighborhood of Chicago for three years, 1971 to 1974. Then she returned in 1977 to follow their paths into the labor market and to discover how the gangs had sustained themselves. Reaffirming the clash of community culture and the wider individualism of U.S. society, she emphasized stasis rather than change. Martin Sanchez Jankowski, who was even more determined to focus on the constant, studied thirty-seven gangs in three cities for ten years (Jankowski 1991). Stints of fieldwork were undertaken and data collected as though they were independent observations at a fixed site. He focused on their common organizational form and their community embeddedness; he was not interested in how the gangs changed over time or varied between cities or how their ties to the political and economic contexts shifted over time. He deployed his long-term field research to reveal the stabilizing effects of another constant—the defiant individualism of gang members. He dwelled on what stayed the same, despite change and through change.

Although technically a serial revisit, Jankowski's goal was replication in both the constructivist and realist senses. As an unobtrusive participant observer, he sought to establish replicable conditions of research, inducing theory from his neutral observations. At the same time he decentered the study of change, whether through internal processes or external forces, in favor of replicating the same result across space and time— the wider the range of cases, the more convincing the result. One might say, paradoxically, he mobilized reflexivity in pursuit of replication.

Although Jankowski made reference to other studies of gangs, it was not to suggest that time and place explained their different conclusions. He could, for example, have drawn on Whyte's (1943) parallel gang study with similar findings to ask what had changed during the intervening forty years. That, however, would have turned Jankowski's study into a "heuristic" revisit, the antithesis of replication.

Framing the Present: The Heuristic Revisit

The rolling and serial revisits return ethnographers to the familiarity of their own field sites. In these revisits memory plays an enormous but rarely theorized role (Mayer 1989). Rolling and serial revisits contrast with the next two types of revisit in which ethnographers compare their own fieldwork with someone else's research, documentation, or study. The first is the heuristic revisit, which appeals to another study—not always strictly ethnographic and not necessarily of the same site but of an analogous site—that frames the questions posed, provides the concepts to be adopted, or offers a parallel and comparative account.

Most heuristic revisits in sociology, like the serial revisits, have a strong realist bent. Thus Mary Pattillo-McCoy (1999) used Frazier's *Black Bourgeoisie* (1957) and Drake and Cayton's *Black Metropolis* (1945) to frame her ethnographic account of the social, economic, and geographical proximity of black middle-class life to the south Chicago ghetto. Mitchell Duneier's (1999) study of street vendors in Greenwich Village goes back forty years to Jane Jacobs's *Death and Life of Great American Cities* (1961), recovering her analysis of the same area and, in particular, the role of public characters. Following Jacobs's example, Duneier regarded the street vendors as "public characters" who, contrary to stereotype, stabilize community relations. With Jacobs's work as his baseline, Duneier considered the broad changes in Greenwich Village—the rising inequality, cultural difference, and crime—and how it came to be a home for the homeless. He traced the vendors to their previous location in Pennsylvania Station and uncovered the political forces that led to their eviction. He practiced what he called the extended place method—realist method par excellence—which attempts to remove all traces of constructivism by striving for an objective record of the behaviors of his subjects and by renouncing theoretical reconstruction in favor of induction.[29]

My final example of a heuristic revisit adopts a more constructivist perspective. Leslie Salzinger (2003) used Patricia Fernandez-Kelly's (1983) pioneering study of women as inexpensive and malleable labor in the Mexican maquiladora industry to frame her own study of the same industry twenty years later. Where Fernandez-Kelly saw only one gender regime, Salzinger discovered a multiplicity, reflecting the expansion of the industry and its changing market context. Stressing indeterminacy of outcomes and reflecting twenty years of feminist thought, Salzinger also made a theoretical turn. Her analysis of production focused on the poststructuralist subjectivity rather than on the political economy of gender regimes. History moves on, but so does theory. Their trajectories are intertwined.

Digging Up the Past: The Archeological Revisit

If the heuristic revisit moves forward in time, from the earlier study to the later one that it frames, the archeological revisit moves backward in time to excavate the historical terrain that gives rise or gives meaning to the ethnographic present. If not strictly a revisit—since there is no reference study known ahead of time—it is a common technique for giving historical depth to ethnography.[30] In the archeological revisit multiple sources of data are used, whether retrospective interviews, published accounts, or archival documents. One could simply triangulate and aggregate all the historical data from different sources as though they measured a singular and fixed reality. This, however, would violate the rules of reflexivity, which demand disaggregating data to reflect their relations of production, namely, relations between observers and participants, and the theories that observers (journalists, officials, witnesses) deploy.

A number of recent sociological studies turn on archeological revisits. Pierrette Hondagneu-Sotelo (1994) explored the historical antecedents of the gendered streams of immigration from Mexico to the United States. To give specificity to the revelations of her fieldwork in a community in northern California, she was led back in time to distinguish immigrants who came before the end of the bracero program in 1965 (the program that channeled single, male migrants into the agricultural fields of California) from those who came after its end. Through oral histories Hondagneu-Sotelo was able to trace the consequences of original migration patterns for the domestic division of labor. Similarly, Rhonda Levine (2001) produced an unexpected ethnography of German cattle dealers in New York State, refugees from Nazi persecution. To understand their participation in the transformation of New York's dairy industry, she uncovered details of their lives in rural Germany before they left. Like Hondagneu-Sotelo, Levine traced the connection between the community of origin and the community of settlement.

Lynne Haney (2002) conducted an ethnography of the social effects of cutbacks in Hungary's postsocialist welfare. To understand the reaction of the poor women she studied, Haney had to reexamine the socialist welfare state, distinguishing the maternalist welfare regime of reform communism from the societal welfare of the early post–World War II period. She turned to archives and oral histories to reconstruct the past, disclosing a novel periodization of state socialism and its aftermath.

It is no accident that so many of the ethnographies of the market and of democratic transitions become archeological revisits, excavating the socialist antecedents of the postsocialist order (Burawoy and Verdery 1999; Kligman 1998; Lampland 1995; Woodruff 1999). As in the case of the postcolonial transition, ethnographers have looked to the character of the previous regime for the source of disappointed expectations. The archeological revisit, however, is not unidirectional, because of necessity the ethnographer tacks back and forth between the past she or he uncovers and the present he or she interprets, rendering all sorts of new insights into both.

The archeological revisit can be used to connect the present to the past, but it may also be used to compare the present with the past. Thus Haney revised our understanding of socialist welfare by stressing its extensiveness and its flexibility. Similarly, Steven Lopez (2003) participated in labor-organizing campaigns in Pittsburgh. He asked why such campaigns were successful in one historical conjuncture but not in another. To understand the conditions of this differential success, Lopez reconstructed an earlier point in time for each campaign from interviews, archives, legal reports, and newspapers. He disentangled how obstacles to organizing were overcome (or not) as a function of both the new context and the cumulative effects of previous campaigns.

In the sometimes desperate search for historical data, the ethnographer is easily tempted to repress data's constructed character. Thus, as I alluded to earlier, historians such as

Stephan Thernstrom have been critical of how community ethnographers reduce history to the mythologies of their participants. With theoretical lenses to guide their investigations, however, ethnographers become sensitive to the constructed nature of historical narrative. Indeed, they are able to exploit its constructedness.

Reporting Back: The Valedictory Revisit

My last type of revisit is what I call the valedictory revisit, when the ethnographer returns to the subjects, armed with the results of the study, whether in draft or published form. The purpose is not to undertake another in-depth ethnography but rather to ascertain the subjects' responses to the reported research and perhaps to discover what has changed since the last visit. Assuming the subjects can be engaged, this is the moment of judgment, when previous relations are reassessed, theory is put to the test, and accounts are reevaluated. It can be traumatic for both sides, and for this reason it is all too rare.

William Foot Whyte (1955) undertook valedictory revisits to Cornerville to find out what, if anything, *Street Corner Society* had meant to the gang members. Doc, his chief informant, showed some ambivalence and embarrassment about the central role he played in the book; Chick was more upset by the way he was portrayed; and Sam Franco was inspired to do fieldwork himself. Whyte was not led to any reassessment of the study itself, for he had had a relatively smooth ride as compared, for example, with Nancy Scheper-Hughes (2001). She was drummed out of her Irish village, An Clochan, when she returned twenty-five years after her original fieldwork.

The inhabitants still remembered her. Many had not forgiven her for her portrait of their weak and vulnerable community. The hostile reception prompted her to rethink the argument in a new prologue and epilogue to her book. It was also an occasion to reflect on changes that had occurred during the intervening period—the impact of Ireland's integration into the European Union, the expansion of the tourist industry, and continued out-migration. In her case rejection by the participants led her to qualify her original interpretations but also propelled her to write an account of historical change. Her valedictory revisit borders on a focused revisit, covering all four principles of reflexivity.

Frequently, the subjects of an ethnography are simply not interested in what the ethnographer has to say until it comes to the attention of adversarial forces. Consider Diane Vaughan's (1996) historical ethnography—itself an archeological revisit that retraced the steps that led up to the *Challenger* disaster of 1986. Contesting the conventional story of human error and individual blame, she uncovered an alternative history of the National Aeronautics and Space Administration (NASA) as it descended incrementally into bad judgment and normalized design flaws. She located the cause of the disaster in the type of technology, organizational culture, and external context. Published ten years after the *Challenger* disaster, her study received much publicity but not a peep from NASA, the object of her investigation. There was no valedictory revisit to NASA until *Columbia* crashed on February 1, 2003, whereupon her *Challenger* study revisited her, and with a vengeance (Vaughan 2006). Her original diagnoses of the problem at NASA found a new lease on life among journalists, engineers, and other experts, prompting her to investigate the *Columbia* disaster. Her comparison of the two disasters figured prominently in a report of the Columbia Accident Investigation Board. Her valedictory revisit turned into a focused revisit that confirmed her earlier conclusions, much to NASA's chagrin. As in the case of Audrey Richards, which I noted earlier, ethnographies have their own history of effects—ignored at one moment, invoked at another—drawn in by the play of external forces.

It is often said that handing a finished product to the subject is the responsibility of the ethnographer. That may be so, but the valedictory revisit also serves a scientific function. This final engagement with the people one studies, confronting them with one's conclusions, deepens both constructivist and realist insights into the world we study. It may be traumatic—for both the participant and the observer—but through pain the cause of reflexive ethnography advances.

WHAT ANTHROPOLOGY CAN LEARN
FROM SOCIOLOGY

The postcolonial world has driven anthropologists back to their early historical and macroperspectives, which they lost in the era of professionalization. As I have tried to argue here, in their inception these moves beyond fieldwork in time and beyond the field site in space were invariably positive. Now, however, these moves often take a self-defeating turn. As anthropologists release their subjects from conceptual confinement in their villages, the anthropologists mimic their subjects' migratory circuits. Bouncing from site to site, anthropologists easily substitute anecdotes and vignettes for serious fieldwork, reproducing the cultural syncretism and hybridity of the peoples they observe (Hannerz 1996).

As they join their subjects in the external world, anthropologists have also all too easily lost sight of the partiality of their participation in the world they study. They begin to believe they are the world they study or that the world revolves around them. Ruth Behar's (1993) six-year dialogue with her single subject, Esperanza, fascinating though it is, brackets all concern with theoretical issues and thus fails to grapple with change in Mexican society. Behar's view of reflexivity reduces everything to the mutual orbiting of participant and observer. It dispenses with the distinction between internal and external: in the constructivist dimension, where anthropological theory is reduced to the discourse of the participant, and in the realist dimension, where there is nothing beyond "multisited" ethnography. Furthermore, the very distinction between realism and constructivism folds into an autocentric relation of ethnographer to the world.

Clifford Geertz, whose recounting of the quandary of the changing anthropologist in a changing world introduced this chapter, similarly fails to address the dilemmas of revisits, dissolving his reflections into a virtuoso display of literary images. In his hands ethnography becomes a mesmeric play of texts upon texts, narratives within narratives (Geertz 1995). By the end of its cultural turn anthropology has lost its distinctive identity, having decentered its techniques of fieldwork, sacrificed the idea of intensively studying a site, abandoned its theoretical traditions, and forsaken its pursuit of causal explanation. Theory and history evaporate in a welter of discourse. Anyone with literary ambition can now assume the anthropological mantle, making the disrupted discipline vulnerable to cavalier invasion by natives and impostors. Once a social science, anthropology aspires to become an appendage of the humanities. Although this is only one tendency within anthropology, it is significant and ascendant—a warning to ethnographer-sociologists as they emerge from their own wilderness.

As the examples in this chapter have shown, ethnographer-sociologists are following anthropologists out of seclusion—more cautiously but more surely. As I have said, within sociology ethnography has had to wrestle with a positivist legacy that was also reductionist—a tradition that reduced the external to the internal (theory induced from observation, context suspended to insulate the microsituation) at the same time that it privileged realism over constructivism (the world is purely external to us). As anthropologists veer toward the center of the universe looking out, ethnographer-sociologists are coming from the margins and looking in. Ethnographer-sociologists may be latecomers to history and theory, but therein lies their advantage. For as they leave their guarded corner they are disciplined by the vibrancy of sociology's comparative history and theoretical traditions. This dialogue within sociology, and with social science more broadly, will help the ethnographer-sociologist retain a balance between constructivism and realism. Such, indeed, are the benefits of backwardness. The ethnographer-anthropologist, on the other hand, has no such disciplinary protection and, unless new alliances are forged, faces the onrushing world alone.

The divergent orbits of ethnography in sociology and anthropology reflect the histories of our disciplines, but they are also responses to the era in which we live. The spatially bounded site, unconnected to other sites, is a fiction of the past that is no longer sustainable. Under these circumstances what does it mean to undertake a revisit, especially a focused revisit? What is there to revisit when sites are evanescent, when all that's solid melts into air? How, for example, might I revisit Allied today—thirty years after my first encounter—if I cannot find it where I left it? One possibility, all too popular, is to simply study myself. I could trace my own research trajectory from Chicago to communist Hungary to postcommunist Russia, reflecting on the world-historical shifts since the mid-1970s. Moving beyond such solipsism, I might follow my work-mates, as Jay MacLeod (1995) did with his two gangs. We might call this a biographically based revisit.[31] Or I could study the homeless recyclers who now, hypothetically, inhabit the vacant lot that used to be Allied. We might call this a place-based revisit. Or I could go off to South Korea where, again hypothetically, Allied's new engine division can be found. We can call this an institution-based revisit. These different types of revisit might all coincide if we were studying the same enclosed village or the old company town, but with globalization they diverge into three profoundly different projects. The only way of connecting them is to look upon each as a product of the same broad historical process, examining, for example, the implications of the shift in the United States from an industrial to a service economy. This could interconnect biographies of workers and their children, the redeployment of place, and the fleeing of capital to other countries.

But we can no longer stop at the national level. Today the recomposition of everyday life is also the product of transnational or supranational processes. A comprehensive revisit might involve following individual biographies, institutional trajectories, and the reconstitution of place, locating them all in regional, national, and also global transformation. Katherine Verdery (2003) conducted such a complex of nested revisits in her ethnography of decollectivization in Aurel Vlaicu—a Transylvanian village she studied under communism and then again during the postcommunist period. She followed individual kin members, specific groups (insiders and outsiders), the village land restitution committee, and different economic organizations (state farms, cooperatives, and individual production), all in relation to the transformation of property relations, which itself makes sense only within the local political economy, the national law of privatization, the conditionalities of the World Bank and the International Monetary Fund, and the global spread of market fundamentalism. With so many parts of the world dissolving, reconfiguring, and recomposing under the pressure of their global connections, ethnographic revisits with a global reach become irresistible. The more irresistible is the global revisit, however, the more necessary is theory to track and make sense of all the moving parts.

Privatization and market transition push ethnography to global extensions, which require not only theoretical frameworks for their interpretation but also historical depth. The only way to make sense of global forces, connections, and imaginations is to examine them over time. In other words, global ethnographies require focused, heuristic, serial, and, especially, archeological revisits to excavate their historical terrains (Burawoy, Blum, et al. 2000). Approaching a global ethnography of Allied today would require resituating the

company of 1973–74 in its global market, in the global connections between the engine division and other divisions, in the
global imagination of its workers and managers—before I
could undertake a parallel investigation. This is how June
Nash (2001) turned a focused revisit into a global ethnography
of the Zapatista movement. Every summer between 1988 and
1993 she returned to Chiapas—the site of her own 1957
study—with a team of students. While acknowledging the
shortcomings of the descriptive anthropology extant in the
1950s, namely, the tendency to insulate communities from
their determining context, she nonetheless partially recuper-
ated that insulation as a political struggle to defend autonomy.
In the early 1990s such defensive maneuvers were no longer
effective. In the face of the North American Free Trade
Agreement, the rollback of land reform through privatization,
the erosion of subsistence agriculture, the attrition of state welfare, and the violation of human rights, Chiapas autonomy
could no longer be defended by withdrawal and insulation. It
required aggressive political organization and the development of an indigenous movement of national focus and global
reach. Nash demonstrated that without history to ground it
and theory to orient it, global ethnography is lost.

The time is nigh for the sociologist-ethnographer to come out
of hiding and join the rest of sociology in novel explorations of
history and theory.[32] We should not forget that Marx, Weber,
and Durkheim grounded their history, as well as their theory, in
an ethnographic imagination, whether of the factories of nineteenth-century England, the religious bases of economic behavior, or the rites and beliefs of small-scale societies. Michel
Foucault founded his originality in a virtual ethnography of

prisons and asylums. Simone de Beauvoir and her daughters set out from the privatized experiences of women, while Pierre Bourdieu launched his metatheory from the villages of Algeria. Thus not only does reflexive ethnography require the infusion of both theory and history, but theory and historical understanding will be immeasurably advanced by the conceptualization and practice of ethnography as revisit.

THREE

Two Methods in Search of Revolution

Trotsky versus Skocpol

> If methodological work—and this is naturally its intention—can at
> some point serve the practice of the historian directly, it is indeed by
> enabling him once and for all to escape the danger of being imposed
> upon by a philosophically embellished dilettantism.
>
> Max Weber, *The Methodology of the Social Sciences*

Sociology has founded its scientific credentials on imitating the
method of the physical sciences as understood by philosophers.
Regulative principles such as Mill's "canons of induction,"
Hempel's "deductive-nomological explanation," or Popper's fal-
sificationism are laid down as *the* scientific method. However,
these principles evolved more from philosophical speculation
than from careful empirical examination of the "hard sciences"
from which they derived their legitimacy. Indeed, when philosophers turned to history and the actual practice of science, they
found their principles violated. New understandings of science

emerged, motivated less by the search for a single abstract universal method and more by the need to explain the growth of scientific knowledge. My purpose in this chapter is to explore the implications for sociology of adopting one of these historically rooted conceptions of science, namely, the methodology of scientific research programs proposed by Imre Lakatos, by comparing it with the standard methodology of induction.[1]

INDUCTION VERSUS THE METHODOLOGY OF SCIENTIFIC RESEARCH PROGRAMS

Organizing and concretizing the comparison requires examples of each methodology that study a similar object in a substantively similar manner. For reasons that will become apparent it is difficult to find pure cases of each methodology, let alone cases that combine comparable theories with different methodologies. I choose Theda Skocpol's *States and Social Revolutions* (1979) and Leon Trotsky's *Results and Prospects* ([1906] 1969) for the following reasons. With important qualifications, they do exemplify the methodologies of induction and research program. Both works deal with the causal logic of social revolutions in comparative perspective, and they dwell on very similar explanatory variables. Both stress the importance of class struggle, the autonomy of the state, and international relations in the causes as well as the outcomes of revolutions. Thus Skocpol stresses politico-military crises of state and class domination; the emergence rather than making of revolutionary situations; the uneven development of capitalism on a world scale; an international system of competing states; organizational and ideological developments between revolutions; and, finally, the state as a potentially autonomous structure and independent actor both at home and abroad (1979: 17–31). These are also the factors that Trotsky lays out, not only in the work cited earlier but in his monumental *History of the Russian Revolution.*[2] Because the similarities are so considerable, the differences can be more easily isolated and attributed to their divergent methodologies.

One merit of Skocpol's *States and Social Revolutions* is that it attempts to follow rigorously Mill's canons of induction. With a resolution unmatched in historiography Skocpol pursues the causes of social revolutions by examining what "successful" ones have in common and then trying to isolate those causal factors that distinguish successful from "failed" revolutions. Her intent is clear: "How are we ever to arrive at new theoretical insights if we do not let historical patterns speak to us, rather than always viewing them through the blinders, or heavily tinted lenses, of pre-existing theories?" (1986: 190).

Induction, then, is the process of inferring causal explanations from "pre-existing facts." Among the philosophers of science, Karl Popper (1959) has been the most celebrated opponent of this view, arguing that without a mechanism for selecting among the facts there is no way of inferring theories. Theories, or, as he calls them, conjectures, are necessarily postulated before the facts that they organize and select. Furthermore, facts are not to be used to verify conjectures but to refute them. Although this is a widely defended position, it is also untenable. Because all theories are born refuted and remain refuted, if we followed Popper's prescription, knowledge would be in perpetual chaos rather than grow. We would have no theories if we always abandoned them when they were refuted by facts (see, for example,

Polanyi 1958; Feyerabend 1975; Kuhn 1962; Laudan 1977; Lakatos 1978; Putnam 1981).

These conclusions led Lakatos to argue that science develops not through refuting theories but by refuting refutations or at least refuting some refutations and ignoring others.[3] Research programs emerge from the attempt to protect the premises of earlier scientific achievements against refutation. Scientists define certain hard-core postulates, which they accept by convention. According to the methodological principle that Lakatos (1976) calls the negative heuristic, refutations of the hard core are not allowed. Scientists defend the hard core of their research program against falsification by various strategies, some of which lead to progressive problemshifts and others to degenerating problemshifts. Protective strategies lead to degenerating research programs when they reduce the empirical content of the core postulates by restricting their scope or by labeling anomalies, that is, puzzles or theoretically unexpected outcomes, as exceptions. Progressive problemshifts, on the other hand, resolve anomalies by introducing auxiliary theories that expand the explanatory power of the core postulates. Here scientists follow the methodological principle that Lakatos calls the positive heuristic, which is a research policy, made up of models and exemplars, for digesting anomalies by constructing theories consistent with the hard core. In other words, a progressive defense of the hard core takes the form of an expanding belt of theories that increase the corroborated empirical content and solve successive puzzles. Scientists should not evaluate one isolated theory against another but rather sequences of theories that make up research programs. According to Lakatos, therefore, scientific revolutions replace degenerating with progressive research programs.

I shall try to show that Trotsky's theory of the Russian Revolution can be viewed as part of a progressive Marxist research program. The main focus will be on his 1906 formulation in *Results and Prospects,* which Deutscher called "the most radical restatement of the prognosis of the Socialist revolution undertaken since Marx's *Communist Manifesto*" (1954: 150). That Trotsky long predated Lakatos is no reason to deny the relevance of the methodology of research programs. Successful science does not depend on following an articulated methodology.[4] Indeed, some would even say that too much methodological self-consciousness is an obstacle to good science. According to Michael Polanyi (1958, chaps. 1, 4, and 6), scientists work with inexplicit "tacit skills" and "personal knowledge" that stem from "dwelling in" a research tradition. This is one, but not the main, reason why the elaboration of the principles of the research program will, of necessity, have a less definitive character than the corresponding elaboration of the principles of induction. More important, the canons of induction claim to apply to all scientific contexts, whereas each research program has its own distinctive principles, or heuristics, as Lakatos calls them. There cannot be any methodological prescriptions that apply across all research programs.[5]

My concern is not simply to compare the two methodologies. I also evaluate them in terms of their capacity to advance the science of sociology. However, we need to be clear about the meaning of "scientific advance." I propose to use Popper's criteria for the growth of knowledge (1963: 240–43). First, a new theory should proceed from some "simple, new, and powerful, unifying idea." Second, the new theory should be "independently testable," that is, it must lead to the prediction of new, unexpected phenomena rather than simply accounting for existing phenomena. Third, we require that the theory "pass some new, and severe tests," that is, some predictions must be corroborated.

How do the two approaches measure up to these criteria? Both Skocpol and Trotsky introduce a "simple, new, and powerful, unifying idea." Skocpol proposes that successful revolutions occur as a result of structural circumstances, whereas Trotsky elaborates his theories of combined and uneven development and of permanent revolution to explain the causes and outcomes of different revolutions. Are their theories "independently testable," and do they "pass some new and severe tests"? Skocpol, as I shall try to show, balks at predicting novel phenomena and so avoids the challenge of severe tests, whereas Trotsky, in 1906, successfully predicts the outcome as well as the outbreak of the Russian Revolution but fails in his anticipation of revolution in the West.

With respect to Popper's criteria of scientific advance, Trotsky surpasses Skocpol. This is particularly surprising because—in contrast to Skocpol's detachment, aspirations to science, and claims to be true to "historical patterns"—Trotsky, as a leading participant in the events he analyzes, casts norms of positivist objectivity to the wind. He does not pursue the "treacherous impartiality" of the historian who would "stand upon the wall of a threatened city and behold at the same time the besiegers and the besieged" (Trotsky [1933]1977: 21).

The question then has to be posed: Why should the one have fallen short and the other succeeded in fulfilling Popper's second and third criteria? One answer is that Trotsky's innate genius allows him to stand head and shoulders above all of us, even Skocpol. But that's not very helpful; there's method even in genius. A second answer, the essential rival to the one given in this chapter, is that the execution of the method rather than the method itself is the source of the differences. This view has two variants. One might argue, as Stinchcombe (1978) has, that there is only one true method, the method of induction, and Trotsky executes it better than Skocpol. Or one might argue there are indeed two methods, but Trotsky carries out his method with greater finesse than Skocpol carries out hers. In this essay I hope to demonstrate the opposite. There are indeed two methodologies that hold different implications for the development of science. Skocpol carries out Mill's canons with consummate skill until the methodology breaks down, whereas Trotsky, at decisive points, deviates from the research program methodology. That is, neither follows a single method consistently—as I shall show, fortunately for Skocpol and unfortunately for Trotsky. Skocpol rises above her method while Trotsky sinks below his, yet Trotsky still makes the greater scientific advance, thereby underscoring the superiority of research programs to induction.

The inherent limitations of Mill's canons of induction compelled Skocpol to violate its principles at crucial points. However, to the extent that she actually does follow Mill's method, her work tends to suffer. The method of induction denies her the possibility of demonstrating the theory she claims to be demonstrating. Far from being a neutral algorithm for deriving theories from facts, the method of induction generates theories independent of facts. The method protects its self-generated theory from falsification and competition from other theories. This is encouraged by two methodological assumptions of induction, namely, that in the final analysis the facts (historical patterns) are uncontroversial and that they converge toward one unique theory. Finally, if the method embraces a conception of a one true history, it also tends toward a history of the past discontinuous with the present, a history that pretends to locate the historian outside history. In other words, I try to show that a grounding in the facts turns out to be a grounding in method that separates her from the facts. All this inhibits prediction of novel phenomena. That Skocpol was still able to develop such a powerful theory of revolutions is a tribute to her macrosociological imagination, which overrode Mill's methods at crucial points.

Trotsky's strength, on the other hand, lies in his implicit commitment to the methodology of research programs. He grounds himself in a Marxist research program that he elaborates in the light of anomalies, leading him to predictions, some of which are corroborated and others refuted. But refutation does not lead to the rejection of the Marxist research program but to the construction of new theories on the same Marxist foundation. By throwing up anomalies history is continually forcing the reconstruction of Marxism, leading, in turn, to the reconstruction of history but also of possible futures. In this conception the historian stands in the midst of history, caught between the future and the past, entering a dialogue with a developing research tradition about the potentialities of the surrounding world. Where Trotsky falls short of the methodology of the research program, it is to the detriment of his analysis. His insistence on the revolutionary character of the Western working class is the most startling case of primitive "exception barring"—the refusal to recognize a global counterexample—and certainly limited his contributions to the Marxist research program.

In short, Trotsky does better than Skocpol on Popper's criteria because Trotsky's modal methodology is that of the research program, while hers is that of induction. Skocpol's analysis shines when she repudiates Mill's canons of induction and pales when she embraces them, just as Trotsky's Marxism flourishes when he adheres to the methodology of research programs but regresses when he departs from its guiding principles. Therefore, emphasizing the inductive features of *States and Social Revolutions* and the research program features of *Results and Prospects*—as I must do in order to make my argument— inevitably presents Skocpol in a poorer and Trotsky in a richer light than is warranted by an overall assessment of their respective works.

The analysis that follows is a conjecture that calls for refutation, that is, for an alternative explanation for Trotsky's relative success. To facilitate such a refutation I have organized this chapter to highlight its general claims. The first part examines Skocpol's work, mainly *States and Social Revolutions,* and the second part examines Trotsky's work, mainly *Results and Prospects.* The two works are contrasted in terms of seven antimonies designed to reveal *the context of discovery*, where I examine how the methodology shapes theory (induction versus deduction, freezing history versus "nonrepeating" history, causal factors versus causal processes); *the context of justification*, where I examine how theories are validated (nonfalsifiability versus falsifiability, no predictions versus predictions); and *the context of the scientist*, where I examine how methodology situates the scientist in relation to the world being studied (history of the past versus history of the future, standing outside history versus standing at the center of history).[6]

SKOCPOL: LET THE FACTS SPEAK
FOR THEMSELVES
1. The Method of Induction

Skocpol writes that comparative historical analysis has "a long and distinguished pedigree in social science. Its logic is explicitly laid out by John Stuart Mill in his *A System of Logic*" (1979: 36; see also Theda Skocpol and Margaret Somers 1980; Skocpol 1984, chap. 11).

> Basically one tries to establish valid associations of potential causes with the given phenomenon one is trying to explain. There are two main ways to proceed. First, one can try to establish that several cases having in common the phenomenon one is trying to explain also have in common a set of causal factors, although they vary in other ways that might have seemed causally relevant. This approach is what Mill called the "Method of Agreement." Second, one can contrast the cases in which the phenomenon to be explained and the hypothesized causes are present to other cases in which the phenomenon and the causes are both absent, but which are otherwise as similar as possible to the positive cases. This procedure Mill labeled the "Method of Difference." (Skocpol 1979: 36)

Skocpol applies these two principles to discover "the generalizable logic at work in the entire set of revolutions under discussion."[7] She defines social revolution as "the coincidence of societal structural change with class upheaval; and the coincidence of political and social transformation" (Skocpol 1979: 4). For the purposes of her analysis of classical revolutions in France, China, and Russia, she reduces social revolutions to two components: political crisis and peasant revolt.

She begins with an examination of the common factors that give rise to a political crisis in France and China:

> [R]evolutionary crises emerged in both France and China because the Old Regimes came under unwonted pressures from more developed nations abroad, and because those pressures led to internal political conflicts between the autocratic authorities and the dominant classes. . . . [A]utocratic attempts at modernizing reforms from above in France and China . . . triggered the concerted political resistance of well-organized dominant class forces. In turn, because these forces possessed leverage within the formally centralized machineries of the monarchical states, their resistance disorganized those machineries. . . . [T]he successful opposition to autocratic reforms inadvertently opened the door to deepening revolutions in France and China alike. (1979: 80–81)

In Russia, however, the dominant classes were much weaker and succumbed to state reforms. "In Russia, a weak landed nobility could not block reforms from above. Yet the agrarian economy and class structure served as brakes upon state-guided industrialization, thus making it impossible for tsarist Russia to catch up economically and militarily with Imperial Germany, her chief potential enemy in the European states system" (Skocpol 1979: 99). But in all three cases the state was caught between international pressures calling for reform and the constraints of the agrarian structure, which obstructed such reform. "[R]evolutionary political crises emerged in all three Old Regimes because agrarian structures impinged upon autocratic and proto-bureaucratic state organizations in ways that blocked or fettered monarchical initiatives in coping with escalating international military competition in a world undergoing uneven transformation by capitalism" (99).

The task now is to show that both international pressure and an "organized and independent dominant class with leverage in the state" were necessary ingredients for political crisis. Her two contrasting cases are the Meiji Restoration (1868–73) in Japan and the reform movement in Germany (1807–15). In both cases, but for different reasons, the dominant class was either not powerful (Germany) or did not have leverage in the state (Japan) and therefore did not create a revolutionary political crisis. So the state was able to introduce reforms without sowing the seeds of revolution. Skocpol writes that "the different fates of these agrarian monarchical regimes faced with the challenges of adapting to the exigencies of international uneven development can be explained in large part by looking at the ways in which agrarian relations of production and landed dominant classes impinged upon state organizations" (Skocpol 1979: 110). So far so good, but note immediately that the contrasting cases do not demonstrate "international pressure" as necessary for the development of a revolutionary political crisis.

In the next chapter Skocpol examines the necessary conditions for the second component of revolution, peasant revolt. She proceeds as in the previous chapter, first with the method of agreement and then the method of difference. She shows how agrarian structures in France and Russia gave autonomy and solidarity to peasant communities, which combined with a political crisis of a repressive state to produce peasant revolt. She now has to demonstrate that both political crisis and peasant autonomy were necessary for peasant revolt. Let us first take political crisis. For long periods of French, Chinese, and Russian history peasant autonomy gave rise only to localized peasant rebellion. Only with a revolutionary political crisis does societal peasant revolt occur. To establish the necessity of peasant autonomy, on the other hand, Skocpol must produce cases where political crisis did not lead to peasant revolt: "Given that revolutionary political crises had deposed the absolute monarchs and disorganized centralized administrations and armies, agrarian class relations and local political arrangements in France and Russia afforded peasant communities sufficient solidarity and autonomy to strike out against the property and privileges of landlords. Conditions so conducive to peasant revolts were by no means present in all countries. And their absence could account for why a successful social revolution could not occur, even given a societal political crisis" (Skocpol 1979: 140). In both the political revolution in England and the failed social revolution in Germany (1848), there was a political crisis, but the crucial ingredient for peasant revolt, and thus for social revolution, was missing—an autonomous peasant community. Finally, Skocpol turns to the complex case of China, where the peasant community was only potentially autonomous. The potentiality was realized only after 1930 under the direction of a peasant army.

It appears that Skocpol has made a convincing argument that a successful social revolution involves an agrarian structure that is paralyzing a state's response to heightened international pressures, leading to a political crisis, which in turn triggers peasant revolt where peasant communities are autonomous and solidaristic. Only by combining her two sets of arguments into a single table do some flaws become visible (see table 5).

Establishing the necessity of community autonomy for peasant revolt depends on showing that where there is political crisis (a necessary ingredient for peasant revolt) but no community autonomy, there is no peasant revolt, that is, Germany in 1848

Table 5. *Skocpol's Arguments*

Y = Yes, Y* = Yes after 1930, N = No

	Method of Agreement for Successful Revolutions			Method of Difference for Unsuccessful Revolutions			
	France 1789	*China* 1949	*Russia* 1917	*Germany* 1807	*Japan* 1868	*England* 1640	*Germany* 1848
International pressure	Y	Y	Y	Y	Y	N	N
Organized and independent dominant class with leverage in state	Y	Y	N	N	N	Y	N
Prosperous agrarian economy	Y	N	N	Y	Y	Y	Y
Solidaristic and autonomous peasant communities	Y	Y*	Y	N	N	N	N
Political crisis	Y	Y	Y	N	N	Y	Y
Peasant revolt	Y	Y	Y	N	N	N	N

and England in 1640. But if there is political crisis in England in 1640 and Germany in 1848, then the original analysis of the conditions for political crisis, based on France, China, Russia, Japan, and Germany in 1807, no longer holds. For, examining England in 1640 and Germany in 1848, we discover that neither international conflict nor "an organized and independent dominant class with leverage in the state" is necessary for the development of a political crisis and therefore of social revolution. In short, the application of Mill's method to peasant revolt in Skocpol's chapter 3 undermines its application to political crisis in chapter 2.

Mill's method doesn't deliver what Skocpol claims for it— namely, a generalizable logic of revolutions.[8] While it is true that in France, China, and Russia the state was unable to respond effectively to international pressures because of constraints imposed by the agrarian structure, there is nothing in the data to suggest that either such agrarian constraint or international factors were necessary for a classical revolution.[9]

I am not suggesting that Skocpol's insight into the structural determinants of revolution is invalid. Not at all. It remains the "simple, new, and powerful unifying idea" that makes her book a classic. I am suggesting that it does not emerge from nor is it confirmed by Mill's principles of induction. Quite the opposite: applying those principles would seem to falsify her theory.

To sustain her conclusions Skocpol has had to drop her comparative historical method and effectively adopt a conjunctural analysis in which political crises have different causes, according to whether the outcome is a social revolution or not. There is, after all, no reason to believe that political crises have a unique set of causes. As I will show, this is an arbitrary assumption that derives from her application of Mill's method.

2. Freezing History

We have just seen how Skocpol's historical intuition gets the better of her proclaimed comparative historical method. At other points, however, her method gets the better of her intuition. In crucial respects her theory is an artifact of the two principles of induction. Method becomes a substitute for theory.

To carry out Mill's method of agreement she has to make several assumptions. First, the French, Chinese, and Russian revolutions are members of the same class of objects. She defines revolution as "the coincidence of political with social transformation" so that these three revolutions do indeed appear as particular examples of a single species.[10] Second, the same causal factors operate in all three revolutions, that is, there is indeed one theory of social revolutions. Third, the causal patterns leading to failed revolutions are different from the causal patterns leading to successful revolutions. That is, the distinction between revolutions that transform political structures and ones that transform social structures is causally salient (see Nichols 1986). These assumptions are tantamount to freezing world history for the three centuries from 1640 to 1947, in the sense that throughout this period revolutions are of a single kind and have the same causes. You might say Skocpol is keeping history constant or controlling for history. As a result, for example, she dismisses the rise of the working class in Petrograd and Moscow in 1917 as necessary for the Russian Revolution because a similar uprising was not found in the other two revolutions (1979: 113). This conclusion is an artifact of her methodology.[11] She does not justify it on the basis of an examination of the events of the Russian Revolution.

The methodological assumption of a common causal logic has a second consequence. It rules out the possibility that one revolution might inaugurate new conditions for subsequent revolutions. Here too Mill's method prevails over Skocpol's own judgment. Before getting on with the actual analysis of the revolutions, she writes in the introduction,

> [A]ttention should be paid to the effects of historical orderings and of world historical change. . . . One possibility is that actors in later revolutions may be influenced by developments in earlier ones; for example, the Chinese Communists became conscious emulators of the Bolsheviks and received, for a time, direct advice and aid from the Russian revolutionary regime. Another possibility is that crucial world-historically significant "breakthroughs"—such as the Industrial Revolution or the innovation of the Leninist form of party organization—may intervene between the occurrence of one broadly similar revolution and another. (Skocpol 1979: 23–24)

One might add, following Sewell (1985), that the French Revolution enlarged political discourse through the introduction of the ideas of revolution and nationalism. But the method of agreement leads Skocpol to smudge out any such historical emulation, borrowings, or breakthroughs. The revolutions have to be constituted as isolated and disconnected events in space and time. They are thereby wrenched out of the organically evolving world history of which they are a part.

3. No Causal Processes

I have argued that the application of Mill's principles of induction to the explanation of peasant revolt undermines its application to the explanation of political crises. On the one hand, in applying the method of difference to the causes of peasant revolt, Skocpol allows political crises to develop out of very different causal contexts. On the other hand, the application of the method of agreement to successful revolutions assumes, without empirical or theoretical justification, that for three centuries the causes of political crises are the same. I will now argue that this same inductive procedure also predisposes toward the central feature of her theory, namely, that revolutions are not "made" but "happen".

According to Mill, "the Law of Causation, the recognition of which is the main pillar of inductive science, is but the familiar truth, that invariability of succession is found by observation to obtain between every fact in nature and some other fact which has preceded it; independently of all considerations respecting the ultimate mode of production of phenomena, and of every other question regarding the nature of 'Things of Themselves'" (1888: 236). In seeking a causal logic of social revolutions one therefore looks for empirical regularities, or what Skocpol calls "causal associations" (1979: 39). That is to say, Skocpol looks for the antecedent conditions common to all successful revolutions and absent in failed revolutions. This use of Humean causality leaves two things unexplained: the existence of the antecedent conditions and the way they cause their outcome.[12] It is precisely these explanatory silences that predisposes toward the view that revolutions "happen".[13]

Her method leads to an account of the factors of social revolutions but not the social processes that make those factors causes.[14] To put it in slightly different terms, the canons of induction aim to discover the necessary conditions but not the processes that make those conditions sufficient for revolution. An examination of those social processes would involve examining how revolutions are made. In short, Skocpol concludes that revolutions "happen" because her method suppresses how they are "made", because it collapses necessary and sufficient conditions.

This is not to deny that Skocpol spends a great deal of energy describing the processes of revolution—in the analysis of the causes of peasant revolts or the perceptions of the French landed classes or the struggles among the landed classes in the explanation of the Chinese Revolution. Indeed, were it not for these rich and compelling treatments of revolutionary process, her book would never have received its well-deserved acclaim. This virtue exists despite, not because of, her declared method. The social processes stand outside that method, incidental to the methodological purpose, and therefore remain untheorized. She has no theory of how antecedent conditions lead to revolutionary processes.

If Mill's method, far from being a neutral instrument for deriving a theory from the facts, smuggles in its own undefended theoretical assumptions, a change in method should give different results. In examining the outcomes of revolutions, Skocpol drops the strict application of the method of agreement and of difference for the looser strategy in which the ways of the old regime collapsed, and in which the timing and nature of peasant revolt, old regime socioeconomic legacies, and world historical events set in motion social struggles among political leaders trying "to assert and make good their claims to state sovereignty" (Skocpol 1979: 164). Her explanations are "overidentified," with more independent variables than cases. With so many explanatory factors to manipulate she cannot fail to account for any variation in state building, particularly when it is defined as vaguely as "the consolidation of new state organizations" (163). If her analysis of outcomes does not have the virtue of boldness and precision, does it at least avoid the pitfalls of her theory of revolutionary causes, namely, the absence of causal mechanisms and the artificial separation of cause and consequence?

In principle, yes; in practice, no. Even such a loose use of the method of agreement and difference compels her to locate the differences and similarities of revolutionary outcomes in the exigencies of the revolutionary crisis. So she is forced to present a picture in which the outcome was already present in the crisis. Stalin's victory was inevitable because, in the circumstances of socialism in one country, his economic and political strategy had greater appeal to political elites. We hear nothing of the struggles between Stalin and the Left Opposition, while the struggle between Stalin and the Right Opposition is reduced to the lack of realism in Bukharin's economic strategy. But why, then, did Trotsky not triumph in 1924, when he was already advocating collectivization and central planning? Why do we have to wait for Stalin to do this in 1929? Although Skocpol acknowledges their importance, her comparative method does not encourage an analysis of the struggles either within the state or outside the state. In her conception, therefore, revolutionary outcomes are immanent in the revolutionary crisis, while revolutions happen as a result of a constellation of structural factors. So history is reduced to either conditional laws or accidents. In both cases the method leaves no room for human agency.

4. Nonfalsifiability

We have seen how the method of induction leads, in some instances to its own rejection (section 1) and in other instances to its own arbitrary explanations (sections 2 and 3). So much for the context of discovery—what about the context of justification? Skocpol immunizes her methodologically induced theory against falsification by two different methodological stratagems: by assuming that only one theory can fit the facts and by refusing to entertain predictions. I deal with the first in this section and the second in the next section.

How does Skocpol claim the superiority of her theory over others? Only in her introduction does she deal with other theories in a sustained fashion. There she argues by assertion. The "purposive image" of revolutions falsely assumes the necessity of value consensus for societal order (Skocpol 1979: 16). Or relative deprivation theory is too general to disprove, although she actually invokes a variant of it herself when she gives an account of peasant rebellions (34, 121–23). There is in fact no adjudication process among different theories. She assumes that if her theory is correct, then others must be wrong, that is to say, she assumes a body of unambiguous "preexisting facts" that, following the right method, uniquely determine theories. The assumption that a body of indisputable facts provides the bedrock of knowledge is fallacious for two reasons. First, facts themselves are not "given." Historical facts, in particular, are created out of a vast body of past events. Second, different theories might fit the same facts equally well.[15] I deal with each fallacy in turn.

Facts are selected. For example, to demonstrate that her own structural theory fits the facts Skocpol pays little attention to historical facts that would address the importance of the legitimacy of states or to the role of political parties. She ignores the very facts that would address the validity of competing theories. But more important, facts are already interpretations. Here Skocpol's work is remarkable for ignoring the controversies that are the bread and water of historians' debates. François Furet's (1981) revisionist treatment of different interpretations of the French Revolution shows just how debates about "the facts" have been orchestrated around political interests in the present. According to Furet himself, the French Revolution was not a revolution at all in Skocpol's sense of a "coincidence of political with social transformation." He would argue that her interpretation mistakes the mythology of the revolution for its reality and that what marks the revolution is not a transformation of social structure but the "collective crystallization" of a new political discourse. The issue here is not who is right, Soboul, Lefebvre, Mazauric, or Furet, but simply that for Skocpol the facts have a certain obviousness that they don't for historians. This becomes particularly problematic when she assumes the existence or non-existence of a societal political crisis or makes claims about "international pressure." The irony is that, while Skocpol follows the method of induction and insists that historical patterns have their own voice, she pays little attention to the controversies that rage around the historical "facts." She is forced into this blindness in order to get her induction machine off the ground.

In relying on the method of induction, Skocpol not only assumes that the facts are unproblematic but also that, once constituted, they give rise to a unique theory. Alternative theories are compatible with the same "facts." For example, Stinchcombe's (1978, chap. 2) reconstruction of Tocqueville's and Trotsky's accounts of the French and Russian revolutions is a variant of the weak state theory. Revolutions happen when regimes become ineffective and alternative centers of power emerge. Does Skocpol provide any evidence that this theory is incorrect?

If it explains both the successful and the unsuccessful cases, then how can she claim the superiority of her theory?

Mill's canons of induction can generate any number of causal explanations from the same facts but cannot discriminate among them on the basis of their truth content. Accordingly, Morris Cohen and Ernest Nagel (1934, chap. 13) conclude that the method is useless as a means of discovery or proof. Instead they suggest that it be adapted to eliminate rather than confirm proposed theories. In other words, Skocpol might have been better off using Mill's method to eliminate Marxist or structural functionalist theories of revolution as violating accepted facts while presenting her theory as a bold conjecture. Instead she does the opposite: dismisses alternative theories by fiat and misconstrues induction as confirming the superiority of her own.[16]

5. No Predictions

Commitment to principles of induction allows Skocpol to protect her theory from competition with other theories, but does she also protect her theory from facts? Does she make predictions that might be falsified? I have already referred to the passage at the beginning of her book where she lays out her goal: "[T]his book is concerned ... primarily with understanding and explaining the generalizable logic at work in the entire set of revolutions under discussion" (Skocpol 1979: 6). At the end she writes: "Such broad resemblances raise the issue of the generalizability of the arguments presented in this book. Can they be applied beyond the French, Russian, and Chinese cases? In a sense, the answer is unequivocally 'no.' One cannot mechanically extend the specific causal arguments that have been developed for France, Russia and China into a 'general theory of revolutions' applicable to all other modern social revolutions" (288). Instead of confronting predictions derived from her explanation of classical revolutions, Skocpol develops the rudiments of an alternative theory of modern social revolutions, suited to the political and economic conditions of 1949–79.

Dividing history into two periods, one that is three centuries long (the era of classical revolutions), in which one set of causal factors operates, and one that is thirty years long (the era of modern revolutions) in which a different set of causal factors operates, is certainly a convenient strategy for saving her theory. But it also threatens to undermine her theory. For how does one justify dividing up the entire period from the English Revolution to the present into two rather than, say, four segments? Why isn't there a different causal logic for each of her classical revolutions? After all, the similarity of causal logic was a methodological rather than a theoretical stricture.

It seems that there are only two ways to justify this freezing of history into two blocks. She could claim that modern revolutions are not social revolutions. Or she could derive a set of more general uniformities that encompasses the logics of both the modern period and the classical period. Skocpol explicitly repudiates the first alternative in her subsequent analysis of the Iranian Revolution. She identifies it as a social revolution and acknowledges that her earlier theory doesn't work: Shi'a Islam was an essential ingredient in an urban-based revolt. "Fortunately [*sic*], in *States and Social Revolutions* I explicitly denied the possibility of the fruitfulness of a general causal theory of revolutions that would apply across all times and places" (Skocpol 1979: 268).

What about the second justification for distinguishing between modern and classical social revolutions? Are there any underlying uniformities that their causal logics share? She recognizes this strategy and draws the following final conclusion from her analysis: "It suggests that in future revolutions, as in those of the past, the realm of the state is likely to be central" (1979: 293). Did she have to undertake such an elaborate historical analysis to come to this conclusion? Indeed, isn't the centrality of the state embedded in her very definition of social revolution?

How might she have proceeded if she were interested in developing a causal logic that would span both modern and classical revolutions? According to Skocpol, one of the critical aspects that separates the modern period from the classical one is the ability of states to counter revolutions with modern military technology and organization (1979: 289). This would suggest making state capacity a critical variable in her theory of classical revolutions. Throughout the text Skocpol does indeed make reference to the ability of states to weather storms of international pressure, resistance from the landed classes, and pressure from peasant rebellions. She notes, for examples, that after 1750 England's war-making capacity was greater than France's and that Prussia was financially and militarily stronger in the 1848 crisis than was France in 1789 or Russia in 1917. She calls attention to the strength of the Tsarist state vis-à-vis its own landed classes and, before the Crimean War, vis-à-vis other major powers. However, she does not theorize the concept of "state capacity" so as to afford her a link between modern and classical revolutions. Such an approach might, for example, have thrown some light on her original interest in the prospects for revolution in South Africa.[17]

Theories can always be rescued when they fail to correspond to some old or new set of facts. Indeed, according to Lakatos (1976), that is the essence of the growth of scientific knowledge. What is important, however, is the way we deal with such counterexamples. "Monster-barring" (redefining the meaning of social revolution, which Skocpol repudiates) or "exception-barring" (limiting the scope of the original theory to classical revolutions) strategies reduce the empirical content of the theory, whereas "lemma-incorporation" (building in an auxiliary theory of state capacity) would enrich the original theory. Skocpol's division of the history of the world into two—one where her theory works and one where it doesn't—is not a stratagem that furthers our understanding of revolutions. But it does follow from induction's suspicion of prediction and even more fundamentally from its interest in improving conjectures by an increase in truth rather than by the reduction of falsehood. Induction seeks to improve conjectures by avoiding refutations. It purges "the growth of knowledge from the horror of counter-example" (Lakatos 1976: 37).

6. History of the Past

We have seen that applying the method of agreement and method of difference does not discriminate among a number of theories and introduces arbitrary and undefended theoretical presuppositions of its own while creating an air of certainty by insulating the theory from both falsification and competition from other theories. These problems derive from the assumption that history is a "corpus of ascertained facts," a bedrock of "irreducible and stubborn facts" (Carr 1961: 6;

Whitehead 1925: 15). This inductivist school of history sees the present as a vantage point of objectivity from which we can infer generalizations about the past. The more remote the region of the past we investigate, the greater the potential for objective history. Insofar as she is committed to induction, Skocpol assumes that the past speaks to us as a single message, or a series of messages that converge on some truth, that we can in fact have a history of the past independent of the shifting present. The barrier she erects between classical revolutions and modern revolutions is only the most startling testimony to her separation of the past from the present. Her refusal to extract any tangible lessons from her analysis of social revolutions equally cuts off the past from the future. But history is inescapably the connection between the past and a future emerging out of the present. "It requires us to join the study of the dead and of the living" (Bloch 1953: 47). The present constitutes the lens through which we can see the past; it generates the problems in whose solution the past can assist; it supplies the vocabulary, the concepts, and the theories through which we translate the past into history. As Croce put it, "All history is 'contemporary history.'"

Even if Mill's method calls for it, Skocpol herself knows better than to separate the past from the present. In the opening page of her introductory chapter she justifies her interest in revolutions as follows: "[They] have given rise to models and ideals of enormous international impact and appeal—especially where the transformed societies have been large and geopolitically important, actual or potential Great Powers" (1979: 3). As ever, Skocpol's strength lies in her repudiation of Mill's canons of induction.

7. Standing outside History

Separating the analysis of the past from the present is necessary to stand outside history as an objective observer. Skocpol, however, makes no such claim to stand outside history. In the preface to *States and Social Revolutions,* she describes the formative experiences that led her to study social revolutions: political engagement in the early 1970s, the puzzle of South Africa, and her exploration of the historical origins of the Chinese Revolution. In her compelling reflections on her career, Skocpol (1988) again emphasizes the historical and biographical context to explain how it was that she came to undertake such an ambitious project for her dissertation.

But these reflections only underline the point I am trying to make. While Skocpol recognizes that both she and her theory bridge the past to the future, this recognition is presented as incidental background information, relegated to the preface, to introductory remarks, or to an autobiographical statement but abandoned as she gets on with the method of agreement and difference.[18] The interaction of past and present, of social scientist and the world she inhabits, is included only to be discounted. It is irrelevant to the scientific process, the serious business of deriving theory from data. And yet we saw in section 1 that her method, far from explaining how she obtained her theory of revolutions, actually refuted that theory. In other words, Mill's canons conceal rather than reveal the source of her theory.

So where does her theory come from? We may now conjecture that wider social and political currents of the civil rights movement and then the post-Vietnam era also insinuate themselves into her theory. It is not farfetched to argue that the emphasis on international factors reflects not just a critical appropriation of Barrington Moore and Marxism but the growing consciousness of the rise and then precipitous fall of U.S. dominance in the international arena, just as the autonomy of the state reflects an executive seemingly beyond the control of the public. Her structuralism could be traced to a reaction to the social movements of the 1960s in which she participated, movements that carried with them illusions of dramatic change. Finally, the very adoption of a conventional scientific mode to present such a challenge to reigning orthodoxies might be seen as a strategic move for an "uppity" graduate student to gain credibility within the sociological profession. The irony is that Skocpol *is* sensitive to currents around her but denies their contribution by falsely presenting their refracted presence in her theory as the product of her method.

8. The Paradox of Induction

States and Social Revolutions is a rich and complex work. It is not univocal but multivocal. At one level it is a careful and determined application of Mill's canons of induction. This is certainly how Skocpol announces her method and organizes her analysis. It is her scientific register. Closer inspection reveals two other, unannounced registers. When the generic method, in which each case is an exemplar of a general law or pattern, breaks down, she substitutes the genetic method in which the causal logic is particular to each case. Second, previously postulated theories insinuate themselves without justification, as though they emerged from the application of Mill's canons or as macrosociological imagination. Ironically, these deviations from Mill's method are the source of her "simple, new, and powerful, unifying idea." Her work suffers to the extent that she rigidly adheres to the method of induction. But for my purposes here her doggedness has the advantage of laying bare the limitations of induction. I now summarize these limitations:

Context of discovery. In pretending that theory emerges from the facts, induction hides other sources of theory, namely, sociological intuitions and methodological rules. Rather than elaborating theory as a logical structure with empirical implications, induction presents it as a summary of the facts.

Context of justification. Should further facts appear to refute the theory, the theory is not reconstructed but simply limited in its scope. There is little attempt to put theories to the more severe test of elaborating their implications for the anticipation of novel facts.

Context of scientist. Because facts are given and relatively unproblematical, they are best grasped through methods that strip the researcher of the "blinders," "lenses," "biases," and so on that stem from identification with historical traditions and involvements in the present.

We are left with two paradoxes. Induction starts out from preexisting facts but ends up with unexplicated preexisting theories. Induction strips the scientist of biases and blinders but overlooks the biases and blinders of method. If preexisting facts are an illusory foundation for social science, does a foundation in preexisting theory fare any better?

TROTSKY: MARXISM IS A METHOD OF ANALYSIS
1. The Method of Deduction

Skocpol situates herself in a positivist tradition and induces her structural theory from "the facts." Trotsky situates himself within a Marxist research program and deduces the direction of history.[19]

> All scientific research programmes may be characterized by their *"hard core."* The negative heuristic of the programme forbids us to direct the *modus tollens* at this "hard core." Instead, we must use our ingenuity to articulate or even invent "auxiliary hypotheses," which form a *protective belt* around this core, and we must redirect the *modus tollens* to *these*. It is this protective belt of auxiliary hypotheses which has to bear the brunt of tests and get adjusted and re-adjusted, or even completely replaced, to defend the thus-hardened core. A research programme is successful if it leads to a progressive problemshift; unsuccessful if it leads to a degenerating problemshift.[20]

Trotsky takes as his irrefutable hard core Marx's famous summary of his studies in the preface to *The Contribution to the Critique of Political Economy*. There Marx describes how history progresses from one mode of production to another. We can divide it into the three postulates of historical materialism:

> At a certain stage of their development, the material productive forces of society come in conflict with the existing relations of production. . . . From forms of development of the productive forces these relations turn into their fetters. . . .
> Then begins an epoch of social revolution. . . . In considering such transformations a distinction should always be made between the material transformation of the economic conditions of production, which can be determined with the precision of

natural science, and the legal, political, religious, aesthetic or philosophic—in short, ideological forms in which men become conscious of this conflict and fight it out. . . .

No social order ever perishes before all the productive forces for which there is room in it have developed; and new, higher relations of production never appear before the material conditions of their existence have matured in the womb of the old society itself. (Marx [1859]1970: 19–23)

This is obviously not the only way of constructing the hard core of a Marxist research program. It is the one, however, that Trotsky defends against refutation through the development of his theory of "permanent revolution" and that leads him to predict that socialist revolution will first break out in a country of the second rank rather than in the most advanced capitalist country, as Marx had anticipated.

In *Results and Prospects,* written in 1906, Trotsky defends the three postulates as follows. First, "Marxism long ago predicted the inevitability of the Russian Revolution, which was found to break out as a result of the conflict between capitalist development and forces of ossified absolutism" (1969: 36). Trotsky describes how Russian absolutism sowed the seeds and then stifled the growth of capitalism in absolutism's attempt to defend itself against European states that had grown up on more advanced economic bases. As international rivalry intensified, the Russian state swallowed up more of the surplus and at the same time was unable to develop the parliamentary forms necessary for the growth of capitalism. "Thus, the administrative, military and financial power of absolutism, thanks to which it could exist in spite of social development, not only did not exclude the possibility of revolution, as was the opinion of the liberals, but, on the contrary, made revolution the only way out" (44).

Second, what was to be the character of the revolution? Following Marx, the revolutionary outbreak "depends directly not upon the level attained by the productive forces but upon relations in the class struggle, upon the international situation, and finally, upon a number of subjective factors." (Trotsky 1969: 63). In Russia the working class is the only class with the capacity and the will to carry out a bourgeois revolution against an absolutist monarchy but, once that is accomplished, it must advance toward socialism, and the success of this is predicated on support from socialist revolution in the West. Therefore, third, the objective prerequisites for socialism are in place in advanced capitalist countries, whereas the subjective prerequisites are to be found in Russia. The theory of the permanent revolution—uninterrupted revolution from absolutism toward socialism in Russia and its triggering of revolution in other countries—coordinates the two sets of prerequisites.

We see that Trotsky's theory of permanent revolution seeks to protect the hard core of Marxism from refutation by the failure of revolution in the most advanced capitalist countries. His theory of permanent revolution focuses on the factors that Skocpol also stresses, namely, international relations and the autonomy of the state. Both also recognize the critical role of the peasant revolt while agreeing that peasants, in Trotsky's words, "are absolutely incapable of taking up an *independent* political role" (1969: 72) or, in Skocpol's words, that peasants "struggle for concrete goals. . . . . . without becoming a nationally organized class-for-themselves" (1979: 114). They differ precisely over the role of the working class. "In order to realise the Soviet state," Trotsky writes, "there was required a drawing together and mutual penetration of two factors belonging to completely different historic species: a peasant war—that is, a movement characteristic of the dawn of bourgeois development—and a proletarian insurrection, the movement signalising its decline. That is the essence of 1917" ([1933]1977: 72). From where does their difference in the assessment of the importance of the working class come?

2. History Never Repeats Itself

Skocpol removes the working class from any critical role in the causes of the revolution through methodological fiat, by assuming that all three revolutions are caused by the same factors. Thus if the working class is not central to one of these revolutions, for example, the Chinese, then it cannot be necessary for the others. Where Skocpol's method leads her to regard the French, Russian, and Chinese revolutions as species of the same phenomenon, having the same antecedent conditions, Trotsky sees different forces operating to produce different outcomes. Where Skocpol freezes history, for Trotsky "history does not repeat itself. However much one may compare the Russian Revolution with the Great Revolution, the former can never be transformed into the latter. The 19th century has not passed in vain."[21]

What lies behind his assertions? What is the positive heuristic, "the partially articulated set of suggestions or hints on how to change, develop the 'refutable variants' of the research-programme, how to modify, sophisticate, the 'refutable' protective belt" (Lakatos 1978: 50)? For Trotsky the central principle that inspires the Marxist problem-solving machinery is the view that history is the history of class struggle. Trotsky adopts as an "exemplar," or "model," Marx's analyses of the abortive revolution of 1848 in France in *Class Struggles in France* and *The Eighteenth Brumaire*. But Trotsky goes beyond them in trying to show how the development of capitalism on a world scale creates a different balance of class forces in different nations.

In the French Revolution the people—petty bourgeois, workers, and peasants—were united under Jacobin leadership to overthrow the feudal order. The French Revolution was indeed a national revolution in which bourgeois society settled its accounts with the dominant feudal lords of the past. But capitalism was still embryonic and the proletariat weak and insignificant. The failed German revolution of 1848 reflected the development of capitalism within a distinctive social structure.

> In 1848 the bourgeoisie was already unable to play a comparable role. It did not want and was not able to undertake the revolutionary liquidation of the social system that stood in its path to power. We know now *why* that was so. Its aim was—and of this it was perfectly conscious—to introduce into the old system the necessary guarantees, not for its political domination, but merely for a sharing of power with the forces of the past. It was meanly wise through the experience of the French bourgeoisie, corrupted by its treachery and frightened by its failures. It not only failed to lead the masses in storming the old order, but placed its back against this order so as to repulse the masses who were pressing it forward. . . . The revolution could only be carried out not by it but against it. (1969: 55–56)

All other classes—urban petty bourgeois, peasantry, intellectuals, and workers—were too weak and divided to carry through a revolution against feudal absolutism. In particular, "The antagonism between the proletariat and the bourgeoisie, even within the national framework of Germany, had gone too far to allow the bourgeoisie fearlessly to take up the role of national hegemon, but not sufficiently to allow the working class to take up that role" (57).

If the development of capitalism in Germany produced a stalemate of class forces, in Russia it shifted the balance of power in the direction of the working class. As a late developer, Russian industry had been infused with foreign capital and nurtured by the state. The state itself, facing international political competition from technically and militarily more advanced states, squeezed the rural economy and suffocated the nascent capitalism. The result was a weak bourgeoisie dependent upon the state and foreign banks. At the same time, by skipping stages of development and transplanting the most advanced forms of industry directly onto Russian soil, capitalism concentrated workers into large factories. Recently torn from their feudal moorings and with only weak craft traditions to contain depredations from the state, the new working class could resist successfully only through revolutionary insurgency. Both the objective necessity of a revolution against absolutism as well as its subjective possibility were laid by the international development of capitalism and its grafting onto the backward Russian social structure.[22]

In explaining the different outcomes of the French, Russian, and failed German revolutions, Trotsky develops his second theory, that of the combined and uneven development of capitalism on a world scale, and how this sets parameters on the form of class struggles. Capitalism continually expands and transplants itself onto foreign soils and combines with different social structures to produce different constellations of class forces, so that revolutionary changes take on distinctive national characters. "It would be a stupid mistake simply to identify our revolution with the events of 1789–93 or of 1848. . . . The Russian Revolution has a quite peculiar character, which is the result of the peculiar trend of our entire social and historical development, and which in its turn open before us quite new historical prospects" (Trotsky 1969: 36). The theories of permanent revolution on the one hand and of combined and uneven development on the other support each other in protecting the theses of historical materialism—the hard core of the Marxist research program.

3. Causal Processes

Earlier I showed how Skocpol's method of induction reduced causal processes to causal associations, causal forces to antecedent conditions. Her method led her to behead the second element of the Marxian negative heuristic concerning the role of objective and subjective forces in history: "Men make their own history, but they do not make it just as they please; they do not make it under circumstances chosen by themselves, but under circumstances directly found, given and transmitted from the past" (Marx ([1852]1963: 15). This is the leitmotif for Trotsky's analysis of history, except that he seeks to develop further Marx's ideas about the development of the conditions handed down from the past, the way these shape class struggles, and how these in turn reshape conditions. Where in Marx the analysis of history as made by people was often separated from the analysis of history as unfolding behind the backs of people, Trotsky brings the two closer together.

In *The History of the Russian Revolution* Trotsky vividly portrays the crumbling of the Russian class structure and the rising fortune of the revolution as the interweaving of micro and macro social processes. There is no space to do justice to Trotsky's majestic analysis here. Arthur Stinchcombe's fascinating rendition of Trotsky's theory stresses the following: The provisional government loses its authority because of declining effectiveness and the development of alternative centers of power in which peasants and workers can participate. The erosion of government authority affects the working class, the soldiers, and the peasantry differently at different times, differences that can be explained in terms of their social, political, or geographical position. As institutions lose their purposive character, they become social fields of open struggle. Finally, Stinchcombe points to Trotsky's diagnosis of the accumulation of microprocesses that change the revolution's momentum at critical junctures as well as opening up new historical possibilities for contending forces.[23]

Instead of Skocpol's artificial detachment of cause and consequence—revolution, its antecedents, and its outcomes—Trotsky focuses on the social process of revolution. "The pulse or event conception of cause, popularized by Hume and by the psychological experiment, fits very uncomfortably with Trotsky's mode of analysis. There is no event that causes the army to be less ready to go into rebellion than the workers, but 'molecular processes' of contrasting speeds" (Stinchcombe 1978: 68). He carries forward Marx's project of establishing the microfoundations of a macrosociology, of understanding how individuals make history but not necessarily in ways of their own choosing.[24]

The molecular processes that set the revolution in motion also propel it into the future. As Trotsky anticipated as early as 1906, in Russia, once the proletariat comes to power with the support of the peasantry, it cannot stop at a democratic revolution but will have to go forward toward collectivism and neutralize opposition from the peasantry (1969, chap. 6). "The very fact of the proletariat's representatives entering the government, not as powerless hostages, but as the leading force, destroys the border-line between maximum and minimum programme: that is to say it *places collectivism on the order of the day.* The point at which the proletariat is held up in its advance in this direction depends upon the relation of forces, but in no way upon the original intentions of the proletarian party" (80). The duality of revolutionary process, namely, the concentration of bourgeois and proletarian revolution in a single process, would define the distinctive problems of the new socialist regime. A ruling caste, a dictatorship over the proletariat, would emerge because the forces of production are underdeveloped, because sections of the peasantry, together with elements of the landed classes, bourgeoisie, and petty bourgeoisie, would combine forces to overthrow the socialist order, and because the working class would be decimated and exhausted in the ensuing civil war, thus allowing the detachment of the communist leadership from its working-class base. This is the scenario Trotsky anticipates in 1906 and paints more vividly thirty years later in *The Revolution Betrayed.*

Thus where Skocpol sees the rise of Stalinism as immanent within the peculiar historical circumstances in which the revolution was forged, Trotsky sees these as the context of struggles, reconstructed in each subsequent critical conjuncture. Indeed, following Deutscher (1963: 110), one can see the end of the New

Economic Policy (NEP) and the subsequent imposition of forced industrialization and collectivization in 1929 and 1930 as continuing the permanent revolution that Trotsky had anticipated in 1906. Already in exile, Trotsky himself did not regard Stalin's left course in this light. He was too strongly imbued with Lenin's vision that once the socialist revolution had taken place, it would evolve toward communism. He saw the continuity of the permanent revolution in its international dimension. Its failure there, however, had driven the permanent revolution inward, where it took the form of Stalin's revolution from above.

Trotsky allows subjective as well as objective factors to pave the way to the future. Soviet Thermidor under the flag of socialism in one country was only one of several responses that emerged in the decade after the revolution. His own position of fomenting international revolution was one alternative, and Bukharin's advocacy of the continuation of NEP was another. Writing in 1936, Trotsky interprets the "zig-zags" in the postrevolutionary period as a social process, enabling him to anticipate the future. "The scientific task, as well as the political, is not to give a finished definition to an unfinished process, but to follow all its stages, separate its progressive from its reactionary tendencies, expose their mutual relations, foresee possible variants of development, and find in this foresight a basis for action" (Trotsky [1936]1972: 255–56).

4. Falsifiability

By taking the facts as given and by assuming that only one theory can fit the facts, Skocpol justifies shunning any trial of validity between her theory and other theories and closing herself off to refutation. Trotsky, on the other hand, roots himself in Marxism and sees his task as resolving the anomalies generated by Marxism, that is, turning counterexamples into corroborations of the Marxist hard-core premises by building new theories. The positive heuristic saves the scientist from drowning in the "ocean of anomalies" that all research programs face (Lakatos 1978: 50). The point is to select among the anomalies those whose solution one expects to advance the research program most successfully. The development of a research program therefore depends on the articulation and clarification of its apparent refutations and on a mechanism for ordering and then digesting them.

Different belts of Marxism are defined by the anomalies they seek to solve. German Marxism had to confront the expanding working-class support for a social democratic party that did not challenge the framework of capitalism. Out of this emerge three major constellations of theory—those of Kautsky, Luxemburg, and Bernstein. Russian Marxism confronted the opposite anomaly: a strong and radical working class in a nation that was economically and politically backward. "In spite of the fact that the productive forces of the United States are ten times as great as those of Russia, nevertheless the political role of the Russian proletariat, its influence on the politics of the world in the near future are incomparably greater than in the case of the proletariat of the United States" (Trotsky 1969: 65).

As I have shown, Trotsky sought to reconstruct Marx's view, explicit in the three volumes of *Capital,* that the most advanced society shows to the more backward societies their future, "De Te Fabula Narratur," and that therefore socialist revolution will occur first in the capitalist country whose forces of production are the most developed. For Marx's linear view of history

Trotsky substitutes the theory of combined and uneven development of capitalism:

> The laws of history have nothing in common with a pedantic schematism. Unevenness, the most general law of the historic process, reveals itself most sharply and complexly in the destiny of the backward countries. Under the whip of external necessity their backward culture is compelled to make leaps. From the universal law of unevenness thus derives another law which, for lack of a better name, we may call the law of combined development—by which we mean the drawing together of the different stages of the journey, a combining of separate steps, an amalgam of archaic with more contemporary forms. Without this law, to be taken of course in its whole material content, it is impossible to understand the history of Russia, and indeed of any country of the second, third or tenth cultural class. ([1933]1977: 27)

The political counterpart to the theory of combined and uneven development of capitalism is his theory of permanent revolution.

If it can be said that Trotsky's two theories contain "simple, new, and powerful, unifying ideas" and that they normalize certain anomalies in the Marxist research program, do they do this by an arbitrary patching up or do they anticipate novel facts? And if they predict novel facts, are these then corroborated? These are Popper's second and third criteria for the advance of scientific knowledge. They also demarcate "mature" from "immature" science, progressive from degenerating research programs (Lakatos 1978: 86–90).

5. Predictions

Trotsky shares none of Skocpol's hesitation about making predictions. Writing in 1906, Trotsky not only anticipated the Russian Revolution but the processes whereby it would take place as well as its outcomes. We have already seen how Trotsky predicted the unfolding of the Russian Revolution as a permanent revolution in which "the proletariat, on taking power, must, by the very logic of its position, inevitably be urged toward the introduction of state management of industry" (1969: 67). But the Russian Revolution had to be a permanent revolution not only in the sense of moving from bourgeois democratic to socialist goals but also in the sense of moving from Russian soil to the advanced capitalist countries of Europe. *"Without the direct State support of the European proletariat the working class of Russia cannot remain in power and convert its temporary domination into a lasting socialist dictatorship.* Of this there cannot for one moment be any doubt" (105; emphasis in original). The fate of the Russian Revolution is tied to the fate of the revolution in Europe.

Trotsky fulfills Popper's second and third criteria for the advance of knowledge and Lakatos's requirement that a progressive research program is one that goes beyond existing facts to predict new ones. If Trotsky is successful in anticipating the Russian Revolution, he is wide of the mark in his anticipation of revolution in Western Europe. Where did Trotsky slip up? He argues that the Russian Revolution could spread into Europe in a number of ways. "The Russian revolution would certainly give a strong impetus to the proletarian movement in the rest of Europe, and in consequence of the struggle that would flare up, the proletariat might come to power in Germany." (1969: 105). The Russian Revolution would most likely spread to Poland, forcing the German and Austrian states to declare war against the new powers. "But a European war inevitably means a European revolution," Trotsky says (1969: 112). Finally, France's implication in the Russian economy would mean that a declaration of state bankruptcy in Russia could create such an economic crisis in France as to lead to revolution there.

Behind the optimism lies the assumption that the working class in Europe was prepared to grab the earliest opportunity for revolution. What evidence does Trotsky offer in 1906? He refers to the growing strength of social democracy. Here he distinguishes between the conservatism of European socialist parties and the radicalism of the workers who therefore would eventually have to take history into their own hands. Deutscher (1954: 293) refers to this view as a "necessary illusion" without which Lenin and Trotsky would never have had the courage to lead the revolution in Russia. Despite setback after setback, Trotsky would retain what Krupskaya referred to as Trotsky's underestimation of the apathy of the working class.

Such revolutionary optimism can also be found in Trotsky's treatises on fascism written while in exile on the Isle of Prinkipo. Between 1930 and 1933 Trotsky's writings predicted the rise of German fascism and the threat this would pose to international peace and the socialist movement. While almost everyone else was belittling changes afoot in Germany, Trotsky saw their true significance in prophetic detail. Relentlessly but without success he fought against the Comintern's identification of fascism and social democracy, a strategy that divided the 4.5 million Communists against the socialists when only their unity could have saved German civilization from barbarism. To the end Trotsky had faith that the German working class would rise up against Hitler and forestall the tragedy Trotsky had anticipated.

History turned out otherwise. Trotsky's analyses were time and again shipwrecked on the rock of the Western proletariat.[25] It would be another Marxist, Antonio Gramsci, who would carry Marxism forward, incorporating Trotsky's understandings into a broader interpretation that would try to come to terms with the failure of the revolution in the West. In his *Prison Notebooks* Gramsci takes Trotsky to task for extending the theory of permanent revolution to modern European societies. The Paris Commune spells the end of a period when frontal assault on the state was possible. After 1870 in Europe generally, the extension of education, elaboration of legal institutions, and, above all, emergence of political parties and trade unions—in short, the development of civil society—require the building up of ideological and organizational forces in a "trench warfare" before conquering the state. Following Gramsci's military metaphors, the war of position takes precedence over the war of movement. Trotsky's theory of permanent revolution reflects "the general-economic-cultural-social conditions in a country in which the structures of national life are embryonic and loose, and incapable of becoming 'trench or fortress. . . . In Russia, the state was everything, civil society was primordial and gelatinous: in the West there was a proper relation between State and civil society, and when the State trembled a sturdy structure of civil society was at once revealed" (Gramsci 1971: 256, 238).

This is obviously no place to enter into a discussion of Gramsci's theory of ideology and politics. But two points are worthy of note. Gramsci's theory throws into relief Skocpol's failure to theorize the differences between modern and classical revolutions. Rather than breaking the past from the present, Gramsci uses the past to highlight what is distinctive about the present and future. Gramsci's theory also demonstrates the progressive development of a research tradition. Gramsci builds a new belt of theory to protect the Marxist core against anomalies generated by classical Marxism of the Second International and Russian Marxism as well as pointing to the future. These anomalies—the biggest was the failure of revolution in the West—are not refutations of Marxism but puzzles requiring the elaboration of the Marxist research program.

My introduction of Gramsci to illustrate the elaboration of a research tradition should not be misunderstood. I am not using Gramsci to load the dice in favor of Trotsky as against Skocpol. Trotsky stands by himself. His superiority cannot be reduced to a sensitivity to molecular processes but involves a self-conscious commitment to a research tradition, forcing him to wrestle with well-defined anomalies and thereby leading him to create new theories with new predictions.

6. History of the Future

In seeking a history of the past separated from the future, Skocpol appeals to "the facts." She is in search of those causal associations that will once and for all explain classical revolutions. Trotsky dialogues with the past in search of a future whose possibilities lie in the present. The reconstruction of history becomes a vehicle for understanding ways out of a continuously changing present. Because it is relative to the future, his history has no permanence. "The absolute in history is not something in the past from which we start; it is not something in the present, since all present thinking is necessarily relative. It is something still incomplete and in the process of becoming—something in the future towards which we move, which begins to take shape only as we move towards it, and in the light of which, as we move forward, we gradually shape our interpretation of the past" (Carr 1961: 161). "Good historians," writes Carr, "whether they think about it or not, have the future in their bones" (143). Trotsky does think about it. He examines the French and failed German revolutions to anticipate the Russian Revolution.

As Marxism tries to grab onto an always changing target, the possibility of socialism, so it too must continually transform itself: "Marxism is above all a method of analysis—not analysis of texts, but analysis of social relations. Is it true that, in Russia, the weakness of capitalist liberalism inevitably means the weakness of the labour movement? Is it true for Russia, that there cannot be an independent labour movement until the bourgeoisie has conquered power? It is sufficient merely to put these questions to see *what a hopeless formalism lies concealed beneath the attempt to convert an historically-relative remark of Marx's into a supra-historical axiom*" (Trotsky 1969: 64; emphasis added). Marxism must keep up with history while maintaining a commitment to its hard-core premises.

History belied Marxism's early optimism, which anticipated socialist revolution in Europe. This led Trotsky to focus on what Marx had overlooked, namely, the combined and uneven character of capitalist development, and from there it was a short move to study the economic and political relations among states, as well as the different ways of fusing class structures. Trotsky was able to anticipate the Russian Revolution but was unable to come to terms with the continuing failure of revolution in the West. Gramsci, by focusing on the different character of state and civil society in the West and the East, anticipated the trajectory of European socialist movements. He helped to lay the foundation of what is today known as Western Marxism, with its stress on ideological factors. As a result Marxists have developed a new appreciation for historical cultural forms.

The strangulation of socialist movements in underdeveloped countries after the Second World War called for new theories of underdevelopment. Armed with such theories, highlighting the international character of the capitalist economy, Immanuel Wallerstein reconstructed the entire history of capitalism. At the end of the twentieth century the collapse of the Soviet Union and its satellites, as well as the capitalist turn in China, far from spelling the end of Marxism, generates a new set of puzzles. This "great transformation" calls for a reconsideration of what was state socialism and more immediately forces us to attend to the dilemmas of making a socialist transition to capitalism, something Trotsky had always regarded as a possibility. I will discuss all this in chapter 4.

As history unfolds, so it throws up anomalies, usually crystallized in epochal events, compelling Marxism, on pain of degeneration, to reconstruct itself but on an enduring foundation. From the reconstruction of Marxism follows the reconstruction of history, as we now see the past through different eyes, from the standpoint of different possibilities in the future.

7. Standing at the Center of History

In seeking an "objective" history of the past, Skocpol propels herself outside history. The self-acknowledged influences of the present are confined to the selection of the problem. Participation in her social world stops precisely where the scientific process begins. Trotsky's "objective" history is of a different sort:

> When we call a historian objective, we mean, I think, two
> things. First of all, we mean that he has the capacity to rise
> above the limited vision of his own situation in society and in
> history—a capacity which . . . is partly dependent on his capac-
> ity to recognize the extent of his involvement in that situation,
> to recognize, that is to say, the impossibility of total objectivity.
> Secondly, we mean that he has the capacity to project his vision
> into the future in such a way as to give him a more profound
> and more lasting insight into the past than can be attained by
> those historians whose outlook is entirely bounded by their
> own immediate situation. (Carr 1961: 163).

Here the historian recognizes that she is standing on the fault
line connecting the past to the future, that engagement with and
in the world is not separate from the scientific process but its
very essence. Thus Trotsky saw his participation in Russian history as integral to the reconstruction of Marxism in order better
to understand the possibilities of socialism.

But such participation proved to be a two-edged sword. I
have focused on Trotsky's theory of revolution in *Results and
Prospects* because of its similarities to Skocpol's work. I might
equally have focused on his famous 1904 piece—*Our Political
Tasks*. It was a vituperative but prophetic attack on Bolshevism
as a form of Jacobinism: "Lenin's methods lead to this: the
party organization [the caucus] at first substitutes itself for the
party as a whole; then the Central Committee substitutes itself
for the organization; and finally a single 'dictator' substitutes
himself for the Central Committee" (quoted in Deutscher
1954: 90).

The irony of history cast Trotsky in the role of executor
and then victim of the direst predictions he made in 1904 and
1906. To the young Trotsky, Marxism and Jacobinism were

diametrically opposed but as a postrevolutionary leader he would be a most ardent defender of Bolshevism as Jacobinism. He would organize the militarization of labor, advocate the destruction of trade unions, and quash the Kronstadt uprising—all in the name of the revolution. He became ensnared in the very forces that he anticipated would be unfurled if the Russian Revolution were not followed by revolution in the West. His practice became a living violation of the Marxism of his youth. Not surprisingly, his understanding of the world around him suffered. For him this was not a period of great prophecy. Only later in exile, as the most celebrated victim of the revolutionary process he had predicted and then participated in, did Trotsky regain some of his youthful flare for Marxist reconstruction. In his struggle against Stalinism he could reconnect to his original Marxist principles. His interpretation of the historical significance of the Russian Revolution, culminating in *The Revolution Betrayed* (whose original title was *What Is the Soviet Union and Where Is It Going?*), was another breakthrough in the history of Marxism. Yet even here Trotsky's analysis is haunted by his involvement in the revolutionary process—the unquestioning endorsement of the Soviet Union's original socialist credentials and a future limited to either capitalism or socialism.

Trotsky's contributions to the history of the Soviet Union suggest that not just any engagement with the world fosters the progressive reconstruction of Marxism but one that is congruent with its principles. His contributions to the study of Western capitalism point to the importance of engagement per se. Although he had an impressive understanding of the distinctive state structures of capitalist societies, he never came to grips with their ideological foundations, the lived experience they engendered. Where Trotsky's horizons stop, Gramsci's begin. Even though he was imprisoned, tortured by illness, with access to few books and forced to write in code to escape his censors, he was able to rebuild Marxism out of reflections on the failure of the "Italian revolution" of 1919–20. In fact, one might say that his imprisonment protected him from the Stalinist purges that dealt such a fateful blow to human lives but also to the development of Marxism.

Trotsky and Gramsci had the advantage of being part of a living intellectual and political tradition in a world they had helped to shape. In quieter times, comfortably protected by the walls of academia, it is easy to forget that we are simultaneously participant in and observer of history. It is second nature for us to believe that our role as observer has a distinctive objectivity. We have seen, however, how illusory that objectivity can be. Skocpol's contribution comes not from its pronounced source—induction from the "facts"—but as passive refraction of changes in the world around her. Her contribution would have had greater scientific importance had she struggled to bring her participation in that world from subsidiary to focal awareness. But such a struggle would have to be disciplined by a commitment to an explicit research program.

CONCLUSION

In terms of the criteria for the growth of knowledge formulated by Popper, I have tried to demonstrate the superiority of the methodology of research program over the methodology of induction. Although the argument used Skocpol's and Trotsky's theories of revolution as illustrations, I constructed general claims organized around the contexts of discovery (induction versus deduction), justification (verification versus falsification and prediction), and scientist (external to or part of the object of knowledge). So long as philosophers of science were concerned to discover *the* scientific method, they could successfully compartmentalize these contexts. However, as soon as they became concerned to explain the development of scientific knowledge, they quickly discovered, as I have shown, that these contexts are irretrievably intertwined. So we require alternative categories for comparing methodologies:

Grounds of scientific objectivity. I have tried to demonstrate that the method of induction stands on a false objectivity. While it claims to generate explanations that map the empirical world, it actually erects barriers to the comprehension of that world. Not "the facts" but methodological premises and arbitrary explanatory hunches become the hidden anchors for theoretical conclusions. The method is at odds with its aims. Paradoxically, the methodology of the research program, precisely because it is self-consciously anchored in a complex of moral values, a conceptual system, models (analogies and metaphors), and exemplars— what Skocpol refers to as "blinders or heavily tinted lenses," what Lakatos refers to as negative and positive heuristics—creates a more effective dialogue with those "historical patterns." Blindness comes not from preexisting theories but from failing to recognize their necessity and then failing to articulate and defend their content.

Problem versus puzzle-oriented science. The method of induction claims to be outside and beyond theoretical traditions. Thus Skocpol reduces the classics of Marx, Weber, and

Durkheim to inspirations, sources of hypotheses, and even to variables out of which a true macrosociology can be forged. "Compelling desires to answer historically grounded questions, not classical theoretical paradigms, are the driving force [of historical sociology]" (Skocpol 1984: 4–5). We select a problem that takes our fancy and induce its solutions from the facts. Since, in the final analysis, only one theory is compatible with the facts, we have no need to go through the falsification of alternative theories or put our own theory through severe tests. The methodology of research programs, on the other hand, is concerned with solving puzzles, that is, anomalies thrown up by its expanding belt of theories, discrepancies between expectations and "facts."[26] The health and vitality of a research program depend not on the concealment, obfuscation, and denial of anomalies but on their clear articulation and disciplined proliferation. Continual dialogue between theory and data through falsification of the old and the development of new hypotheses with predictions of novel facts is the essence of a progressive research program. Trotsky's prophetic powers all originate in, even if they are not determined by, his commitment to Marxism—a recognition of its anomalies and the need to solve them in an original manner.

Internal versus external history. The method of induction regards the facts as irreducible and given; the problem is to come to an unbiased assessment of them. Science grows by the accumulation of factual propositions and inductive generalizations. This is its internal history. "But the inductivist cannot offer a rational 'internal' explanation for why certain facts than others were selected in the first place" (Lakatos 1978: 104). Problem choice, as I said earlier, is part of the "external" history relegated to footnotes, prefaces, or to the "sociology of knowledge." By contrast, the methodology of research programs incorporates into its internal history what is branded as metaphysical and external by inductivists, namely, its hard-core postulates and its choice of puzzles. What is reconstructed as scientifically rational in the one appears as scientifically irrational in the other.

Although what is constituted as rational in research programs encompasses much more than the rationality of induction, nevertheless even here external forces necessarily influence the scientific process. This is particularly so in the social sciences, where the object of knowledge autonomously generates new anomalies that the positive heuristic has to absorb. External forces can be seized upon as opportunities for the rational growth of knowledge, but they can also be the source of irrationality. Thus research programs become degenerate when they seal themselves off from the world they study or when that world wrenches the research process from its hard core. Marxism is particularly sensitive to external history. Where it seeks to change the world, it is more likely to be sensitive to anomalies than where it is a dominant ideology and thus more vulnerable to the repression of anomalies.

Obviously, the methodology of research programs has its own distinctive problems that energize its development. Is it possible to identify a single core to a research program or is there a family of cores and how does the core change over time? What is the relation between positive and negative heuristics? How easy is it to distinguish between progressive and degenerating research programs? How do we know that an apparently degenerating program will not recover its old dynamism? How does one evaluate the relative importance of progressive and degenerating branches of the same program? Is it possible to stipulate the conditions under which it is rational to abandon one research program in favor of another? Such problems notwithstanding, I hope I have made a case for the superiority of the methodology of research programs over the methodology of induction as a mode of advancing social science.

FOUR

Multicase Ethnography

Tracking the Demise of State Socialism

One of the most insistent laments of my teacher, the anthropologist Jaap van Velsen, was aimed at Marxists who damned capitalism with utopian socialism. This, he averred, was a false comparison, comparing the reality of one society with an idealization of another. He demanded a comparison of like with like—actually existing capitalism must be compared with actually existing socialism. Comparing the reality of one society with the utopian version of another was a categorical mistake. It was irresponsible of Marxists to let the Soviet Union or Eastern Europe off the hook. His voice boomed all the louder as Marxism became the fashion in the 1970s. When I completed my own study of the capitalist labor process based on eleven months of working as a machine operator in a south Chicago manufacturing plant (Burawoy 1979), he targeted his wrath at me. He was right: lurking behind my text was an unspecified utopian socialism, the hidden foundation of my critique of capitalism.

His remonstrations were enjoined by Robert Merton, who reproached me for the false imputation that mistakes industrialism for capitalism. He was criticizing an essay I wrote in 1982 about the industrial sociology of his recently deceased student Alvin Gouldner. I claimed that Gouldner's classic, *Patterns of Industrial Bureaucracy* (1954), missed the specifically capitalist character of industrial bureaucracy (Burawoy 1982). His mock bureaucracy and his punishment-centered bureaucracy were both shaped by the exigencies of wage labor and the competitive pursuit of profit, while his representative bureaucracy was simply unrealizable in capitalism. Merton responded by saying that I had not demonstrated my claims, which would require comparisons of industrial bureaucracy both within and between capitalist and noncapitalist societies.

To atone for my sins of false comparison and false imputation, I resolved to take actually existing socialism far more seriously. I decided against the easy road of Western Marxism, which dismissed the Soviet Union and its satellites as a form of statism or state capitalism, unrelated to the socialist project. Instead I began a twenty-year journey into the hidden abode of actually existing socialism, the last ten years of which were unexpectedly devoted to following the painful Soviet transition to capitalism. Ironically, in evaluating this Soviet leap into capitalism— the experiments of shock therapy and big bang—I now turned the tables on the avatars of market freedoms. I accused them of false comparisons, as they damned the realities of socialism with an idealization of capitalism, and of false imputations as they assumed the pathologies of Soviet societies would evaporate if its socialist character were destroyed. They forgot the transition costs, all the higher in a global order dominated by capitalism, as well as capitalism's very own pathologies. The economists thought they were shopping in a supermarket and could just grab whatever combination of institutions they wanted and then walk out without even paying. Indeed, the Russian transition proved to be looting on a grand scale. After being under the heel of state socialism, the population at large colluded in this unrestrained expropriation, to its own detriment. To be sure, Russians never saw themselves in a supermarket but in a prison. They had been there all their life, so they assumed that life on the outside could only be better. For many it turned out to be another sort of prison.

The life-and-death costs of a capitalist transition, guided and justified by such false comparisons and false imputations, were no less horrific than those borne of similar errors during the period of agriculture's collectivization and the planned economy. Just as Stalinism eclipsed its atrocities by proclaiming the new order as the realization of "communism" and by imputing perversions to pernicious capitalist legacies, so the neoliberal economists hid the horrors of the capitalist transition behind the labels of the "free market" while imputing perversions to the obdurate inheritance of communism or totalitarianism. Behind the social science errors of false comparison and false imputation there lies a mountain of political (ir)responsibility and guilt.

In this essay I reflect on my own attempts to grapple with the challenges of comparison and imputation in a journey that, in the 1980s, took me from workplace to workplace in Hungary and, then, in the 1990s, from workplace to community in Russia's market transition. What was peculiar, I asked, to work organization and working-class consciousness in the "workers' state," that is, under actually existing socialism, and with what consequences for the demise of the old order and the genesis of the new? And now I must also ask, what are the lasting lessons we can draw from socialism-as-it-was?

THE MULTICASE METHOD

How does an ethnographer compare capitalism and socialism without falling into the traps of false comparisons and false imputations? The old-style anthropologist, alone in his village, focuses on the here and now and, cut off from the world beyond, has little to offer. No better is the old-style symbolic interactionist or ethnomethodologist, working with the minutiae of face-to-face social interaction, searching for formal theory in social process, suspending both time and space, suppressing the historical contexts of capitalism and socialism.

Breaking out of these traditional genres of ethnography, seeking to grasp social meaning in the age of globalization, is the appealing idea of multisited ethnography—ethnography that connects different sites across national boundaries. Multisited ethnography sets out from a rejection of classical anthropology's spatial incarceration of the native, immobilized within and confined to a single place (Appadurai 1988). It rejects the enforced coincidence of space, place, and culture (Gupta and Ferguson 1992). Today borderlands, migration, cultural differences within communities, and the postcolonial condition all point to ties and identities that have to be explored across and among multiple locales. In one of the early programmatic statements George Marcus (1995) regarded multisited ethnography as the way to get inside the process of globalization rather than seeing it as an external system imposing itself on the life-world. He catalogues the techniques of multisited ethnography: tracing the movement of people as in the study of immigration; following the flow of things as in commodity chains or the spread of cultural artifacts; discovering the changing manifestations of metaphor as in Emily Martin's notion of flexibility; or unraveling a story, as in the pursuit of social memory or the trajectory of life histories across boundaries.

Multisited ethnography works well in following flows, associations, and linkages across national boundaries, but it is still marked by a reaction to conventional anthropology. Just as the village or the tribe used to be a "natural" entity, so now the "site," albeit connected to other sites, speaks for itself as a natural essence that reveals itself through investigation. Abandoning the idea of a preexisting site, I turn to cases, that is, from natural empirical objects to theoretically constructed objects. We have to be self-conscious about the theory we bring to the site that turns it into a case of something—in this chapter a capitalist factory or socialist factory. What is a factory? What is a capitalist factory? What is a socialist factory? These are not innocent questions whose answers emerge spontaneously from the data but come packaged in theoretical frameworks.

Constituting distinct sites as cases of something leads us to thematize their difference rather than their connection, which, then, poses questions of how that difference is produced and reproduced, in other words, how capitalist and socialist factories are different and then how that difference is produced and reproduced. Instead of the connection of sites to examine networks or flows, we have the comparison of cases constituted with a view to understanding and explaining their difference. Instead of multisited ethnography we have multicase ethnography. In short, the "case" is doubly constituted: realistically by the social forces within which it is embedded and the social processes it expresses, and imaginatively by the position we hold in the field and the theoretical framework we bring to bear. Only then, when we have constituted the case, can we think about connections.

Following the principles of the extended case method that I outlined in previous chapters, I begin with factories in specific places, a factory in the United States and one in Hungary, but then the factories have to be constituted as cases reflecting the worlds in which they are situated—the worlds of capitalism and socialism. The factories have to be rooted in their broader political and economic context, in the field of social forces of which they are a product. This is the first step, to see the microprocesses as an expression of macrostructures. The second step is to recognize the dynamics of change within each order. Capitalism and socialism are not static orders but dynamic societies, and in comparing the two we have to pay attention to how they change over time. But not only over time—over space, too. We have to recognize both the changes that take place within factories and the variety of factories that can be found within each system—complexities expressive of the character of each order. Just as there is not a singular capitalist factory, so there is not a singular socialist factory. Thus each case dissolves into multiple subcases from which we reconstruct what they have in common, what makes them part of a capitalist or socialist order.

So much for the realist dimension of comparison—the real forces and social processes at work that comprise the case. But there is also a constructivist dimension to comparison. Any complex site looks different from different places within it. A factory, whether capitalist or socialist, looks very different according to whether we take the standpoint of the manager or the worker, just as a village looks different through the eyes of Dalits or Brahmins. As ethnographers we don't have access to some Archimedean standpoint; we are always inserted somewhere in the site, which has grave consequences for what we see. Even the "outsider within" is a distinctive place with distinctive properties—blindnesses as well as illuminations. Moreover, once inserted into a specific location, the competences of the ethnographer play a crucial role in how she or he is viewed and in turn views others. Some attributes are learned while others are ascribed. Depending on the specific context, race, gender, age all affect the way others see a person and interact with that person. I call this first constructivist dimension *positionality.* In making comparisons among factories, it is important to recognize the embodiment and biography of the ethnographer as well as his or her location. Positionality, as I will show, is important in the constitution of the case.

The second constructivist moment refers to the theoretical suppositions and frameworks necessary to make sense of our sites. All three moments—context, process, and positionality—are heavily saturated with theory. The very categories of context, capitalism and socialism, presume a theoretical framework of some sort. The dynamics of such systems, that is, social processes, cannot be examined empirically without understanding potential internal variation, and this requires previous conceptualization. Even comprehending the significance of position is not simply an empirical problem, since significance is also theory laden—significance for what? Indeed, we might say that theory is necessary to keep us steady within the field, giving us bearings on our positionality. To put it more generally and

Table 6. *Four Moments of the Multicase Method*

	Exogenous	Endogenous
Realist	Context	Process
Constructivist	Theory	Positionality

bluntly, the world is complex: We cannot see anything without lenses that make it possible to focus. We carry around lenses that are so much a part of us that we don't notice we have them, yet as social scientists our task is to bring those lenses to consciousness, compare one with another, and to develop from them other more detachable lenses, which we call social theory, so that we can get on with the business of studying the world. Theory is an inescapable moment in the discovery and constitution of the difference between capitalism and socialism.

It is impossible to concentrate on all four moments of comparative ethnography at the same time, so it is necessary to proceed moment by moment, from case study to case study, but in such a way that each step responds to anomalies created by the previous steps. The cases do not spring ready-made, like a phoenix out of the ashes, but develop through successive approximation. The Hungarian case studies, trying to grapple with the peculiarities of socialist working-class consciousness and work organization, are based on synchronic comparisons with capitalism. I move from context to process and from process to positionality and finally to theory. The Russian case studies are a diachronic analysis of the transition to capitalism. They proceed in the opposite direction: from process to context and from there to theory and finally to positionality. In both sets of studies the realist analysis precedes the constructivist analysis, but each moment always

Table 7. *The Trajectory of Successive Case Studies*

Hungary: Synchronic Case Study		Russia: Diachronic Case Study	
Context	Process	Context	Process
Theory	Positionality	Theory	Positionality

presupposes the necessary existence of the other three moments. The two sets of studies diverge in the order in which the moments are problematized, but each enters serially into dialogue with the others as, indeed, do the two series themselves.

The ethnographer is not a lone figure, observing the natives in isolation, recording their every move in his private notebook. The ethnographer is in dialogue not only with the participants but with various informants and collaborators, active participants in the process of construction and reconstruction. Here I am drawing on the plot of Paul Rabinow's *Reflections on Fieldwork in Morocco* (1977), which traces the anthropologist's dialogue with a succession of informants, as he moved from periphery to the center, moving from superficial to deeper truths. In contrast to Rabinow, however, I make no presumption of increasing depth as ethnographer engages with collaborator or adversary, nor is there the separation of the dialogic process between informant and observer from the scientific process, which is a second dialogue between theory and data, the dialogue within the academic community. They work together—the two dialogues are themselves in dialogue. From beginning to end dialogue is the essence of this reflexive approach to ethnography.

SEARCHING FOR SOCIALISM IN HUNGARY

I had already turned my attention to the Soviet Union and its satellites in Eastern Europe when Poland was struck by the Solidarity movement (August 12, 1980–December 13, 1981). This, or so it appeared to me, was the first society-wide revolutionary working-class movement. Why should it take place in a "communist" society rather than a "capitalist" society? I watched with amazement as the movement unfolded, sweeping more and more of Polish society into its orbit, refusing to succumb to the party-state as other such movements before it had done—East Germany in 1953, Hungary in 1956, Czechoslovakia in 1968. I had recently completed *Manufacturing Consent,* which had sought to demonstrate that the Marxist anticipation of working-class revolution under capitalism was stymied not at the level of superstructures—education, ideology, state, and the like—but in the workplace, that is, in the very place where it was supposed to congeal.

My south Chicago ethnography, based on eleven months of working at Allied in 1974–75, draws out a model of advanced capitalism in which "hegemony was born in the factory," and consent was produced by the very way that work was organized and regulated. Work was constituted as an absorbing game that eclipsed the conditions of its existence: the internal labor market and grievance machinery constituted workers as individuals ready to play games, while the internal state coordinated the interests of those individuals with those of management in the pursuit of profit. Could it be that work was organized and regulated differently in Eastern Europe, so much so that dissent rather than consent was the product? This was the abiding question that motivated the succession of comparative factory studies. It began as a comparison of my own experiences in the United States with those of Miklós Haraszti in Hungary, and it continued as an examination of the specificity of Haraszti's experience as a factory worker, based on studies conducted first by others and then by myself.

Context: Advanced Capitalism versus State Socialism[1]

It was with amazement that in 1979 I read Miklós Haraszti's *A Worker in a Worker's State* (1977). A dissident who in 1971–72 had been punished by the state with factory labor, Haraszti turned this to his advantage by writing a moving and detailed account of his experiences at Red Star Tractor Factory. But it was serendipity that found us in different parts of the world yet in similar machine shops of enterprises that produced similar vehicles, using similar technology. I immediately recognized the array of mills, drills, and lathes that surrounded him, but whereas I was a miscellaneous machine operator, which meant I moved from one machine to another, Haraszti was riveted to the two mills that he ran simultaneously. We both worked on a piece rate system that paid workers for how much they produced. Indeed, the original Hungarian version of *A Worker in a Worker's State* was called *Piece Rates*. In both factories workers were divided into operatives, like ourselves, who ran the machines, and auxiliary workers who facilitated production— clerks, inspectors, truck drivers, set-up men, and so forth, who could be the bane of our lives.

What was extraordinary to my capitalist eye was the intensity of work under Hungary's socialism. I estimated that Haraszti was actually working, and was supposed to be working, twice as hard as my co-operators at Allied. He had to run two mills at once, whereas that was unheard-of at Allied. Now there was the puzzle—if there was one right that state socialist workers had won, it was the right not to work hard. Or so conventional wisdom had it. To be sure, there was the socialist competition and the Stakhanovite movement of the 1930s, but now with full employment workers never feared loss of job and thereby commanded considerable power on the shop floor. So how come Haraszti was working so much harder than I had?

My first answer to this question lay in the political economy of advanced capitalism and state socialism. I dissected Haraszti's representation of his lived experience in order to compare it with my own. He lived under the oppressive rule of the foreman, the party, and the trade union as well as petty clerical staff. He was subjected to what I called bureaucratic despotism. All this was so different from the hegemonic regime of Allied, where the trade union was a guardian of the rule of law, enforced the contract, and administered a grievance machinery that protected the rights of individuals. At Allied there was an "internal state," but it was not the arbitrary exercise of power that Haraszti faced. Rather, it was a regulated form of power that possessed a measure of legitimacy and elicited consent to the factory order. Moreover, the internal labor market gave workers with seniority the opportunity to move away from hated bosses by simply bidding on other jobs. Haraszti had no such escape hatch.

But what had Haraszti to fear? Why did he work so hard, how was he forced to run two machines at once? Answering this question requires going beyond the regulatory order of bureaucratic despotism to its material basis, the piece-rate system. The hegemonic regime under which I labored guaranteed a minimum wage so that if the rate for a job was impossible, we were still assured a reasonable wage. This economic security gave rise to two types of output restriction: goldbricking when we took it easy on a difficult job because we were guaranteed a minimum wage unattainable on the basis of piece rates, and quota restriction in which we collectively agreed to adhere to a maximum of 140 percent so that management would not be alerted to gravy jobs. At Red Star, on the other hand, there was no minimum wage, no security against speed-up. There was therefore no goldbricking but neither was there quota restriction, because the setting of piece rates had no rhyme or reason, and workers engaged in no collective enforcement of a ceiling on output. Haraszti was defenseless against the dictatorship of the norm; he could not establish counternorms to protect against the intensification of work. Bureaucratic despotism pulverized the workforce, making wages dependent on a battle with the norm, so workers could not develop any countervailing power. At Allied, on the other hand, the security offered by minimum wage, unemployment compensation, and an elaborate bumping system that protected workers against layoffs called forth a hegemonic order in which managers had to coax and bribe rather than coerce workers into the expenditure of labor. Workers were allowed to organize work as a game of making out, and the game turned life on the shop floor from arduousness and boredom into an exciting challenge to the operator's ingenuity, measuring his status by the success with which he met but did not exceed management's output targets.

In describing these regimes of production I was also explaining their divergent politics. In the case of hegemony workers were constituted as individual citizens with rights and obligations, and because of rewards to seniority and collective bargaining their economic interests were coordinated with those of the enterprise. Instead of galvanizing opposition, capitalism elicited the consent of its exploited toilers. In the case of bureaucratic despotism, workers faced the arbitrary power of the state in the form of a collusive arrangement of management, trade union, and party. Workers responded to palpable exploitation and repression by carving out secretive realms of autonomy and creativity— Haraszti's "homer"—that could burst forth in a rebellion against the entire political system, as it did in 1953, 1956, and 1968. State socialism, I concluded, seemed more vulnerable to working-class rebellion than advanced capitalism. The following year Solidarity would demonstrate precisely my point, or so it seemed.

Social Process: Variations in Despotism and Hegemony[2]

This was the first step in developing a comparison of actually existing socialism and advanced capitalism, namely, a comparison of my experiences at Allied and Haraszti's experiences at Red Star in which each factory stood for the respective type of political economy. The project assumed that each society was internally homogeneous and unchanging. The next step was to explore variations of and within capitalism and state socialism to see if there was any basis to the claims I had made. Perhaps these were simply two anomalous factories?

The most difficult task was to determine whether the bureaucratic despotism found at Red Star was typical of socialist

Hungary and then why Solidarity sprung to life in Poland rather than Hungary (not to mention the Soviet Union). A second, easier task was to examine whether the hegemonic regime was representative of the United States and whether U.S. production politics was distinctive among advanced capitalist countries. A third task was to pose the question of despotism—how did the bureaucratic despotism of Red Star compare with the market despotism of early capitalism? This is where I began.

The conceptualization of hegemonic regimes under advanced capitalism and of bureaucratic despotism under state socialism both implied a contrast with market despotism of early capitalism.[3] The hegemonic regime was built on a double supposition: first, that the reproduction of labor power (wages, social security, etc.) was independent of the expenditure of labor and, second, that the nation-state set limits on the way management could wield its power by regulating a relatively autonomous "internal state." Comparisons among machines shops, or similar work processes, in Japan, Sweden, England, and the United States substantiated the idea of a hegemonic regime's association with advanced capitalism, although the regulation of industrial relations and the extent of the welfare state gave rise to different types of hegemonic regimes. But what they shared as hegemonic regimes separated them from the despotic regime of early capitalism. Here my point of departure was Marx's characterization of manufacturing as a form of market despotism in nineteenth-century England, wherein the livelihood of the worker was directly dependent upon the expenditure of labor in the factory and subject to the arbitrary whim of the overseer. If the foundation of despotism in nineteenth-century England was the economic whip of the market, then the source of despotism in socialist Hungary was the bureaucratic power of the party-state.

Marx provided the model of market despotism, but the reality of nineteenth-century industry was rather different, operating as it did through family patriarchy as a mode of recruitment and regulation or through the company town, which assured the binding of community to workplace and was ameliorated by the skill of the craftworker, who could not be replaced at will. Examining various secondary accounts of factory work, I could compare patriarchal and paternalistic regimes in the English cotton industry with the paternalism of the New England mills and the artisanal regimes of the Russian textile industry. What distinguished the prerevolutionary Russian case of despotism from its English and U.S. counterparts was the greater regulatory presence of the state at the site of production, which created a clear object of struggle. Just as workers could identify the state as exploiter and oppressor at Red Star, so the same was true in the prerevolutionary factories of St. Petersburg and Moscow. Both repressive orders were therefore vulnerable to insurrectionary struggles from workers. Through these successive historical comparisons I was able to determine the specific characteristics of bureaucratic despotism that distinguished it from market despotism.

Bureaucratic despotism might be vulnerable to the shared dissent of the workers it dominates, but why did the actual mobilization take place in Poland rather than Hungary? After all, Hungary, not Poland, had been the scene of the most dramatic worker uprising in 1956. Perhaps Red Star—or Haraszti's portrait of Red Star—was not a typical Hungarian factory. But how to find out? Just as I knew that in the United States hegemonic regimes of the monopoly sector coexisted with more despotic regimes of the competitive sector, I asked what the corresponding variation within a state socialist economy was. The most obvious counterpart to the monopoly and competitive sectors of advanced capitalism was the position of different enterprises with regard to central planning—the existence of key enterprises that received closer attention and more resources than the more marginal ones. Heavy industry had traditionally been given priority, whereas the consumer goods sector was underprivileged. Yet there was no evidence to suggest whether or how this affected work organization and its regulation. The few Hungarian studies that were available, by Héthy and Mako, documented a center and a periphery *within* the enterprise, with workers in the core having a more privileged existence on the shop floor than peripheral workers, who were subject to much greater hardship and labor intensity. This would begin to explain why Haraszti, a new and peripheral worker, was under such intense pressure to produce.

Further digging around revealed that Red Star Tractor Factory was also under the gun of economic reform when Haraszti was working there. This monster of a factory was subject to harder budget constraints as attempts were made to introduce economic criteria for efficiency. The pressure from the state to tighten up the factory's finances translated into pressure to work harder on the shop floor. Here was another reason why Haraszti might be working harder than workers in other socialist factories as well as workers in the United States. The enigma was beginning to unfold.

Positionality: American Worker in a Socialist Factory[4]

A Worker in a Worker's State was intended to be a general representation of all work under state socialism. At no point does Haraszti acknowledge that his experience might be specific to a particular factory (in crisis), to a particular time period (the beginning of reforms), to a particular country (Hungary), or even to his particular position within the factory. I had been trying to reconstruct the historical and locational specificity of his experience from theoretical explorations and secondary data. Because the evidence was thin, I decided to examine the question by taking a job in a Hungarian factory myself. Of course, it would be a decade later but nonetheless worth the effort.

I was fascinated by the development of the Solidarity movement, which seemed to support the conclusions of my first essay on *A Worker in a Worker's State,* and I planned to go to Poland. By the time I managed to secure a leave of absence and was learning Polish, however, Gen. Wojciech Jaruzelski had staged his coup and Solidarity went underground. Instead I readily accepted the invitation of Iván Szelényi to accompany him to Hungary in the summer of 1982—his first trip back since being exiled to Australia. Coincidentally, his expulsion was in part due to his role in publishing Haraszti's book. During our two-week trip I learned of Hungary's burgeoning sociology of labor and labor markets. I returned the following summer for six months, learning Hungarian and working first on a state farm that produced champagne and then in a small textile shop located on an agricultural cooperative. During this period I began my collaboration with János Lukács, then a young industrial sociologist at the Institute of Sociology in the Academy of Sciences.

The following summer (1984) I landed a job as a machine operator in the manufacturing plant that we called Bánki, which is analogous to Allied and Red Star. It wasn't easy to secure the position because the fate of the working class was perhaps the most heavily guarded secret of state socialism. While not overly enthusiastic, the director of the enterprise was willing to go along with the idea of my working on the shop floor, so long as all the "authorities" would endorse the project. The Academy of Sciences supported my request, and Lukács used a contact in the Central Committee to secure the support of the party. It was a tortuous process, but in the end permission was granted. I could enter the hidden abode of socialist production. I recall the look of glee on the shop superintendent's face when he was told to give me a job. He led me to an old radial drill that no one used. I soon learned why: it was not just old but dangerous. I'd never run a radial drill in my life, but for two months that's what I tried to do. In fact, it assumed a superhuman form, running me rather than being run by me.

Much of what I had inferred from Haraszti and the few industrial sociologists who had studied state socialist work was true. The party, the trade union, and management were in cahoots, although they were not necessarily the oppressive presence described by Haraszti. When I tried to file a grievance with the union for nonpayment of overtime, everyone laughed at me. The union—they are *nulla nulla* (nothing). And, yes, the piece-rate system worked much as Haraszti described it, with no security wage. The rates weren't easy, at least for me, but they were nowhere near as tight as at Red Star, which reinforced my supposition that Red Star was indeed a victim of the economic reforms of the immediate post-1968 period.

The most distinctive difference was our conception of social relations on the shop floor. Haraszti painted a picture of atomized individuals, and here I think he was projecting his own (unreflected) placement within the factory. As a dissident, a Jew, and an intellectual, he was shunned by his coworkers. He was thrown into competition with them, he was ruled by them, and he was most certainly not one of them. To be sure, I was not one of them either—but my strangeness had an appeal. They laughed at my inept Hungarian, at my incompetence as a machine operator, and I was embraced as an exotic foreigner. Within hours of hitting the shop floor I was ringed by workers asking me about the United States. From my vantage point I could see and experience the spontaneous cooperation that made production possible in the socialist factory.

Here I drew on the work of the great Hungarian economist János Kornai (1971, 1980) and his theory of the socialist economy as a shortage economy. In an economy of centralized (re)distribution, enterprise managers continually bargain with the state for resources, as a result of which they are always in short supply. But Kornai was not one to fall into false comparisons. He understood that market economies have their own disequilibria, not in the direction of shortage but in the direction of surplus. Each economy had its own (ir)rationality—the one constrained from the side of supply, the other from the side of demand. That explained a lot. For, to be effective, socialist work organization had to improvise in the face of the fluctuating quantity and quality of inputs on the one side and the pressure from plan targets on the other. I saw such flexible cooperation all around me at Bánki, and, curiously, its work organization was far more efficient than at Allied, where incomplete engines lined the aisles, where management was always demanding that "hot jobs"—a sort of rush work—take precedence over everything else. In other words, it was not that capitalism was rational and socialism irrational but that each system had its own (ir)rationality.

I concluded that Bánki looked more like the stereotype of a capitalist workplace, while Allied exhibited features of the stereotypical socialist workplace. The reason lay in the character of a multinational capitalist corporation, which is itself a planned economy generating its own internal shortages. There was a reverse embeddedness—a corporate enterprise within a market economy in the United States and a marketized enterprise within a corporate economy in Hungary. Just as U.S. enterprises compensated for market exigencies with bureaucratized internal labor markets, so Hungarian enterprises experimented with market-driven inside-contracting systems to address the exigencies of central planning.

From my vantage point in production I was able to see more clearly the differences and similarities between advanced capitalist and state socialist production. Haraszti's account made no attempt at comparing socialist and capitalist work but rather was aimed at the yawning gap between ideology and reality, between the workers' paradise projected by the state and the reality experienced on the shop floor. Still, even that experience on the shop floor was colored, in ways he did not reveal, by his own biography, his embodiment so much at odds with his fellow workers'—a difference that set him apart from the working-class community. Concerned with debunking state ideology, he had no interest in the peculiarity of his own experience, whether the product of who he was (manifestly a novice and outsider) or where he was (in a factory subject to fiscal pressures). My own difference, on the other hand, brought me into the community so that I could, with the help of my experiences at Allied, explore the specificity of state socialist production.

Extending Theory: Western Marxist Meets Eastern Dissident[5]

The last stage of my Hungarian odyssey took me into the heart of the working class—the Lenin Steel Works situated in the industrial city of Miskolc. Between 1985 and 1988 I worked there as a furnaceman on three occasions that totaled about a year in all. The importance of shop-floor autonomy in the face of a shortage economy was even more apparent here in the production of high-quality steel. I was again working with Lukács, who spent time interviewing management, and we observed the clash of two principles—management's bureaucratic regulation and workers' spontaneous collaboration. Often we observed how senior management's interference disrupted the capacity of the shop floor to adapt to the fluctuating quality of materials and unreliable machinery. When Lukács and I reported our findings to management, a party meeting was called in which our research was denounced and we were told to do it over.

Because I was firmly integrated into the October Revolution Socialist Brigade, I was able to focus on the class consciousness of socialist workers. Again, this was not a question of much concern to Haraszti, yet his own perspective as a dissident was not that different from those of my coworkers. Compelled to participate in rituals that proclaimed socialism to be just, efficient, and egalitarian, what I called "painting socialism," my coworkers were only too keenly aware of the injustices, inefficiencies, and inequalities that pervaded their life. This led them, so I argued, to embrace the idea of socialism but as an immanent critique of the party-state that governed their lives. Finally, I was approaching the question of the Polish Solidarity movement—the question that had brought me to Hungary.

I worked with Konrád and Szelényi's (1979) theory, which regarded state socialism as a system of central appropriation and redistribution of goods and services, a system in which intellectuals play a key role in defining societal needs to be realized in the plan. State socialism, which justifies open and transparent domination and exploitation, has a legitimation problem. A system that requires legitimation is always vulnerable to being held accountable to its ideology. State socialism is vulnerable to immanent critique, demanding that the party-state live up to its promises. Whereas this led Haraszti to cynical dismissal of the whole enterprise, it led workers to demand the proclaimed fruits of socialism. Through this lens Solidarity was not an attempt to overthrow the state but to force the state to take its own ideology seriously. It did this by keeping its distance from the state, opposing it with a burgeoning, self-regulating civil society.

But the puzzle remained: Why Poland and not Hungary? Here the question was not so much one of a class-in-itself becoming a class-for-itself, that is, the capitalist question of consciousness raising, but rather a different question: How could class consciousness become a material force? In Hungary the development of a market economy to compensate for the dysfunctions of planning—the cooperatives both inside and outside production—led to a competitive individualism. In Poland, on the other hand, the lesser development of the second economy on the one side, and the umbrella of the Catholic Church on the other, created the propensity and the resources for collective mobilization.

As I was busy working out the conditions for the working-class challenge to state socialism and the possibilities for a transition to democratic socialism, history took its revenge. Hungary's socialism did not capitulate from below but collapsed from above, and the transition was not toward some democratic socialism but toward market capitalism. This was not without some resistance. My own shop steward in the October Revolution Socialist Brigade took part in an effort to resurrect the council system that had sprung up in 1956, by turning the struggle over privatization into a struggle for worker control of industry. My collaborator, János Lukács, inspired by what he saw of ESOPs (employee stock ownership plans) in the United States, sought to introduce parliamentary legislation that would favor workers taking over their factories. But in the end this was all to no avail, as managers grabbed the profitable parts of socialist enterprises, leaving the state to subsidize the rest.

I and the workers around me were completely unprepared for the transition to capitalism precisely because we were so focused on production. The transition game was being played at the political level, slowly but surely, bringing in its train privatization and devastating consequences for the Lenin Steel Works as well as many other industries. Whereas the Lenin Steel Works would slowly disintegrate over ten years to become a black dwarf, Bánki would be completely rebuilt by its German partners. When I returned for a visit in 1999, I discovered the old, gray, noisy, oily, and dirty socialist factory had been turned into a bright and polished high-tech plant run by neatly clad technicians who were nursing numerically controlled machines with a barely audible hum.

How could I have been so blind? As a Marxist I came to Hungary in search of the potentialities of socialism, but now

I faced the unexpected transition to capitalism. To help me uncover the potentialities of socialism, I had compared state socialism with capitalism, never thinking that one would morph into the other. To be sure, I had reconstructed Marxism to accommodate the past, a working-class revolt under state socialism. I had recognized that whereas capitalism might organize the consent of workers, state socialism was far more fragile and was as likely as not to generate dissent. In the end, however, the party leadership's loss of faith in its own ideology resulted in the crumbling of the socialist edifice and the imposition of capitalism.

While theory was indispensable for the comparative analysis, it also limited what I could see. Haraszti suffered a similar fate. He too revised his theory of state socialism in the 1980s. He now saw state socialism not as a repressive order but as a more smoothly running panopticon, absorbing rather than punishing dissent (Haraszti 1987). Dissidents were no longer shot, jailed, exiled, or even sent into factories. They were watched by giving them space to make their criticisms, a far more powerful and effective mechanism of control. Like me, he did not anticipate the collapse of this order, and like me he was heavily invested in state socialism—his identity as a dissident relied on its continued existence. In the aftermath he became no less estranged than I was. Like other dissident intellectuals, he would enter politics but, as in so many cases, this was not for long. Dissidence was in his blood, just as Marxism was in mine.

THE TRAUMA OF THE CAPITALIST TRANSITION IN RUSSIA

While all eyes were on the disintegration of state socialism in Eastern Europe, my attention turned to the Soviet Union. Now, in the full flow of perestroika and glasnost, a country hitherto off-limits was opening itself to the sociological eye. I'd been to the Soviet Union on five occasions during the 1980s—two conferences on U.S. and Soviet labor history and three extraordinary trips with Erik Wright to launch a Soviet version of his survey of class structure. It was all too clear to me that the Soviet Union was politically inhospitable to ethnographic studies, but additionally this was not something Soviet sociologists would ever take seriously. It simply wasn't science. I was very skeptical, therefore, when I received an invitation, while on sabbatical in Hungary in 1990, to spend ten days on the Volga River lecturing to a boat full of industrial sociologists. Still, I accepted, as I had never even seen the Volga and was always looking for new adventures, not to mention the distraction it afforded from the ongoing Hungarian debacle of the transition to capitalism. As it turned out, it was quite an adventure. The politically courageous organizer, Nina Andreenkova, let me (and three other social scientists from the United States) loose among about 130 sociologists and personnel officers from a diverse array of organizations, including military plants, from all over the Soviet Union.

On that boat, fittingly called the *Gogol,* I met Kathryn Hendley, then a political science graduate student at Berkeley, and Pavel Krotov, a sociologist from Syktyvkar, capital of the Komi Republic in the far north of European Russia. With Kathie I would collaborate on a study of a Soviet rubber factory, known as Kauchuk, during the following winter (1991) and with Pavel I would develop a ten-year partnership, studying the capitalist transition in Komi.

The theoretical framework that I had developed in Hungary came up against all sorts of challenges at Kauchuk, where we stumbled upon civil war. The study of these internal struggles in a Moscow factory was followed, later that spring, by a study of the timber industry in Komi, beginning with my own participant observation in a furniture factory. Here, Krotov and I looked more carefully at the character of the transformation of the economy as a whole, a move to what we called merchant capitalism.

In the first post-Soviet decade that followed, I teamed up with other sociologists in Komi, most notably Tatyana Lytkina, to examine the process of economic and social involution as it affected family life. This called for a major overhaul of my theoretical framework, a shift from Marx to Polanyi. I would leave Komi with a whimper rather than a bang as my attention was turned back to the fate of American sociology.

Social Process: Between Perestroika and Privatization[6]

My introduction to working-class life in Hungarian socialism came by way of the lyrical account of Miklós Haraszti; my introduction to the Soviet landscape was more dramatic and visceral. Kathie Hendley and I insinuated ourselves into an old "political" enterprise—Kauchuk, a rubber factory that had begun production in 1915. We arrived in January 1991, when Russia had already plunged into political turmoil. The party had formally relinquished its monopoly of political power, and the Baltic Republics, inspired by the path taken in Eastern Europe, were asserting their autonomy. The struggle between Yeltsin and Gorbachev, between the Russian Federation and the Soviet Union, was intensifying. On the one side were the forces for privatization and a market economy while on the other side were apparatchiki still invested in the continuity of the planned economy. The crisis that engulfed the Soviet Union became a fault line running through Kauchuk itself.

Mode of entry always says much about the place being entered. Whether because of the changing times or because of Soviet specificities, access to Kauchuk was very different from access to the Hungarian enterprises. In the latter case Lukács had to enlist the support of a range of powerful authorities in state and party, national and local, as well as enterprise management. Here we gained entry through a deal that we struck with the trade union leadership. If we provided computers for their kindergarten, we could have carte blanche access to the enterprise and its personnel. So that's what we did, notwithstanding opposition from Soviet customs officials. And, with the assertiveness of a corporate lawyer, Kathie got us access to almost everything we desired. Much to my disbelief, we even got into the morning planning meetings, where all managers assembled to discuss the state of the enterprise, the bottlenecks, the breakdowns. The dysfunctionality of the Soviet enterprise was laid out before us—until we were banned from those meetings.

From this privileged vantage point Kauchuk looked vastly different from the Hungarian enterprises that I had studied. First, I had finally stumbled on the true economy of shortage. Kornai insisted that, reforms or no reforms, socialist enterprises suffered from shortages, but there are shortages and shortages. They were not so palpable at Hungarian enterprises, but Kauchuk was awash with shortages, not least because of the collapsing Soviet infrastructure and the factory's dependence on materials from all over the Soviet Union. The manager of supplies was regularly vilified in the planning meetings, and it remained a mystery not only how he survived in that position but also how he actually secured basic supplies during the winter of 1991. We finally managed to interview him, but he was an astute and wily customer who gave away no secrets of his trade.

In some ways the external turmoil exaggerated the pathologies of the Soviet enterprise, and yet, paradoxically, at the same time it also exaggerated tendencies in the opposite direction, reminiscent of the entrepreneurial moments of the Hungarian enterprise. Turbulence in the wider economy deepened the problem of shortage but, equally, created the opportunity for a complex network of cooperatives that thrived within the protective shell of the formal enterprise. The Hungarian second economy— the inside contracting cooperatives—was sedate, transparent, and restrained compared with the wild entrepreneurship we observed at Kauchuk. All the workshops contained their own cooperatives or even "small enterprises" (as they were then called), where the real money was made. Funneling labor, machinery, materials, and social contacts into their ventures, chosen managers and selected workers were able to make a killing at the expense of the official enterprise. I'd seen all this at the Lenin Steel Works but only after 1989. At Kauchuk we saw this spontaneous privatization from below within the fast-eroding Soviet economy, although we didn't know that its collapse was just around the corner.

The internal economic transformation of Kauchuk was reflected in schisms cutting through its political regime. Managers could not hide from us the open warfare between the director and his henchmen on the one side and the younger technicians and engineers on the other. The old guard, connected to the ministries, resolutely defended the Soviet planning order, while the young Turks defended the encroaching market system

and, in what was a political reflex of the same project, the autonomy of the Russian Federation from the Soviet Union. We witnessed public meetings in which the young Turks attacked the
director's private accumulation of wealth (through the cooperatives), while the director and his supporters condemned the
young Turks for sabotaging the enterprise to pursue their own
careers. The party apparatus within the enterprise was supposed
to be the keeper of the peace, but it had already effectively dissolved. Nothing could restrain an all-out struggle for control of
the enterprise. I had seen workers use guerrilla tactics on
Hungarian shop floors, but this was the first time I had seen two
alternative political-economic systems vying for power within a
single enterprise.

This was my introduction to the Soviet economy. We were
there for two months before I moved out of Moscow and
trekked north to the Komi Republic, where I began a quite
unexpected ten years of research into the processes and repercussions of economic decline.

Exploring Context:
From Merchant Capitalism to Economic Involution[7]

I got a job at Polar Furniture in 1991 through a rather circuitous
route. Pavel Krotov, whom I met on the *Gogol,* was the first
Soviet sociologist I came across who exhibited the ethnographic
instinct. He came from a poor background, knew the life of the
down-trodden, and was fearless in exploring it. One of his
friends was a Korean entrepreneur who had recently left the
local university, like so many in late perestroika, to set up a small
business. He, in turn, was a good friend of the young leader of

the republic's Labor Federation—part of a new generation of politicians that would come to power after the fall of the Soviet Union. Through the offices of the official trade union Pavel and I spent a month visiting all the main enterprises in the city. We hit it off with the personnel manager of Polar Furniture as he showed off his new model factory, which made wall units, the staple furniture of every Soviet apartment. So we inquired whether I could work there. The old man who was director—a known public figure—laughed and said why not. So I began working there, once again drilling holes, while Krotov talked with management for two critical months—May and June 1991—and then we spent another month trying to construct the linkages among the different enterprises of the Komi timber industry.

Kauchuk, which was at the heart of the Soviet system and dependent on supplies from all over the country, was far more vulnerable to the turmoil in the economy than the furniture company was. Polar Furniture was situated in the periphery and able to capitalize, at least for a short time, on the disintegration of the planning system. Management formed a unified bloc, cleverly taking advantage of the new uncertainty. Space for maneuvering opened up as the power of the central planning agencies evaporated. Polar had many advantages: it was well placed in the local timber consortium that organized the local industry, it depended on local supplies of timber and other materials, and it had a monopoly in the production of a needed consumer item—wall units. While shop-floor life was still subject to shortages, and I experienced many moments of production standstill as well as end-of-month rush work, it did not have the chaos of Kauchuk. Indeed, workers and management had struck a bargain. The various shops took responsibility for meeting the production plan, while management was responsible for making sure that supplies arrived, for which end they had a precious commodity to barter, namely, wall units. Management could also use wall units to barter for timber supplies, lacquer, or whatever other materials were needed but also for places in summer camps for children of employees or for sugar, which was then being rationed.

As the political superstructure of state socialism peeled away, and as the centralized distribution system disintegrated, enterprises were left to fend for themselves and those who could exploited their monopoly position in the emergent market. Time horizons shrunk, and no one was thinking about capital investment. Instead they were turning to a primitive prebourgeois capitalism based on booty, adventure, speculation, or piracy. Instead of capital accumulation, we found asset stripping. As Max Weber insisted, such a capitalism, what we called merchant capitalism—seeking profit in exchange rather than production—is a revolution away from modern bourgeois capitalism. Yes, the market was stepping in to replace the planning mechanism but with disastrous consequences.

The collapse of the Soviet Union at the end of 1991 only consolidated the perverse effects of the market. At the beginning of 1992 prices were liberated and astronomical inflation was the immediate result, fueling barter and the invention of new currencies. Voucher privatization, represented as a democratic way of sharing the public wealth, proved to be a peaceful and effective system of looting by the powerful. In the summer of 1992 we went up to the coal mines of Vorkuta, the site of militant strikes in 1989 and 1991, which, together with miners from

Siberia and Ukraine, played an important role in bringing down the Soviet Union. In Vorkuta a syndicalist fever had gripped the workers. They thought that the demolition of the party-state and their taking over the mines would install a new order of plentitude. Instead they would become the victims of mine closures as coal became more expensive with the spiraling price of transportation and as the demand for coal fell with the collapse of the metallurgical industry. From 1991 to 1998 the Russian economy seemed to be in free fall. The only dynamic sectors involved natural resources (gas and oil) and the realm of exchange where the mafia, banks, or newfangled intermediaries were gouging the rest of the economy. There was neither revolution nor evolution but economic *involution,* a gradual hollowing out of production by exchange. It was a process of primitive disaccumulation.

To underline how catastrophic the transition to the market was, I extended my study even further beyond the factory, comparing the Russian and Chinese transitions. To be sure, my knowledge of China was limited but the argument seemed compelling to me. The Russian transition to capitalism was a replica of its earlier transition to socialism—dominated by revolutionary intent. Western economists were also preaching the quickest transition possible—big bang and shock therapy—to forestall any political backlash against the market. The Bolshevik transition to capitalism argued for the most rapid destruction of all that was socialist, specifically, all the levers of central control, on the assumption that the market would rise spontaneously. But there is no market transition to a market economy without the creation of supporting institutions (financial, legal, material infrastructure). This was the lesson of China, where a market economy was incubated under the supervision of the party-state. If in Russia there was political transition without economic transformation, in China there was economic transformation without political transition.

Theory: From Marx to Polanyi[8]

To study a small furniture factory in northern Russia and draw conclusions about the transition to capitalism will appear preposterous to those who think social science proceeds through induction from fact to theory. If, however, we recognize that facts are always theory laden, and we therefore must begin with theory, then science progresses through the reconstruction of theory. We have to be self-conscious about the theory we carry into our studies. I began with a theory—developed in my research in Hungary and before that in the United States and Zambia through (real and imagined) dialogue with others such as Szelényi and Kornai—of how the Soviet economic system worked. Kauchuk and then Polar Furniture became the vehicles for extending this theory to the transition to a market economy. In other words, the theory constitutes the case and the case in turn helps to reconstruct theory.

However, the theory I worked with was manifestly Marxist, focusing on the political economy of state socialism. From Szelényi I had elaborated the class character of state socialism, based on "teleological redistributors" who appropriated and then redistributed surplus in a transparent fashion. These redistributors—planners, if you will—needed a justifying ideology, which in turn set in motion immanent critique. Capitalism was very different. It hid its exploitative practices and secured the

coordination of interests between conflicting parties. Its domination became a hegemony based on the consent of workers and
intellectuals. State socialism, on the other hand, had to legitimate its central appropriation, its barefaced exploitation. It
therefore always faced a potential legitimation crisis that threatened to bring down the system as a whole. State socialism was
always a fragile order, which was why it had such frequent
recourse to force. The success of the Hungarian system lay in the
effort to build hegemony alongside and in support of legitimation.

From Kornai I derived the distinctive character of work and
its regulation. A shortage economy required a spontaneous and
flexible specialization on the shop floor that gave rise to solidari-
ties that could fuel a working-class movement against state socialism. I was, of course, wrong. State socialism dissolved from above
rather than below. The legitimators themselves could no longer
believe in their own legitimation; they lost confidence in the
capacity of the party-state to deliver on its socialist promises. Like
rats they fled their sinking ship for an imaginary one, dragging
with them a population also victim of its own hallucinations.

This revised Marxist theory could make sense of the collapse
of the old order—the veritable forces of production had collided
with the relations of production, a collision most forcibly felt by
the political directorate. But Marxist theory had greater difficulty making sense of the genesis of the new capitalist order,
especially as industrial production soon disappeared altogether.
With the unleashing of market forces, what we were observing
in Syktyvkar was the retreat to an economy of barter, reciproc-
ity, and household production. The strategy of research had to
change dramatically. Instead of working on the shop floor with
Krotov interviewing managers, I turned to the workers who

were losing their jobs, trying to comprehend how they were surviving. I teamed up with a brilliant interviewer, Tatyana Lytkina, and together we visited households of those who had worked at Polar Furniture and at a local garment factory. We learned the importance of social networks of exchange, political resources that garnered benefits from the state, especially pensions, and the economic significance of subsistence production. Women became the center of household production and men hangers-on. Men were more likely to have lost their wage-labor jobs and were singularly ill prepared to do anything else, whereas women held on to their jobs in the service and retail sectors and were much better able to adapt to the exigencies of a barter economy—they inherited those skills from state socialism, and they shouldered the responsibility for children. The story is a familiar one in different parts of the world undergoing structural adjustment.

The market transition required a new body of theory, and for this I turned to the work of Karl Polanyi, who became a key figure in transition studies. *The Great Transformation* (1944) engaged the dangers of market fundamentalism—the view that left to themselves markets could solve all economic problems. Polanyi argued that when certain entities—land, labor, and money in particular—are fully commodified, they can no longer perform their function. Exchange values destroy use value so that fully commodified land can no longer support agriculture, so that fully commodified workers can no longer contribute their labor, so that fully commodified money can no longer serve as a medium of exchange. Markets cannot survive if they are not embedded in social relations that regulate and sustain limited commodification.

If that's the general principle, the power of *The Great Transformation* lies in its historical treatment of market society. First, Polanyi shows the crucial role of the state in creating and then sustaining market capitalism in eighteenth- and nineteenth-century England. In short, there is no market road to a market economy. Second, if market forces are unregulated, they generate a reaction precisely because they threaten the very existence of society—and the reaction takes different forms in different societies. So Polanyi claims that the countermovement in the nineteenth century was largely due to the spontaneous revolt of labor—the development of trade unions, cooperatives, friendly societies, and the factory movement to limit the length of the working day. In the twentieth century the countermovement revolved around the nation-state, reacting to global markets: social democracy in Scandinavia, the New Deal in the United States, but also fascism in Italy, Spain, and Germany; and Stalinist collectivization and planning in the Soviet Union. For Polanyi reactions to the market can easily erode the freedoms of liberal democracy and therein lies its danger. *The Great Transformation* spelled out the dangers of the liberal creed, what we now call neoliberalism. What, then, is the character of this third great transformation?

What better foundation than *The Great Transformation* for exploring the consequences of the market transition in Russia? Working with Polanyi's theory, I asked what sort of countermovement to market fundamentalism did Russia exhibit? All my research pointed to the absence of a countermovement from below—the working class had been decimated and its morale deflated. The Soviet working class was in full flight from the market, defending itself against the on-rushing market tide.

There was no evidence that, driven to extremes, it would spontaneously turn against the tide as Polanyi imputed to the English working class. Rather, reaction was more likely to come from above by way of a repressive state. Putin fit the role perfectly, personifying the authoritarian response to market fundamentalism.

Positionality: The Ethnographer Out of Place

When studying capitalism in the United States, Africa, Hungary, or even Russia in 1991, the site of production was still at the center of the world. It disclosed the physiognomy of the social formation in which it was embedded. Just as the market transition called forth a shift in theoretical perspective from Marx to Polanyi, from production to exchange, from exploitation to commodification, so it also called forth a fundamental ethnographic repositioning in all three dimensions: location, embodiment, and biography.

When plants were closing down and production was in free fall, taking someone's job was not only immoral but also not the place from which to study the new order. The energy of the new order came from the sphere of exchange that was replacing planned distribution. In the winter of 1993 Krotov and I devoted ourselves to the investigation of Komi banks in Syktyvkar. In the Soviet era banks were largely accounting centers, an epiphenomenon of the planning system, but now they became a fulcrum of transition. But how to study a bank as an ethnographer? We tried for five months and, while this afforded us all sorts of insights into the dilemmas of the new companies serviced by the bank, understanding the bank itself was far more challenging.

Once one gains entry into a factory, it is no longer hidden; its functioning is there for all to observe. Production is tangible. Not so with a bank. This is not a productive entity but a transactional entity, and transactions have no firm place in space or time. We could talk to everyone in the bank, except the person who was making all the decisions, and miss all that was crucial. Precisely because its transactions are invisible, it can be the vehicle for the wholesale movement of resources from the realm of production to the realm of exchange and from there into all sorts of surprising outlets. On reflection I think we were rather fortunate not to discover much, as we might never have lived to tell the tale. At that time banking was a hazardous occupation as its leading cadres were the target (or source) of much criminal activity. Bankers were routinely being imprisoned or shot—an indication that something important was at stake.

If location in the field was the problem we faced in the bank, it was the combination of location and embodiment that obstructed the study of survival strategies of families of the now-unemployed or semiemployed workers. Short of living with them, it was almost impossible to grasp how they survived, and they certainly, with the best will in the world, could not articulate their tacit, nondiscursive knowledge. Even had I lived in families, I think it would have been difficult to comprehend what they were up to. The complexity of their lives would have been inaccessible. I simply did not have the categories, the concepts, or the theory with which to interpret what I heard and saw. All this was made amply clear to me when I worked with Tatyana Lytkina. I watched with awe and amazement how she unraveled, layer by layer, the household strategies that our informants recounted. She knew when and how to probe, she knew what was justification and what was cause, what was surface and what was deep. It might take her several long interviews, but she always managed to ferret out from our informants things they did not comprehend themselves that were so much a part of their unexamined life.

After every interview, during which I generally remained silent, she would interrogate me to see what I had understood. Hard as I might try, I invariably failed the test. It was not simply my language skills but the unfamiliarity of the practices embedded in that language. Our informants knew that Tanya understood their lives—she was from their class, she grew up in a rural community and migrated to town like so many. She went through the same struggles as they, trying to keep her own family together. She shared with them the language of life, a very specific life that was inaccessible to me. I was fascinated by the confidence and assertiveness with which she interrogated her interviewees and how trusting were their responses.

Gender, of course, was central to the picture. From her own life she understood what it meant to be the main breadwinner and manager of the household. She understood what so many men could not. Indeed, when we tried to interview men about strategies of survival, we quickly landed in a cul-de-sac. Even under Tanya's prompting—and she was an expert interviewer with many arrows to her bow—men simply did not know what was going on in their own household; they abstained from the very process, had become parasites and burdens. In their depression they had also become inarticulate.

It was not just my gender but my nationality and, indeed, my profession that posed serious problems in the field. Not just with regard to families but also with regard to our studies of enterprises—whether it be the timber, coal, or construction industries—our interviews became more difficult over time. In the beginning managers were full of hope for the future, happy to embrace a sociologist from the United States, proud of the possibilities of their enterprises in the newly found freedom of the market. But as they struggled to survive, as the economy plunged into depression, so the mood of the managers also changed. Rather than greet me as a long-lost friend, they wondered what I was doing, returning year after year. I often wondered myself. To be sure, my coworkers from Polar, at least those who had managed to find jobs elsewhere after its closure, were happy to greet me in their homes. But working-class Syktyvkar was a decaying society in which social research became daily more difficult.

It is interesting indeed to think about my reception in different workplaces, my biography of engagement. At Allied, where the workforce was fragmented by age and by race, and workers came from all over the South Side of Chicago, workers had little tolerance for my incompetence. My experiences there were perhaps more similar to Haraszti's at Red Star. When I came to Hungary, the situation was reversed and my incompetence was a source of amusement, eliciting sympathy and even affection from my coworkers. There I would go out drinking with my brigade and visit its members in their homes—the only problem was when to write my field notes. Especially at the Lenin Steel Works, the more I drank, the more I had to write, the less time I had at my disposal, and the more difficult it was to concentrate.

Russia, however, was more like Chicago. Here my exotic qualities redounded against me. Syktyvkar had been a "closed" city, more or less cut off from the outside world, so my coworkers had never seen an American before, let alone a professor laboring on their machines. I felt my every move was being watched, and I was excluded from shop-floor rituals. This was also the time of Gorbachev's campaign against alcohol consumption so it was difficult to break the ice with alcohol. Instead a few workers took pity on me and invited me to play dominoes during breaks and downtime. As I discovered years later, that was not the only problem. The forewoman in my shop had exploited my presence, continually warning workers that they had better come to work on time because there was an American watching!

Finally, there was the age factor. When I began my ethnographic odyssey in Chicago, I was twenty-seven, toward the lower end of the age spectrum. There were people my age, and I could stand to work for eight, ten, and even twelve hours a day. Ten years later it was already more difficult—but added to that, transactions were conducted in shop-floor Hungarian, and one never gets used to rotating on shifts. By the time I got onto the Russian shop floor I was forty-four—not that old for a real worker but arduous for an itinerant one like me. Moreover, learning yet another language at that age, for someone who is not good at languages in the first place, was an uphill struggle. As it turned out, Russian industry more or less shut down so I didn't have to ever work again. For me it was a blessing, for others a catastrophe.

So we see how the very processes of involution that had expelled my coworkers from the factories, expelled me from my place in the field. Like them, I had become a parasite on female labor, female skills. Marked by gender, nationality, and redundant skills, I had become an ethnographer out of place, ready to ignominiously exit the field.

CONCLUSION: COMPARISONS, CONNECTIONS, AND COLLABORATIONS

Of late there has been much talk of "counterhegemonic global-ization," the idea of an incipient movement of globalization from below that connects labor movements, feminist move-ments, racial diasporas, or nongovernmental organizations across national boundaries. It's never clear what *counter* or *hege-monic* signifies with regard to these movements, in what way they contain the seeds of any alternative hegemony or how they challenge "globalization from above," which is itself left largely unexamined. More likely, *counterhegemony* is wishful thinking or illusory phrase mongering. Counterhegemony is the roman-tic side of multisited ethnography, based on fictitious solidaristic connections or flows across the world and imagining the fiction to be an emancipatory political project.

This chapter has shown, at least for the case of labor, that existing patterns of domination leave little room for alternative hegemonies from below. If and when they have existed, as in the case of Polish Solidarity, they are based on national struggles of limited duration. If we want to approach "globalization from below," let alone counterhegemony, we have to first think through the ways labor is trapped in more local containers—factories, communities, and nations. One might say that the rel-evant "fields of force" stretch vertically from the labor regime rather than horizontally across labor regimes. We must move from the empiricism of multisited ethnography to the theoreti-cally driven multicase ethnography of "factory regimes."

This chapter has described my attempts to study such factory regimes, first in state socialist Hungary and then in post-Soviet

Russia, in search of the conditions and possibilities of "Solidarity" and kindred movements against state socialism. The first stage of the research, 1982–89, began in a synchronic mode, comparing the bureaucratic despotic regimes of state socialism to the hegemonic regimes of advanced capitalism and to the market despotisms of early capitalism. In the second stage of the research, 1991–2002, carried forward on the wave of dissolving state socialism, I turned from a synchronic comparison to a diachronic analysis of the Russian transition to capitalism, a process of economic involution.

Methodologically, I undertook what one might call a stepwise sampling in which one comparison led to the next. I didn't select a sample of cases and then investigate them together but instead pursued them serially in a succession of comparisons. Thus in the first comparison I contrasted my own experiences at Allied with Haraszti's account of Red Star, locating each in its distinctive political economy. This raised the question of variations over time and space within state socialist Hungary—how typical was Haraszti's experience? Here I uncovered the effects on production regimes of economic reforms, of position within the overall Hungarian economy, and of the dualism created within socialist factories.

These were the "realist" moments of the extended case method, but what about the ways Haraszti's portrait of shopfloor life was affected by his relations with his coworkers? To establish an appropriate comparison I needed to partake in the state socialist labor process myself. With János Lukács as my collaborator and guide, I made my way into Bánki from where I conjectured that Haraszti's account of atomism and oppression was in part the product of his own specific outsider status. By contrast, my own outsider status brought me into close connection with the collectivist dynamics of the shop floor. From Bánki, Lukács and I moved to the Lenin Steel Works, where a much longer stint of working allowed me to develop the second moment of constructivism—theoretical reconstruction. As a Western Marxist I looked for working-class opposition to state socialism, focusing on its collective basis within the steel mill, in contrast to Haraszti, the dissident who saw the workplace through the lens of totalitarianism.

The four moments of the extended case method—two realist and two constructivist—are inseparable because we can know the world only through our relation to it. Yet we cannot focus on all four moments simultaneously, so we aim our focus on one while, so to speak, holding the others constant. Since I am interested in the real world and its transformation, that is where I always begin. In the case of Hungary I chose to locate the different work organizations at Allied and Red Star within their respective overall political economies. This was possible only by "holding constant" social process, positionality, and theoretical framework, which were subsequently problematized.

In the case of Russia, Kathie Hendley and I did not begin with a structural (micro-macro) analysis of the Soviet political economy in flux but with the examination of internal processes, the civil war we encountered at the Moscow enterprise, Kauchuk. Yet this was possible only on the basis of preexisting theories of the Soviet enterprise, in particular the framework I had developed in socialist Hungary—theories that were also challenged by our experiences and observations. When I trekked north to Syktyvkar with Pavel Krotov, the wider transformation of the Soviet economy became more visible as we studied the internal and external forces buffeting a small furniture factory. In the final analysis, however, the transition from socialism to capitalism demanded a new theoretical approach that focused on markets rather than production, and the logic of that theory led us out of the factory, first into the realm of exchange (banks) and then into the home, and with it came a new and unfamiliar positionality, as I orbited around my collaborator Tatyana Lytkina. The movement from case to case was rarely ruptural but represented a shift in focus from one moment of the extended case method to another.

We know the world only through our relation to it: sometimes that relation obscures the world, while sometimes it brings it into the light. In *Manufacturing Consent* I argued that the way workers were inserted into the world, that is, their relation to the world, mystified the working of that world—capitalism systematically obscured from its participants their exploitation. As an ethnographer I did not elaborate the "good sense" of my coworkers at Allied but rather broke with their "bad sense." I made little attempt to connect my emergent reconstruction of Marxism to their folk understanding of the world. Very different was my experience in Hungary, where workers were inserted into production in a way that allowed them to see how that system worked. Their exploitation and subjugation were transparent to them. Here I could build my theory of state socialism on the basis of their "good sense," and so I found myself collaborating in the joint production of knowledge. János Lukács became a central figure in this collaboration, and indeed I ended my Hungarian stint by studying him as he tried to introduce employee-owned enterprises under the rubric of privatization.

In the Soviet Union it was more difficult to gain access to the worlds of workers, even while I toiled on the shop floor at Polar Furniture. When the collapse came, I became dependent on my collaboration with Krotov and Lytkina. For much of the research we spent time with managers and entrepreneurs who were steering Russia through the market inferno, developing their own barter schemes, their own banks, and even their own currencies. Workers were indeed passive onlookers, suspicious of the machinations of the new grasping, speculative bourgeoisie. As the workers used to joke, all that the communists taught about socialism was wrong, all that they taught about capitalism was right. From the beginning I found myself critical of the taken-for-granted but false comparison of this Russian merchant capitalism with ideal-typical capitalism, as though the former would naturally evolve into the latter. Those who did recognize the abyss that separated the two fell into the trap of a false imputation—that the obstacles to the Russian transition were to be found in the legacies of communism. Harboring illusions of another radiant future, no one wanted to listen to the ravings of this alien Cassandra.

I began my socialist escapade in an optimistic vein, searching for the roots of Solidarity and the possibilities of a democratic socialism. I ended up in a pessimistic vein, recounting the eclipse of the very idea of socialism, dissolved in a primitive, marauding capitalism. Such are the dialectics of ethnography—you never end up where you begin, if only because this is research in real space and time. History takes its own course, which defies the very theory that makes it intelligible.

Conclusion

The Ethnography
of Great Transformations

The twentieth century was strewn with the corpses of unrealized ideals—freedom, equality, and self-realization. In thwarting their realization, as Eric Hobsbawm writes, no century has been more brutal or more violent—it was indeed an age of extremes (Hobsbawm 1994). As the inheritors of the twentieth century, we can blame the specific ideals and seek out others whose realization might be less recalcitrant. Alternatively, we can blame idealism itself, banish ideals, and make the best of the existing order as the only possible world. But there is a third possibility. We can hold on to the old ideals, seeking new ways for their realization, ways informed by examining the social processes that led to their initial defeat. It is this third road that I have chosen.

The third road beckons us to refuse the nihilism that sees the twentieth century as a succession of events that piled wreckage upon wreckage and instead to step into the storm in order to take a closer look, turning a chain of catastrophes into distinctive processes of social transformation. The twentieth century began with transitions from capitalism to a socialism that then betrayed its own ideals. By the end of the twentieth century socialism-as-it-was collapsed under its own weight, returning its exhausted subjects to an unbridled capitalism. In between we witnessed the transformation of capitalism at its center and an anticolonial revolution at its periphery, each with its own alarmingly destructive variants. These four transformations defined the experience of the twentieth century and laid the foundations of the twenty-first century. Together these four transformations have exercised my attention, and this conclusion briefly assembles what I have learned.

In this book my approach to these social transformations has been first and foremost methodological. In trying to show how the horizons of ethnography are not limited to the here and now of field research, in chapter 2 I developed the idea of the ethnographic revisit to understand history. I now return to the ideas of that chapter to show how I investigated each transformation: the postcolonial transition through digging up the past in an archeological revisit and returning my research to its subjects in a valedictory revisit; the transformation of capitalism by comparing two ethnographies of the same place separated in time, that is, in a focused revisit; the transition to state socialism by framing it in terms of previous revolutions, what I called a heuristic revisit; and finally the transition from state socialism to capitalism in a succession of ethnographies, or a serial revisit. Great transformations are not just historical but societal; they involve the transformation of the relation between state and civil society or civil society and the economy. Studying a great transformation means considering not only the broad swathe of history but extending beyond the field site to national institutions, that is, from the microprocesses to the macroforces shaping them. If my point of departure has been mines and factories, my destination has been of much broader scope, seeking to understand the economy, the state, and society within which they are embedded, and through which they are transformed.

There are perils in this endeavor. If, in recent years, much has been made of the danger of romanticizing the subjects of ethnography, there is also the obverse danger of reifying the world beyond the field as unchanging and homogeneous. As I will suggest, I have been all too guilty of this second error in my treatment of market and state, not recognizing that they too are sites of human action, sites of contradictory processes, sites with their own dynamics.

Errors are always in abundant supply. They become the spice of science, when we interrogate them carefully. In making predictions we are bound to make mistakes; that is why we make predictions—to put our theories to the test so that we can then improve them. Improving theory requires obsessing about its failings. Science proceeds by correcting falsehoods rather than by capturing final truths. That is, science proceeds not by being boringly right but by being brilliantly wrong. Reflecting on the errors I made in these studies has allowed me to push theory forward.

In other words, there is more to methodology than method. From the beginning method is inextricably bound up with theory; it cannot operate without theory. As Karl Popper warned, and as I showed in the case of Skocpol's account of revolution (chapter 3), to put the induction machine into motion without the fuel of theory leaves us where we were, standing still. We need to begin with theory if we are to end with theory, so best pick theorists that we find worth developing. Thus Frantz Fanon was my lens for Africa, Antonio Gramsci for advanced capitalism, Leon Trotsky for the Russian Revolution and its Stalinist fallout, Iván Szelényi for the transformation of state socialism, and Karl Polanyi for its demise. Each theorist was an inveterate participant in the societies he studied, so he therefore had a distinct advantage over social science at a distance. These theorists never hesitated to make predictions, to map out roads into the future, which made them great but fallible scientists.

THE POSTCOLONIAL TRANSFORMATION

If methodology is not theoretically innocent, then for it to be an asset rather than an impediment we need to be theoretically self-conscious from the beginning. It took me many years to come to this realization, so I have not always followed this precept myself. My first study, conducted between 1968 and 1972, the study of Zambianization, was the most unreflective, both theoretically and methodologically. It expressed the pure undisciplined joy of social research. Even here, however, Frantz Fanon hovered in the background as a guide to postcolonialism. His class analysis of the colonial and postcolonial racial formation informed *The Colour of Class on the Copper Mines.* Zambia was not Algeria—it was not a settler colony, and its economic basis was not agrarian but industrial—so this called for a reconstruction of Fanon's theory of postcolonialism for an enclave economy based on copper. In Zambia the national bourgeois road to postcolonialism—the one in which the color of class changes but not the class structure—remained largely unchallenged by any radical visions of liberation that were among the responses to the settler colonies of Africa.

To understand the class forces behind the reproduction of the racial order in the copper mines, specifically, the principle that no black shall have any authority over any white, the principle of the color bar, I conducted an archeological revisit. I excavated the colonial history of African advancement, that is, the ways Africans were slowly advanced into positions in the industrial hierarchy hitherto monopolized by whites—a process of fragmenting and parceling out parts of white jobs to African successors but always under the guiding rule of the color bar. I concluded that the capitalist foundation of Zambia's economy set the parameters for racial succession in both periods. If anything, independence rationalized the domination of capital *and* the racial order upon which the mining industry rested. As Fanon had warned, the postcolonial transition proved to be less radical than its rhetoric. If the national liberation road to democratic socialism was blocked, then, he surmised, postcolonial rule would degenerate from democratic pluralism to one-party democracy to military dictatorships and one-man despotisms.

After my departure in 1972 the trajectory of Zambia and its copper mines was, indeed, tragic. As part of the nationalist project the Zambian government nationalized the copper mines in 1971, and in return the multinational companies received a handsome management contract. Soon after nationalization the international price of copper began to fall, turning profits into losses, but the mines were kept open as a major source of employment. Moving heavily into debt, the Zambian government took a structural adjustment loan from the International Monetary Fund (IMF) that was conditioned on reprivatization of the mining industry. During the 1970s and 1980s Zambians had advanced to the highest positions in the industry, but under privatization expatriates were pulled back into management positions from different parts of the world to make the mines a more appealing purchase on the world market. We might call it a recolonization. After some initial interest from one of the old multinationals, the Anglo American Mining Corporation, Chinese and Indian capital began taking over the industry in the twenty-first century. The story of the 1980s and 1990s was a falling price of copper that plunged the Zambian mining industry and thus the country into debt and its people into poverty and disease. Ironically, once the government off-loaded its losing investment, the price of copper shot up to four times what it was in 2002, bringing in windfall profits.

I had made at least two errors in my analysis of the copper industry and its racial order. First, in assuming that "the state" preferred the line of least resistance and so would not touch the color bar, I had homogenized the interests of the state. I did not see the state as a contradictory set of institutions in which some might pursue racial justice even at the expense of short-term economic disruption. The extended case method is in danger of reifying the external forces that shape the social processes under observation, not recognizing (because not seeing) those forces as themselves the product of uncertain social processes. I saw the errors of my ways when I undertook a valedictory revisit, that is, when I presented my ethnography to the ruling powers and unexpectedly found considerable support from the very state that I had so vehemently criticized.

My second error was to limit the macroextension to the national configuration of class forces, thereby excluding global forces, be they the price of copper or what would be the structural adjustment of the IMF. This was a deliberate reaction against the ruling elite's ideology that pointed to "neocolonialism" as the cause of continuing underdevelopment, masking its own domestic class project. While the ruling elite did promote and disguise its own interests behind the rhetoric of neocolonialism, global forces were nonetheless real. Both errors might be traced to Fanon's *The Wretched of the Earth*. I had reconstructed some parts of his theory but not others.

Disillusionment with postcolonialism has inspired new perspectives in social theory. Subaltern studies, originally developed in India, are one of its best expressions. The universality of postcolonial depression called into question the original project of independence, a project ensnared by the same metropolitan notions of nationalism that had driven colonial subjugation. Subaltern studies began to recover indigenous projects buried in the anticolonial struggles of India's peasantry and working classes. Debates raged about the alternative represented by Gandhiism. Of the two tasks—the critique of Western discourses and the recovery of counterhegemonic projects—it was the former that increasingly preoccupied subaltern studies, but it was also the one that was more easily assimilated into Western academia. In denouncing Fanon's nationalism, subaltern studies, perhaps deliberately, lost sight of his emancipatory concerns and the investigation of historically suppressed alternatives. As I shall argue later in this conclusion, today we are in desperate need of a sense of alternatives to capitalism.

THE TRANSITION TO ORGANIZED CAPITALISM

Shifting from the colony to the metropolis, the second great transformation treated in this book is the one that brought organized capitalism into existence. If the Zambianization study showed how social processes reproduced themselves despite wider changes aimed at their disruption, the second study traced small but significant changes on a factory shop floor to systemic changes in the character of capitalism.

I found my way into a machine shop in south Chicago, the engine division of Allied Corporation, a large multinational corporation, only to discover that it was precisely the same factory that had been studied by the famous Chicago ethnographer Donald Roy. He had worked there as a radial drill operator in 1944–45, and I worked there as a miscellaneous machine operator in 1974–75. At first I was stunned by how little had changed (which was why I was led to identify the plant as the one Roy had studied), but then, as I settled into his dissertation, I found small but significant changes, not so much in the technology but in the way work was regulated, what I called the internal labor market and the internal state. Broadly speaking, during the thirty years the regime had moved along the continuum from despotism to hegemony, that is to say, the balance of force and consent had shifted in the direction of consent.

It was the reconstruction of the new Marxism of the 1970s—theories of the economy, of state, and of politics influenced, especially, by the writings of Antonio Gramsci—that first allowed me to focus on this shift in the regime of production and then allowed me to explain and interpret that shift. I had been especially interested to investigate and elaborate Gramsci's claim that in the

United States hegemony was born in the factory. Specifically, the thirty years saw the consolidation of a dual economy—on the one side a monopoly or corporate sector with workers organized into unions and a production regime increasingly monitored and regulated by the state, and on the other side an unregulated competitive sector of unorganized workers. Allied Corporation had bought up Roy's Geer Company, moving it from the competitive to the monopoly sector, at the same time that the monopoly sector had itself adopted a more hegemonic regime of production.

Very different from the archeological revisit of the Zambianization study, in which I dug up the past, the Chicago study was a focused revisit—a detailed comparison of two distinct ethnographies of the same place separated in time. Theoretical reconstruction allowed me to extend—or, more precisely, to project into history—the specific differences between Geer and Allied in an account of the transition from competitive capitalism to organized capitalism. In early capitalism life depended on work, whereas under organized capitalism the dependence of life on work was mediated by the state—a state that gave certain guarantees to those without work whether because of age, infirmity, or redundancy. Since workers were less fearful of losing their jobs, they had to be persuaded rather than coerced into cooperating with management. At the same time that the state gave workers certain welfare guarantees, it also held management accountable to procedural norms in the treatment of workers. The result was a hegemonic regime of production in which coercion was applied in a regulated manner and was itself the object of consent.

The persuasion of organized capitalism was not always of a gentle kind. It could also be coercive as under fascism, and in the late 1970s a more despotic regime—hegemonic despotism—was emerging in the core sectors of U.S. industry. The hegemonic regime, which I mistakenly saw to be so stable, represented only a brief moment in history. The recession of 1974 signaled an impending double offensive against organized labor: on the one side from global capitalism that would destroy the industries of south Chicago and on the other side from the state, initiated in 1981 by the Reagan administration's firing of striking air traffic controllers. Competition from overseas manufacturing turned south Chicago into an industrial wasteland, an enormous ghetto, a warehouse of surplus population, ejected from Chicago's housing projects, themselves pulled down to make way for real estate development. As in the Zambian case study, I missed the storm of global capitalism waiting on the horizon but also the contradictory character of the state. The state is not a reified object of constant effect but itself the product of unfolding social processes. What we have witnessed, therefore, since the late 1970s is a broad erosion of labor protection and a return to the brutality of early competitive capitalism but now operating on a truly global scale, aided and abetted by more or less neoliberal states. As in Zambia, so in Chicago unfettered markets wrought their misery.

THE SOVIET REVOLUTIONS

We come now to the second set of transformations that has defined what used to be called the second world: first the transition to state socialism and then the transition to market capitalism. Methodologically, my study of the postcolonial transition involved a reconstructive projection into history based on archives and reports, whereas the analysis of the transition to advanced capitalism was based on a revisit to a plant studied thirty years before. The third transition, ostensibly of a different character, concerns the Russian Revolution. Here I rely on another participant observer, Leon Trotsky, whose analysis first anticipated and then reflected on the revolution and its denouement, an analysis that was originally based on a heuristic revisit, or retrospective reconstruction of the understanding of the French and failed German revolutions, a reconstruction that also involved the transformation of Marxist theory.

Long before the October Revolution, Trotsky was wrestling with the Marxian conception of history, according to which revolution would first occur in the most advanced capitalist countries, because there both contradictions and class struggle were the most mature. Trotsky countered this classical Marxism with an alternative account in which the world capitalist order actually concentrated contradictions in semiperipheral countries, thus creating the seeds of revolution in those countries first. Faced with competition from states built on more developed economic foundations, the Russian absolutist state sought to extract surplus more coercively and as a result stifled rather than incubated the productive forces. The percolating economic crisis coincided with the formation of a militant proletariat, militant because it was recently ripped from the land and herded into large-scale modern factories built with foreign capital. At the same time that revolution became an economic necessity, the only class capable of carrying it forward was the working class— the bourgeoisie was weak and dependent on French and German finance. The balance of forces favoring the working class distinguished the Russian Revolution from the French

Revolution, where the emerging bourgeoisie prevailed, and from the failed German Revolution of 1848, where bourgeoisie and working class were in equilibrium.

If the working class became the leading political force in Russia in 1917, its instincts and interests, so Trotsky argued, would drive it forward to socialism—improved working conditions, democratic control of production, shortening of the working day, and so on. Yet all these were impossible, given the underdevelopment of the productive forces. The success of the Russian Revolution depended on triggering revolution in Europe, which was most likely to break out in Germany. Failing that, the Russian Revolution would inevitably degenerate. Here Trotsky's perspicacity shone—his anticipation and then analysis of Stalinism was without parallel for his time, yet his continuing anticipation of an imminent revolution in the West was deeply flawed. Other Marxists would have to come to terms with the failure of revolution in the West and the stabilization of organized capitalism.

Trotsky was the supreme participant observer, allowing him to develop theory and practice alongside each other, leading him to participate in what came to be a self-destroying revolution. His interested participation in the Russian Revolution and its denouement was not an obstacle but an asset to his analysis and the grounds for his imaginative reconstruction of Marxism. As a revolutionary he had to get his science right—this was no academic exercise but a matter of world historical importance. So when it came to understanding Russia, Marxism was not a dogma but a body of theory that had to be refashioned in accordance with and alongside Trotsky's participation. By the same token his distance from the European theater of class struggle and class compromise led to a more stunted analysis of the West, following a more conventional Marxism.

WITHER STATE SOCIALISM?

In his analysis of the Soviet transitional period in the 1920s, as well as in his analysis of Stalinism, Trotsky already posed the question of whither the Soviet Union: socialism or capitalism? With the consolidation of Stalinism, especially during the Second World War and the post-Stalin thaw, the question of socialism or capitalism divided the world but not the future of the Soviet Union. State socialism seemed to be here to stay. To be sure, it faced challenges on the periphery: East Germany in 1953, Hungary in 1956, Czechoslovakia in 1968, but these rebellions were quickly quashed. Moreover, they aimed at the reform of state socialism rather than a transition to capitalism. The Polish Solidarity movement of 1980 and its self-limiting revolution, however, went far deeper into society and lasted much longer (sixteen months). The movement contained divergent tendencies, but even here its guiding vision was the democratization of state socialism.

Although I was not able to make my way to Poland before General Jaruzelski seized power, the Solidarity movement whetted my interest in state socialism and its potentialities. Locked out of Poland, I began a series of ethnographies, a serial revisit, that took me from factory to factory in Hungary and then into the heartland of Russia. When I embarked on this twenty-year odyssey in 1982, I was in search of the seeds of democratic socialism. Little did I expect to be a participant in or observer of the transition to capitalism. My Hungarian journey began in a champagne factory on a collective farm and moved to a textile factory of an agricultural cooperative, and from there I made my way into an industrial plant similar to Allied. Finally, I reached the heart of the socialist working class, landing a job in a steel mill. Between 1985 and 1988 I worked there for more than a year.

Just at the very moment that I thought I had discovered a working class with a socialist consciousness, the entire order fell apart and descended into capitalism. I gazed upon the broken pieces of a socialist imaginary—justice, equality, and efficiency— won against the mendacity and false promises of the party-state and founded on solidarity produced in the workplace. I took seriously the argument of Konrád and Szelényi that legitimacy was the lynchpin of state socialism but also, so I claimed, the source of its vulnerability. It generated a working class that demanded that the state make good on its claim to be a workers' state. Working with János Kornai's theory of the shortage economy, I drew the conclusion that the pathologies of the socialist workplace required the collective self-organization of work. Thus, paradoxically, it was the political and economic vulnerability of state socialism that inspired visions within its working class of a democratically empowered and economically efficient socialism. My socialist imaginary, however, proved to be more imaginary than socialist.

Why had I been so wrong, so misguided, in believing that state socialism could usher in democratic socialism rather than market capitalism? In part it was wishful thinking, in part I was simply looking in the wrong place—the transition did not come from within the bowels of production but spread down from the political superstructures of society. The ruling elites had lost confidence in their ability to reform state socialism. Once again the problem with the extended case method lay in the reification of forces beyond the ethnographic site, as though they were natural and eternal. The party-state, the planning ministries, may appear as impervious forces from the standpoint of production but in reality they too are the product of social processes and strategic action, albeit hidden from production. Another source of error lay in the question that propelled my investigations— why would the first working-class revolution occur in state socialism, and why Poland and not Hungary? I was asking about the basis of Solidarity so as to understand the conditions for its reenactment, whereas the ruling elites were way ahead of me. Having diagnosed those conditions, they were determined to transform them precisely so there would be no reenactment.

At the same time that Hungarian state socialism was disintegrating from above, the Soviet Union became the site of burgeoning social movements from below. A fateful trip to the Soviet Union in 1990 led to a decade of fieldwork, beginning in early 1991. The developing schisms in Soviet society, which were very different from those in Hungary, *were* very visible from within the factory. In the first study conducted in a Moscow rubber factory, the colliding forces—plan versus market, Soviet Union versus Russia—divided management into warring factions, whereas a few months later in northern Russia I witnessed the emergence of a new form of capitalism—what we called merchant capitalism—that would destroy the existing economy in a process of primitive disaccumulation. The Soviet transition to a market economy was neither revolutionary as the big-bang theorists prescribed nor evolutionary as the institutionalists desired, but instead it was involutionary—a process in which the market expanded at the expense of production. As a result Russia experienced a precipitous economic decline, unparalleled in the twentieth century, that continued unabated until 1998. My theory of merchant capitalism and its consequence, economic involution, offered accurate depictions of the first decade of the market transition. Together with Pavel Krotov and Tatyana Lytkina I traced the reverberations of involution in the timber, coal, and construction industries and in the survival strategies of formerly working-class families.

Unlike my studies of Zambianization and hegemonic regimes of production that called for a deliberate reconstruction of the past, I had become a participant in a historical process that became the object of analysis. As with Trotsky there were two phases—a more optimistic phase of late Hungarian socialism and the more depressing phase of Russian decline and degradation. The second phase called for a profound revamping of Marxist theory, a shift away from production to a focus on the destructive power of the market. Here I took up the ideas of Karl Polanyi, who had devoted his life-work to the dangers of market fundamentalism. Many have drawn from Polanyi the idea that markets have to be embedded in society and, furthermore, require the regulation of the state. For me what is more interesting is Polanyi's historical analysis, that if taken too far markets generate countermovements: in the nineteenth century the countermovement was from society, involving the factory movement and the creation of trade unions, cooperatives, and voluntary associations, while in the twentieth century it was the reaction of states—social democracy and New Deal but also fascism and Stalinism. Given the traumatic reactions of the twentieth century, Polanyi believed that the liberal creed had exhausted itself and that socialism, formed by a collectively self-organized society subjugating market and state to itself, was on the agenda. But he was wrong. Market fundamentalism rose for a third time—a veritable cyclone destroying everything in its path.

That indeed has been the aftermath of the great transformations I have studied for thirty years. We see in Zambia, and Africa more broadly, the devastation wrought by structural adjustment. Even postapartheid South Africa, with its long history of socialist struggles, has turned to the market, privatizing utilities and services, opening itself up to cheap commodities from abroad, allowing the accumulation of wealth on the one side and the destruction of the social wage on the other. We see it in south Chicago, and the industrial heartlands of the United States more generally, which have become wastelands for warehousing surplus populations. We see the political side of market fundamentalism in the calamity that struck New Orleans, a security state that failed to prevent death and misery even though it had been long anticipated, a state that failed to organize relief measures once the storm had struck, and, finally, most amazing of all, a state that has failed to rehabilitate the population in the aftermath. Moving farther afield we see it most brazenly in the embrace of shock therapy by Russian elites aiming to destroy all vestiges of the planned economy by taking a revolutionary road to the market economy. The Stalinist terror of primitive accumulation achieved through collectivization and central planning has turned into its opposite—the primitive disaccumulation of privatization and unbridled markets. We have yet to see the fallout of the (so far) more successful, regulated transition to the market in China.

FROM THIRD WAVE MARKETIZATION
TO REAL UTOPIAS

Karl Polanyi's *The Great Transformation* concerns itself with the transition to a market society—a transition fateful for all humanity that no place in the world escaped. His account stretches from the end of the eighteenth century to the end of the Second World War. Where he sees one long transformation, I see two distinct waves of marketization—the first stretching through the nineteenth century and the second spanning the period from World War I to the middle 1970s. Today we are in the midst of a third wave of marketization that Polanyi never anticipated, one that took off in the last quarter of the twentieth century and has since enveloped the globe.

One of Polanyi's distinctive contributions lies in the analysis of the countermovements to marketization that protect society from unregulated commodification. We can discern a distinctive countermovement for each wave: the reaction to the first wave took the form of local organizations that were responding to the commodification of labor, the reaction to the second wave took the form of distinctive state formations (New Deal, social democracy, fascism, Stalinism) reacting to the commodification of money, while the reaction to the third wave is assuming a distinctively global character, reacting to the commodification of nature, especially land and natural resources. We can look upon the succession of waves as a dialectical progression in which the institutional basis of the countermovements are, at least, partially inherited from one wave to the next—civil society (including labor unions and political parties) from the first, regulatory states from the second. Equally, labor and money continue to undergo commodification in the third wave, but nature assumes increasing centrality in public debate and social movements.

The Soviet Union was shaped by all three waves. The revolution of 1917 was a late reaction to first-wave marketization, while the Stalin revolution of collectivization and central planning, beginning after the failure of the New Economic Policy, was the Soviet reaction to second-wave marketization. The collapse of the Soviet Union and its satellites in the last decade of the twentieth century marked the demise of statist response to second-wave marketization while also consolidating third-wave marketization. The transition from competitive to organized capitalism represented the reaction to second-wave marketization in the core, while the postcolonial transition represented its counterpart in the periphery.

What is striking is how all these great transformations succumbed to third-wave marketization. Whether it be Zambia, south Chicago, Hungary, or Russia, the advent of third-wave marketization has brought devastation and inequality unanticipated in the studies I undertook, except in the Russian case, where the writing was on the wall. In the other studies I missed the global context in part because its impact was still relatively episodic but also because the theories I worked with, and classical sociology more generally, were focused on national social formations. To be sure, third-wave marketization was mediated by national social formations, but it was also often aided and abetted by the nation-state. It struck with such devastating force, a weapon of mass destruction, that it swept away many protective levees.

While I was at pains to bring the state back in, I failed to elucidate its internal contradictions and dynamic processes. In focusing on the vulnerable and the downtrodden, entering the hidden abode of production and working-class communities, I too easily adopted their view of the state, either exaggerating or underestimating its power. I was taken in by the spontaneous common sense of production and paid too little attention to social theory. The state and the ruling class are not the mechanical objects but strategic actors, well versed in exploiting crises, absorbing challenges, and, when necessary, taking offensives against subordinate classes. In each of my cases of great transformation I would have done well to have adopted and adapted Gramsci's concept of passive revolution—a molecular transformation orchestrated from above to absorb challenges from below.

Even as I underestimated the strategic sense of the state and ruling classes, I also exaggerated the power of these macroforces. With the exception of Trotsky's analysis of the Russian Revolution and its aftermath, the ethnographies that I describe here are all concerned with changes in the microcontext, occurring as a result of changes in the macrocontext, that is, the macrofoundations of microprocesses. There is a presumption that the logic of history is given at the macrolevel, that there is a rationality to that history, and that history is on our side. If only we understood those laws of social change, we would be able to assure ourselves a better world. There are no such guarantees, and history never escapes its dark side, the result of intended and unintended consequences of deliberate action. Under third-wave marketization the early gains of postcolonialism, organized capitalism, and even post-Stalin state socialism are reversed. We would do well to dispense with laws of history, whether Marxian or liberal, and leave behind the associated ruptural or catastrophic theories of social transformation.

So what, then, are the implications of this analysis for the ethnography of social transformation? Given that twentieth-century attempts to achieve freedom, justice, equality, and democracy were blocked and even reversed, how should we approach their realization in the twenty-first century? If we cannot rely on laws of history to deliver a better society, and if ruptural revolutions endanger the values we treasure, we have to foster prefigurative institutions that instantiate desirable values. The ethnographer now assumes the special role of social archeologist.

Instead of looking at the field site as a way to understand the laws of history, we look upon it as the foundation of an alternative order. Therefore we don't look for typical institutions but for those odd institutions such as cooperatives or experiments in democratic governance that harbor greater freedom and security. The ethnographer as archeologist concentrates on digging up the subaltern, understood as alternative institutions, and examines their internal contradictions, their dynamics, and their conditions of existence. In seeking out such concrete experiments—real utopias, as Erik Wright calls them—we keep alive the ideals of social and political justice that are in danger of being lost or neutered in capitalist accumulation.[1]

In this context ethnographic extension can move in two directions. On the one hand we can extrapolate small-scale institutional innovation to the national or even global level. If participatory budgeting can occur in one city, say, Porto Alegre, how can we think of this at a national or even global level? What are the implications and possibilities of extending its scale? On the other hand, we can think of extension as joining together different microexperiments in an emerging transnational movement.

Can cooperatives, for example, be linked together to form a global cooperative movement, and, if so, what entity might perform this bridging task? In both tasks of extension—extrapolation and bridging of real utopias—intellectuals have an analytical task, diagnosing what is possible, but they also have an ideological function, galvanizing the critical imagination—simultaneously diagnosing the limits of capitalism and sustaining the idea that another world is possible.

Epilogue

On Public Ethnography

As social scientists we are part of the world we study. Typically, we insulate ourselves from the dilemmas this creates. We barricade ourselves in the ivory tower, relying on data gathered by others, accessing the empirical world at a distance, burying ourselves in archives, or even corralling our subjects into laboratories. As participant observers we cast these protections aside and plunge into the world beyond, which forces us to think more deeply about our relations to that world—relations that both are specific to the immediacy of the communities we study and extend to our responsibilities and obligations as social scientists more generally, independent of the techniques we use. As an extreme form of research, participant observation helps us think about the tensions between accountability to the world we study and obligations to the academic community.

Caught between the world of the observer and the world of the participant, the ethnographer faces a host of practical problems. In gaining entry to a site ethnographers have to justify their intense surveillance, their prying into the lives of others. Not surprisingly, communities often put up barriers to the outsider, causing us to create elaborate justifications for our presence. Gatekeepers effectively shield their sites from intruders, so that sometimes entry can be accomplished only through covert means, as in the case of my Zambian study, or through elaborate negotiation with "authorities," as in my Hungarian studies. The rich and the powerful have more to hide and do not readily consent to our scrutiny. It is easier to study the poor and weak, who are defenseless against our encroachments in their space and time. There is a deep bias in the human subjects protocols.

Not just in entry but in day-to-day involvement, our presence is continually being questioned, both by those with whom we interact and by us, because we are aware that our business is symbolic violence, exploiting the goodwill of others for our own ends. We can assuage our guilt by developing a gift economy, bribing our subjects, offering advice, but also by representing the community to the outer world. Here we are entering dangerous territory since communities are rarely unified, so which faction should we represent—workers or managers? Brahmins or Dalits? Teachers or students? In the end, to whom are we accountable? We can easily lose our moral compass and, like the military anthropologist who helps stabilize foreign occupation, become a hired expert for dubious causes.

These questions are no less salient once we leave our site, and leaving often proves as problematic as gaining entry. Having established relations, it is difficult to cut them off just because the study is technically complete. We might say there are two types of ethnographers, those who return to their communities and those who don't, those who establish an enduring human connection and those who negotiate a more instrumental relation. There are, of course, also those who create such turmoil in their sites that they are expelled, never to be allowed to return.

There are no simple answers to such ethical and existential dilemmas that the participant observer confronts in the field. The participant observer cannot escape the contradictory poles of participation and observation. Whereas texts on participant observation see these dilemmas in narrow individualistic terms, as problems faced and resolved by the individual ethnographer, I want to embed these dilemmas in two broad questions—questions connected to the fourth element of the extended case method, that is, in the extension, elaboration, reconstruction of theory. From the side of observer we must ask whose theory we refute or reconstruct, and from the side of the participant we must ask which audience we address with our reconstructed theory.

The first question, then, is, whose theory do we reconstruct? I take the view that everyone is a theorist in the sense that some coherent account of the world is necessary to live in community with others. We all have tacit theories of how the world works, leading us to anticipate the behavior of others. We stop at a red light because a watching police officer might give us a ticket, or because we don't want to get hit by a car coming the other way, or because we have learned to do this ever since we could walk. Contained in that very act is a theory or range of theories of how the world functions, a theory that remains tacit and unexamined. As ethnomethodologists have taught us, such nondiscursive, taken-for-granted theories are exposed when our anticipations are violated, when, for example, a driver runs through a red light. Such tacit theories may be short on mechanisms, indeed may be shorthand for inaccessible processes, processes that are the concern of the explanatory theory of social science.

Therefore we can distinguish two types of theory. On the one hand there is the theory of the people we study, namely, folk theory, buried in common sense and sometimes elaborated into ideology. On the other hand, there is the theory of the philosophers and social scientists, that is to say, of intellectuals, what I call analytical theory, which we can also call science. I assume that folk theory, while it has to contain some truth, a practical truth, is not as adequate as the truth of analytical theory, scientific truth. This is an act of faith, perhaps, but also the raison d'être of our scholarly existence. As sociologists, therefore, we may think of ourselves as breaking with or elaborating folk theory, but in either case we are moving from folk theory to analytical theory.

Just as academics too often take for granted that the object of transformation is our own analytical theory rather than the folk theory of our subjects, so equally we cannot assume that the people we address are also social scientists. The second question, therefore, is, to whom is our theory addressed? Are we addressing academic audiences—our home community of scholars, specialists in the production of theory—or are we focused on lay audiences? In principle one can be doing both simultaneously, but these discursive communities tend to be distinct, calling for different strategies of engagement. Within each category there is a broader and a narrower audience. Within the academic world one can address a narrow community of specialists or a broader community of scientists, just as beyond the academy we may be focused on the people we studied or on wider publics.

Table 8. *Public and Academic Ethnography*

	Academic Audience	Extra-academic Audience
Analytical theory (science)	Professional	Prophet
Folk theory (ideology)	Critic	Interpreter

Answers to the two questions—theory from whom? and theory to whom?—are independent of each other, which means we can draw up a two-by-two table (table 8). The true public ethnographer, what I have called the interpreter, uses his or her science to elaborate and transform the folk theory of the participants but makes the result accessible and relevant to publics. Here lies Nancy Scheper-Hughes's (1992) report on the desperate circumstances of mothers in the favelas of Brazil, Margaret Mead's (1928) interpretation of the sexual practices of adolescents in Samoa, or Diane Vaughan's (2006) revelations about the organizational biases of NASA. The professional ethnographer does the opposite. Here the object of our social science is to transform, build, and improve academic theory. Examples abound, but they would include the classic anthropologists of kinship such as Radcliffe-Brown or Evans-Pritchard. Within the world of sociology professional ethnographers often also become interpreters— think of Kathryn Edin and Laura Lein's (1997) work on welfare mothers, Mitchell Duneier's (1999) work on street vendors, Elliot Liebow's (1967) work on unemployed men, Arlie Hochschild's (1989) work on the domestic division of labor, or William Foot Whyte's (1943) work on gangs.

Professional ethnographers become prophets when they seek to transmit their analytical theory to wider audiences, turning social science insight into the fate of humanity. We think here of the anthropologists Clifford Geertz, Max Gluckman, or Edmund Leach or the sociologist Robert Bellah, when they took on the role of public educator. Finally, we have the critics, who take folk theory as the object of elaboration but deploy it against existing analytical theory held by academics. The critic tries to demonstrate that not just lay knowledge but social science itself is in the grip of folk theory. One thinks of Karl Marx's analysis of commodity fetishism, a generalized lived experience of the market that holds in thrall not just workers but academics, too. Equally, Pierre Bourdieu shows how the mystification of domination through distinction affects social science as well as everyday life.

Of the four studies that I examined in this book, the study of Zambianization is the only truly public ethnography, where I played the interpreter. The study was constructed as an engagement with the government's Zambianization report, which declared all was well in the copper mines—Africans were replacing expatriates. But these figures hid from view the organizational manipulations that maintained the color bar. I drew on and reconstructed the sociological theories of Alvin Gouldner and Frantz Fanon to understand the social forces working to uphold the racial order, but *The Colour of Class on the Copper Mines* (1972a) was written for a public audience. In addition to being accessible, it touched different interests, as demonstrated by the initial opposition of the mining executives and the enthusiasm of the government's chief of Zambianization. Indeed, when it did appear, it attracted considerable media attention.

Yet in the end, the mining executives used the report to discipline their own mine managers, instructing them to get their

Zambianization house in order. The effect of the report was thereby neutralized. Here lies the problem with "traditional" public ethnography in which the scientist broadcasts her or his discoveries and interpretations but has no control over their deployment on behalf of the powerful. If I had worked more closely with grassroots organizations, and followed Dorothy Smith's (2007) institutional ethnography or participatory action research, my broad criticism of Zambian economic development might have been sustained. Still, for all its shortcomings, this was a case of public ethnography, taking government ideology as its point of departure, discovering the social processes behind it, and bringing those findings into the public realm.

Manufacturing Consent (Burawoy 1979) took the diametrically opposite approach. I adopted an instrumental approach to the field site. As a graduate student I was preoccupied with the academic world, bent on a critique of sociology and developing Marxism based on my experiences on the shop floor. I was a disciple of structuralist Marxism and saw science as simultaneously a rupture with and explanation of common sense. I was intrigued by my coworkers, who labored so hard yet at the same time denied they were doing so. If industrial sociology had conventionally focused on restriction of output, why workers don't worker hard, I inverted the question—why do they work as hard as they do? If traditional industrial sociology didn't ask the question, Marxism assumed the answer lay with coercion and material incentives. Marxists missed the organization of consent on the shop floor, thinking this took place only in political and civil society.

I never thought of convincing my coworkers that they were working hard or that Marxism bore any relation to their lives.

Marxist structuralism, a product of the French Grandes Écoles and a reaction against the intellectual sterility of the French Communist Party, became the rationale for devoting myself to the transformation of social science. I was not alone in this endeavor but part of a 1960s generation, in the United States and elsewhere, that considered the immediate task was to bring sociology out of the dark ages or to simply replace it with Marxism. Following Alvin Gouldner's *The Coming Crisis of Western Sociology* (1970), we claimed that the sociology we inherited from the 1950s and 1960s was out of sync with the mobilization of society, manifested, especially, in third world movements both within the United States and elsewhere. Academic Marxism was a project of intellectuals that made little effort to directly address the working class. Somehow scientific truth would benefit all. In this regard it was different from much of second-wave feminism and the new interdisciplinary programs (African American studies, Chicano studies, Native American Studies) whose raison d'être lay in publicizing and addressing the plight of marginalized communities.

Marxism has not always been cut off from the subjects of its analysis. Leon Trotsky is a case in point. He would find academic Marxism an oxymoron or, more likely, a petty bourgeois deviation. Immersed in the Marxist debates of the time, Trotsky was, at the same time, always determined to address the broadest possible audience. He was a spectacular orator and, of course, a virtuoso organizer, most notably of the Red Army during the civil war. Marxism's claim to knot theory and practice together for social transformation made it an appealing philosophy. Trotsky was unusual among the classical Marxists in that his writings were indeed accessible to all. But this did not mean they were any less theoretical. Wrestling with the specificity of the Russian experience, immersed in a project of revolutionary change, he gave an original twist to Marxism by recognizing the rhythm of world capitalist development and its implications for national transformations.

As Isaac Deutscher portrays him in his majestic three-volume biography (1954, 1959, 1963), Trotsky was indeed a rare prophet. His magnum opus—*The History of the Russian Revolution* ([1933] 1977)—is shaped by his theoretically inspired participation in those events, allowing him to see macrotransformations in the microprocess. He was committed to an emancipatory socialism and recognized this could be accomplished in the Soviet Union only if it triggered revolutions elsewhere. There could be no socialism in one country. His perspective was no innocent academic conclusion but the essence of his ideological and political difference with Stalin. For Trotsky the fate of the revolution rested on the adoption of strategies informed by theory, one might say a naive belief in the correctness of a refashioned Marxism. His arguments still rested on the illusory belief that the Western working class was ripe for revolution—an assumption he never abandoned but that other Marxists—Gramsci in particular—would call into question.

This brings me to the last stance—the critic who starts with folk theory but aims its interrogation and demystification at other academics. Many reasons combined to drive me to Eastern Europe, but the theoretical impulse came from my own claims that a capitalist working class could not arrive at revolutionary self-understanding. Was this true of all working classes or only the capitalist working class? Solidarity suggested that the socialist working class might have such a revolutionary potential.

Furthermore, whether the West's working class was revolutionary or not, it was surely incumbent on Western Marxists to understand the character of actually existing socialism and not simply dismiss it as a statism, irrelevant to the Marxist project. It was simply too easy to harp on the pathologies of capitalism and assume that they would be rectified in a socialist heaven, letting socialism on Earth off the hook. So I ventured to Eastern Europe in the hope of finding a working class with socialist aspirations. Sure enough, I found traces of socialism, nurtured in the womb of production and expressed as a critique of the party-state for failing to live up to its promises—failings to which it drew attention through its political and ideological practices of self-justification.

In Hungary, as in Chicago, I was not keen to display my Marxism since for critical intellectuals it was a bankrupt ideology and for workers it announced itself as betrayal. There was a moment of genuine optimism in 1989 when I thought that the collapse of state socialism prefigured the rise of a democratic socialism, as I wrote in an article titled "Marxism Is Dead: Long Live Marxism!" (Burawoy 1990a). I still believed this as late as 1990, when I lectured on the contradictions and paradoxes of state socialism to South African audiences. The South African Communist Party had just begun a painful interrogation of its past and launched a debate about the possibilities of socialism, a debate that became dying embers once the African National Congress assumed power. My own hopes for socialist renewal took a beating in Russia's catastrophic transition to capitalism. I took up cudgels against the new reigning ideology of market fundamentalism, watching powerlessly as unbridled commodification devoured the productive forces, leaving large swaths of the population in desperate poverty and degradation. I had no audience in Russia, so I became a Marxist critic at home, a critic of market ideology within social science, showing how untamed markets led to disaccumulation, or what I called the great involution. Yet it was becoming difficult enough to defend Marxism within the academy, let alone outside.

For twenty years—from 1982 to 2002—I had taken a detour through socialism. It was time to return to capitalism, perhaps a little wiser but no less Marxist. Marxism after communism would have to finally jettison its laws of history—history as the succession of modes of production, history as the rise and fall of any given mode of production, history as the history of class struggle. The transition to socialism can no longer be understood as rupture with capitalism but instead as the emergence and stringing together of smaller-scale alternatives, what Gramsci called a war of position. Marxist social science has now to base itself in the trenches of society, seeking out embryonic institutions, real utopias that might challenge capitalism, keeping alive the very idea of alternatives. Marxism thereby necessarily becomes public ethnography in so far as it enters into a dialogue and collaboration with the organizers of real utopias. Marxists forsake their grand theories of history to become interpreters and transmitters of the conditions of possibility of alternatives to capitalism, alternatives struggling for survival in the interstices of society.

The collapse of communism may not spell the end of socialism, but it has certainly intensified third-wave marketization around the globe. As third-wave marketization erodes civil society, it threatens all institutions outside market and state, the foundations of real utopias. The very idea of the social is in abeyance, threatening the existence of the *social* sciences, including human geography, anthropology as well as sociology, but not the economic sciences or political sciences that have become ever more asocial or antisocial. In the postcommunist era Marxism and sociology become collaborators in the defense of the social. Indeed, we can go further and declare that sociology itself is fast becoming a real utopia, providing a concrete imagination for an alternative world incompatible with capitalism. As such we need a reflexive ethnography to propagate the sociological imagination, the prophetic glue that can bind real utopias together while holding at bay the destructive forces of market and state. Sociology, if it is to survive, may have no alternative but to go public.

NOTES

INTRODUCTION

1. Outside sociology Victor Turner and Raymond Smith knew all about the Manchester School, and, just as I was leaving the University of Chicago, John Comaroff and Jean Comaroff arrived.

CHAPTER ONE

Acknowledgments: This chapter was twenty years in the making. Earlier versions are unpublished and barely recognizable. Two people in particular helped me bring this endeavor to a close. Erik Wright plied me with dozens of pages of intense argumentation to the effect that there can be only one model of science, while Peter Evans insisted that I persist despite all opposition. And opposition there was plenty, from hostile receptions in talks to dismissive reviews from journal referees. My ideas took shape in heated courses on participant observation and while working with Berkeley graduate students on two books, *Ethnography Unbound* and *Global Ethnography*. Teresa Gowan, Leslie Salzinger, Maren Klawiter, and Amy Schalet were intent on holding me accountable for what I said, while Raka Ray, Jennifer Pierce, Charles Ragin, Michael Goldman, Raewyn Connell, Nora Schaeffer, and especially Linda Blum provided more gentle stimuli over the years. My greatest debt is to Jaap van Velsen, my first sociology teacher, who, as an anthropologist, exemplified the extended case method, although he'd recoil in horror at the formalization to which I have subjected it. Finally, Craig Calhoun braved the opposition to first steer this into print when he was editor of *Sociological Theory.*

1. For an overview of the Manchester School's approach to anthropology, see Kingsley Garbett (1970). For commentary on the Manchester Method by its leading figure see Max Gluckman (1958, 1961a, 1961b, 1964). Major expositions of the extended case method include Clyde Mitchell (1956, 1983); A.L. Epstein (1958); and van Velsen (1960, 1964, 1967). Andrew Abbott (2007) has written a fascinating and erudite critique of my appropriation of the extended case method, rightly distinguishing it from the original Manchester version.

2. On racism and labor markets see Liebow (1967) and Bourgois (1995). On urban political regimes see Whyte (1943), Susser (1982), and Haney (1996).

3. Dorothy Smith (1987). On family ethnographies see Stacey (1990), DeVault (1991), and Hondagneu-Sotelo (1994). Dorothy Smith's paradigm-breaking "sociology of women," originally written in 1977, begins by debunking abstract, decontextualized, and universalistic sociology as the ideology of ruling men and turns to the concrete lived experience of women as its point of departure. The microstructures of everyday life, which women direct, become the foundation and invisible premise for macrostructures controlled by men. This looks like the extended case method, but whereas Smith justifies it on the ground of the "standpoint of women," I ground it in an alternative conception of science. In this regard I am closer to Sandra Harding (1986, 1990), who works the terrain between androcentric science and postmodern dismissal of science. Rather than surrender science to men, Harding calls for a successor science. In her

subsequent writings Smith turns this opening rupture with mainstream sociology into a methodological universal. Thus her institutional ethnography, what Smith (2007) calls a sociology for people, pursues the link between local and extralocal by accentuating lived experience, relations of ruling, and their mediation through texts. She dismisses all other approaches to ethnography and ignores preexisting sociology, including feminist sociologies since the 1970s, except those that are done by her students, pretending to start afresh with every problem she tackles and thereby reproducing what we already know. She identifies problematic aspects of the extended case method, namely, the reification of external forces and the arbitrary invocation of theory, issues I take up in this chapter, but she has difficulty identifying any problematic aspects in her own methodology. All methodologies, like all theories, are limited, and they develop by openly recognizing and engaging with those limitations.

4. See A. L. Epstein (1958) for a description of the system at Luanshya Mine in the 1950s.

5. In chapter 2 I describe another study (Burawoy 1979), this time of a factory in South Chicago. Here I found myself in the same plant that had been studied by another sociologist thirty years earlier. I could have tried to show why his theory of "output restriction" was wrong, but instead I used it as a baseline from which to extend my own study back into history.

6. Just how difficult is it to control context effects can be seen in ethnographically sensitive survey research. In order to reduce "interview effects" survey research matches the race of interviewer and interviewee, but this can exaggerate respondent effects and field effects. Sanders (1995) shows that the wider racial field invades the interview so much that some black respondents imputed whiteness to their black telephone interviewers. Moreover, those blacks who identified their interviewer as white adopted more conciliatory attitudes. In their pen experiment Bischoping and Schuman (1992) show that the divergent polling results before the Nicaraguan election of 1991 were the result of the respondents' perception that the polling organization

was partisan. Bischoping and Schuman (1992) conclude that this was an artifact of the polarized situation in Nicaragua, but exactly how that field affected the responses remained unclear.

7. Stinchcombe (1980). In regard to social situations I am appealing to a methodological situationism (Knorr-Cetina 1981; Cicourel 1964) to replace a methodological individualism. Survey researchers might try to build social situation in as a variable, examining, for example, how a person's race is affected by situation, but that is very different from methodological situationism in which the situation rather than the individual is the unit of analysis. Thus Cicourel (1982) raises the problem of "referentiality"—what can we know about a given situation from a conversation that takes place in another situation?

8. See Clark and Schober (1992). In an inventive move Sniderman and Piazza (1993) try to build dialogue into their surveys by presenting respondents with predetermined counterarguments. For example, respondents are first asked whether they approve of government support for blacks. If respondents approve of spending increases, then they are asked whether they would feel the same way if blacks were singled out for special treatment. If, on the other hand, respondents do not approve of more spending, they are asked if they would feel the same if this meant that blacks would continue to be poorer than whites. The data show that 44 percent of whites were "talked out" of their original position. In the case of affirmative action only 20 percent changed their minds in the face of counterarguments. It is not clear why there should be such changes, whether Sniderman and Piazza are tapping context-specific attitudes, whether attitudes of whites toward race are pliable and superficial, or whether this is simply an artifact of the interview situation itself in which the respondent flows with an expected answer. Whatever else, these changes in responses suggest the importance of studying the interview itself as a social situation.

9. This distinction can be extended to the natural sciences. There are philosophers of the natural sciences, such as Michael Polanyi (1958), who refuse the separation of subject and object. His theory of personal knowledge gives centrality to the natural scientist who makes contact

with and dwells in "nature." Similarly, Evelyn Fox Keller (1983, 1985) makes the case that natural scientists, like social scientists, may also be part of the world they study, that they have a human relation to the objects under investigation. In her feminist view what is distinctive is not the objects of science but the gendered way we approach them. Finally, from a realist standpoint Roy Bhaskar (1979) insists on intervention and experiment as central to both the natural and social sciences. The distinction between reflexive and positive science does not have ontological foundations; it does not depend on the nature of the world being studied. The distinction between the two models lies not in its object (human as opposed to nonhuman) but in the relation of scientist to object.

10. In other words, I follow Abbott (1992, 1997) and Somers and Gibson (1994) in distinguishing the "narrative" of social process from the causality of social forces, but where they want to replace the second with the first, I insist on retaining a place for social forces as methodological expedient and experiential reality, framing and confining social processes.

11. Anthony Giddens (1984) has made structuration the leitmotif of his work. He seeks to transcend the dualism of subject and object, agency and structure, micro and macro by substituting the notion of duality in which practices simultaneously reproduce the conditions that enable them. He stresses how structure facilitates rather than constrains action, much as language allows speech. In the end, intuitive notions of structure evaporate and we are left with a voluntarist vision that emphasizes the control we exercise over our worlds. I return to a more conventional notion of structuration in which "structure," or "social forces," really do confine what is possible, although they are themselves continually reconfigured. What he understands as structuration is closer to what I call process, but even here I will give more centrality to structures of micropower that are beyond the control of individuals.

12. A substantial body of philosophy of science, informed by historical exploration of the growth of knowledge, argues that science

moves forward through the absorption of anomalies within paradigms (Kuhn 1962) or research programs (Lakatos 1978), as well as through competition among paradigms or research programs.

13. Rebecca Emigh (1997) has made the critical distinction between "deviant case" analysis, in which the outliers increase the generalizability of our theory, and "negative cases" analysis, which increases the "empirical content" of theory, what I have called theory reconstruction.

14. Again, Anthony Giddens (1992) has made much of this interchange between academic and lay theory, arguing that sociology appears not to advance because its discoveries become conventional wisdom. The reflexivity of social theory, he argues, is one of the distinctive features of modernity.

15. My position here is not unlike John van Maanen's three "tales of the field" (1988)—realist tales that privilege the participant, confessional tales that privilege the observer, and impressionist tales that accent the interaction of the two. The last, which is the one he favors, is parallel to the interventionist approach that I am advocating here.

16. Giddens (1984) and Sewell (1991). Still, I am closer to Bourdieu and Foucault than Giddens and Sewell, who have little to say about how power enters into the constitution of the conditions of our existence.

17. There is a large literature here starting from Rosabeth Kanter's (1977) analysis of organization processes to Ruth Milkman's (1987) analysis of the forces shaping the position of the gender line to Linda Blum's (1991) class analysis of the contending forces of affirmative action and comparable worth (parallel to the two meanings of *African advancement*).

18. Starting from tensions within Weber's analysis of bureaucracy and refusing Weber's monolithic characterization, Gouldner (1954) develops three types of bureaucracy—mock, representative, and punishment centered. In so doing Gouldner brackets the context of his gypsum plant and misses the historical specificity of his ideal types. The extended case method would have tried to locate the plant in its political, economic, and geographical context. See Burawoy (1982).

19. James Clifford's (1988, chap. 2) study of the French anthropologist Marcel Griaule highlights the strategies of power, the panoptic techniques of surveillance that the outsider uses in documenting the recalcitrant colonized. Ethnography depends on an unabashed power struggle between observer and participant. Clifford contrasts this with Griaule's subsequent initiation into Dogon life by one of its chiefs. Griaule becomes the interpreter of "authentic" Dogon culture, an ambassador who would defend their interests in a colonial world. From willful resister and liar the informant becomes colleague and teacher. But in neither case is there joint symmetrical construction of an ethnographic portrait. Power suffuses both dramaturgies.

20. The colonial encounter provides especially vivid examples of this close link between knowledge and power. See, for example, Mitchell (1988) and Stoler (1995).

21. See, for example, Alain Touraine's "action sociology," which insists on social scientists' working together with participants in a social movement (Touraine 1983, 1988) or "participatory action research" that designs the coproduction of knowledge to contest deep-rooted power inequities.

22. For a nuanced survey and evaluation of different approaches to "qualitative methods" that inclines toward postmodern approaches but without being dogmatic, see Denzin and Lincoln (1994).

23. Elsewhere I have elaborated the distinction between the extended case method and grounded theory (Burawoy, Burton, et al. 1991, chap. 13). A contemporary exemplar of grounded theory is Martin Sanchez Jankowski's (1991) *Islands in the Street*—a ten-year study of thirty-seven urban gangs in three metropolises. It is a remarkable, sustained commitment to positivism. Jankowski constitutes himself as ethnographer and outsider. He tries to minimize his own involvement, although this could never be complete if he was to survive. In seeking general claims across the three cities about gang organization, business activities, patterns of violence, as well as relations to the community, to the criminal justice system, local politicians, and to the media, he has to standardize his evidence and his categories, leading to thin rather

than thick description, correlations rather than processes. In making the cases comparable, he brackets the geographical and historical context—both the importance of the specific urban context and changes during the ten-year period of the study. He homogenizes space and time. In building up his theory from the ground, he systematically codes and classifies all the evidence. He tends to reject (or sometimes endorse) other theories but rarely enters into sustained dialogue with them.

24. Feminists have also explored this clinical or dialogical approach to interviewing. See, for example, Oakley (1981) and De Vault (1990).

25. Even the very best of methodological texts compound these different levels. Charles Ragin's (1987) comparison of "variable" analysis and "case study," while overlapping with some of the distinctions between survey research and the extended case method, assumes there to be a single model of science, one that we all share and therefore not requiring explication.

26. Burgess (1927: 114) writes: "The case-study method was first introduced into social science as a handmaiden to statistics." He was referring to such early sociologists as LePlay, who used monographic studies to prepare the basis for greater statistical studies. But, Burgess continues, there is nothing inherently unscientific about the case study "provided that it involves classification, perception of relationships, and description of sequences" (117). He, of course, sees these as two techniques for getting at the truth and not two methods corresponding to two visions of social science.

CHAPTER TWO

This chapter was launched in a dissertation seminar where it received spirited criticism from Bill Hayes, Linus Huang, Rachel Sherman, and Michelle Williams. On the road it picked up comments and suggestions from many, including Julia Adams, Philip Bock, Patricia Clough, Mitchell Duneier, Steve Epstein, Jim Ferguson, Maria Patricia Fernandez-Kelly, Marion Fourcade-Gourinchas, Herb Gans,

Tom Gieryn, Teresa Gowan, Richard Grinker, Lynne Haney, Gillian Hart, Mike Hout, Jennifer Johnson-Hanks, Gail Kligman, Louise Lamphere, Steve Lopez, Ruth Milkman, Sabina Neem, Sherry Ortner, Mary Pattillo, Melvin Pollner, Leslie Salzinger, Ida Susser, Joan Vincent, Loic Wacquant, Ron Weitzer, and Erik Wright. I also thank the four reviewers from the *American Sociological Review,* in particular Diane Vaughan, whose inspired commentary led to major revisions, and Chas Camic, whose persistent critical interventions kept my argument on an even keel. This venture was made possible by a year at the academy's Arcadia, the Russell Sage Foundation, to which revisits are rightly, but sadly, barred.

1. As I will show in chapter 4, reflexive ethnography can also be developed through synchronic comparisons—comparing two factories, communities, schools, and so on—in different spatial contexts, as well as through the diachronic comparisons of the temporal revisit that form the basis of this chapter.

2. Or, even worse, the same ethnographer will have divergent interpretations of the "same" event. Thus Van Maanen (1998) describes his fieldwork among police on patrol successively as a realist tale that strives for the "native point of view," as a confessional tale that is preoccupied with the fieldworker's own experiences, and as an impressionistic (from the art school of impressionism) tale that brings the fieldworker and subject into a dynamic relationship. Margery Wolf (1992) similarly presents her fieldwork on shamans in Taiwan in three different ways: as field notes, fictional account, and professional article. While recognizing the importance of experimental writing and the contributions of the postmodern criticism of ethnography, Wolf ends up defending the professional article with its rules of evidence and interpretation. Such polyphony calls for a vocabulary and framework beyond "replication."

3. Abbott (1999, chap. 7) argues that the Chicago School ethnographies were "historical" in that they were concerned with process. In my view Chicago ethnographies were largely bereft of process, let alone history. If process or history entered the Chicago School, it was

in the form of the general cyclical theories of social change associated with Robert Park.

4. At least in one area sociologists practicing participant observation have embraced history, theory, and context. Science studies began as a reaction to grand Mertonian claims about the normative foundations of scientific knowledge. It turned to the daily practice of laboratory life (Latour and Woolgar 1979)—a resolutely microanalysis drawing on strains of ethnomethodology. These laboratory studies then relocated themselves in the wider context that shaped science and its history but without losing their ethnographic foundations. See S. Epstein (1996), Fujimura (1996), and Latour (1988).

5. *Manufacturing Consent* (Burawoy 1979) is the published version of my Chicago doctoral dissertation.

6. Roy (1952a, 1953, 1954). I was familiar with a number of other studies of piece rates that showed similar patterns of "output restriction" (see, especially, Lupton 1963).

7. According to Chapoulie (1996: 17), Everett Hughes considered Roy's dissertation "one of the best he had supervised."

8. Merton (1957). When a finding is controversial, replication might pay off. A case in point was the heated and seemingly everlasting debate between pluralist and elite perspectives on community power. Hunter (1953), whose reputational study (an ethnography of sorts) of Atlanta in 1950 led the charge for the elite perspective, revisited Atlanta in the early 1970s to confirm his original finding (Hunter 1980). The very different conditions he found in Atlanta (emergence of a black elite, expansion of the downtown, importance of information technology, etc.) made the replication all the more persuasive. The more diverse the conditions under which a finding holds, the more robust it becomes. Because the conditions of Roy's ethnography and mine were so similar, replication was less interesting than was the explanation of small changes.

9. Similarly, Howard Becker (1998: 89) reduces my revisit to studying the "same problem" under "new conditions." In so doing he misses the distinctiveness of my extended case method. First, I didn't study the

same problem but the opposite problem. That is, he ignores my inversion of Roy's theoretical framework (from the human relations question— why people don't work harder—to the Marxist question—why people work so hard). Second, he misses the historical focus of the study, namely, my attempt to explain changes on the shop floor between 1944 and 1974. Therefore, third, he overlooks my examination of external forces as the source of such change. The problem with both Roy and Becker is not their critique of *Manufacturing Consent* but their anodyne assimilation of the study to a methodology it opposes: the methodology of Hughes (1971), thematized by Becker (1998), that searches inductively for what is common to the most disparate of cases rather than explaining divergences. To be sure, there are insights to be gleaned from showing the similarity between janitors and physicians, but there is also much to be gained by examining why medical and janitorial services have each changed over time or why each varies from place to place.

10. I am here referring to the Manchester School of social anthropology and its extended case method (see chapter 1 and Van Velsen 1967).

11. There have been numerous criticisms of *Manufacturing Consent,* most recently in a symposium edited by Gottfried (2001). These and other criticisms include excellent reanalyses, but few bear directly on my revisit to Geer.

12. Abbott (2001, chap. 3) has written a delightful account of how constructionism and realism reproduce each other. Each is incomplete without the other; each corrects the other.

13. Bourdieu (1990). It should be clear that, like Bourdieu and Wacquant (1992) or Morawska (1997), I do not reduce reflexive ethnography to the relationship between observer and informant (as Rabinow [1977] and Behar [1993] do in their accounts). First, a reflexive ethnography is reflexive in the sense of recognizing not only the relation we have to those we study but also the relation we have to a body of theory we share with other scholars. Second, a reflexive ethnography is ethnographic in the sense that it seeks to comprehend an external world both in terms of the social processes we observe and the external forces we discern.

14. This strategy of indicting one's adversaries by stressing their extrascientific motivation or their nonscientific practices is not confined to the social sciences. In *Opening Pandora's Box* Gilbert and Mulkay (1984) show how biochemists, entangled in disputes about "the truth," deploy two types of discourse: an empiricist discourse that deals in "the facts" and a contingent discourse that attributes errors to noncognitive (social, political, and personal) interests. Scientists apply the empiricist discourse to themselves and the contingent discourse to their opponents. We find the same double standards in type 1 revisits. The revisitor's research is beyond reproach, while the predecessor's research is marred by flawed fieldwork, by biases resulting from biography, location, or embodiment. In these cases of refutation, as for the scientists studied by Gilbert and Mulkay (1984), revisitors exempt themselves from such biases or inadequacies in their own fieldwork— but the grounds for such exemption are more presumed than demonstrated. Critics easily turn the tables on the revisitor by playing the same game and revealing his or her biases.

15. Journals devoted special sections (*American Anthropologist* [1983]: 908–47; *Current Anthropology* [2000]: 609–22) or even whole issues (*Canberra Anthropology* vol. 6, nos. 1, 2 [1983]; *Journal of Youth and Adolescence* vol. 29, no. 5 [2000]) to the controversy. A number of books have appeared (Caton 1990; Freeman 1999; Holmes 1987; Orans 1996), a documentary film was made (Heimans 1988), and a fictionalized play was produced of this high drama in the academy (Williamson 1996).

16. In her comments as a reviewer, Diane Vaughan made this point. So did Richard Grinker in private remarks to the author. Grinker (1994, 2000) revisited the Central African sites of the famous and controversial anthropologist Colin Turnbull.

17. Vincent (1990, chap. 4) situates Lewis's critique of Redfield in much broader moves toward historical analysis that preoccupied postwar anthropology in both England and the United States. I also note, parenthetically, that Redfield was deeply influenced by the Chicago School of urban ethnography, at that time dominated by Robert Park and Ernest Burgess. Indeed, Redfield married Park's daughter and

started out studying Mexicans in Chicago under the direction of Burgess. So one cannot be surprised by his ahistorical, acontextual approach to historical change.

18. In a further revisit to Tepoztlan in 1970 Bock (1980) focuses on the continuing potency of the symbolic life, generating yet another type 2 revisit, reconstructing the interpretations of both Redfield and Lewis.

19. In 1948 Redfield (1950) actually conducted his own revisit to a village he had studied seventeen years earlier. *A Village That Chose Progress* reads like a Durkheimian fairy story of a community moving along the folk-urban continuum or, as Redfield puts it, taking "the road to the light" (1950: 153)—and the light is Chicago. This is an unreal realist revisit of type 3.

20. Even apparently robust internal explanations of social change, such as Michels's "iron law of oligarchy" ([1910] 1962), have been subject to punishing criticism for bracketing historical context. Schorske (1955), for example, showed how the bureaucratic tendencies of the German Social Democratic Party, the empirical basis of the iron law of oligarchy, were a function of a range of forces emanating from the wider political field. Coming closer to ethnography, I (Burawoy 1982) inveighed against Gouldner's (1954) classic case study of the dynamics of industrial bureaucracy for bracketing the external economic context of his gypsum plant.

21. Leach (1954), Barth (1959). David Nugent's (1982) reanalysis of *The Political Systems of Highland Burma* showed that changes in the region were a product of political instability in neighboring China, changing patterns of long-distance opium trade, and contestation between British and Burmese armies as much as they were a product of internal processes. Before Nugent, Talal Asad (1972) had shown the limitations of Barth's Hobbesian model of equilibrium politics by refocusing on class dynamics, in particular, the secular concentration of land-ownership and how this was shaped by colonial forces beyond the immediate region.

22. Later in this chapter I call this type of historical digging an archeological revisit.

23. Another explanation of Lynd and Lynd's (1937) focus on Family X is that Robert Lynd was criticized by residents for omitting it from Middletown I. Bahr (1982) goes so far as to imply that Lynd drew his ideas about the importance of Family X from a term paper written by a resident of Middletown, Lynn Perrigo, that was critical of the first Middletown study. Merton (1980) wrote a letter to Bahr, questioning his insinuations of plagiarism and suggesting alternative reasons for Lynd's change of focus in Middletown II. (See also Caccamo 2000, chap. 4.)

24. The original surveys in Middletown I were not replicated by Robert Lynd in Middletown II, in part, I suspect, because of the absence of Helen Lynd.

25. As Robert Lynd himself wrote: "The current emphasis in social science upon techniques and precise empirical data is a healthy one; but, as already noted, skillful collection, organization, and manipulation of data are worth no more than the problem to the solution of which they are addressed. If the problem is wizened, the data are but footnotes to the insignificant" (1939: 202). Mark Smith (1984) reviewed the Middletown III studies as betraying Robert Lynd's project of critical sociology. Caplow (1984) responded that he and his colleagues were just good social scientists, examining hypotheses put forward by the Lynds and describing the complex social changes since 1924.

26. In the extensive literature on replication, of particular interest is Bahr, Caplow, and Chadwick's (1983) discussion of the problems of replication with respect to their own Middletown III studies.

27. Macdonald (2000) writes about the effects of Firth himself on her own revisit to Tikopia. The Tikopians would cite Firth back to her as the authentic interpretation of their society, and they treated her as his daughter. The chiefs in particular embraced the portrait that Firth had painted of a proud and independent people, captured in the title to his first book, *We, the Tikopia* (Firth 1936).

28. Foster et al. (1979). See Phelps, Furstenberg, and Colby (2002) for a parallel collection of studies that engages some strikingly similar methodological issues in quantitative longitudinal research.

29. Needless to say, Duneier's engagement with Jacobs is already a form of theoretical reconstruction—an externally imposed lens.

30. The archeological revisit goes back to Thomas and Znaniecki (1918–20), who used letters written to Polish immigrants in Chicago to construct the social structure and malaise of the sending communities.

31. Or, since most have retired, perhaps I should study the occupations of their children in a generationally based revisit? This is what Sennett implicitly does when he moves from his account of blue-collar workers in *Hidden Injuries of Class* (Sennett and Cobb 1972) to studying the new service workers in the *Corrosion of Character* (Sennett 1998).

32. As we know from Adams, Clemens, and Orloff (2005), who have compiled a wonderful compendium of novel explorations, comparative historians are ready to embrace ethnography, so ethnographers can only gain from taking their exploration in comparative and historical directions.

CHAPTER THREE

Acknowledgments: I wrote the first, crude version of this chapter in the fall of 1985 for my dissertation seminar. Soon Kyoung Cho, Linda Blum, Vedat Milor, Gay Seidman, Louise Jezierski, and Brian Powers greeted it with bewilderment, dismay, and even horror. Had their adviser gone mad? After that I moderated the argument many times under the influence of their comments as well as those of Vicki Bonnell, Carol Hatch, Elizabeth Nichols, Michael Liu, Charles Tilly, Ira Katznelson, Arthur Stinchcombe, Jerry Karabel, Adam Przeworski, Wally Goldfrank, Wolfgang Schluchter, Erik Wright, Alan Sica, Kathleen Schwartzman, Reinhard Bendix, Julia Adams, Ron Aminzade, Barbara Laslett, Bill Sewell, Perry Anderson, Rick Biernacki, Rebecca Scott, Bill Rosenberg, and Jeffrey Alexander. I should also like to pay tribute to the patience of Bill Form, the editor of the *American Sociological Review,* and his battalion of six referees who, over a period of two years, instigated two major revisions and more than sixty pages of written exchange. Although in the end our differences proved too great to bridge, I believe the essay has benefited substantially from their objections. The essay was eventually published in *Theory and Society* in 1989. Of the two anonymous referees I should particularly like to thank the one who provided a superb set of criticisms of my handling of Skocpol, forcing me to revise the argument once more. Finally, the issues I address here were central to the methodology course (before it was banished) that tainted four consecutive cohorts of graduate students who entered the Berkeley Department of Sociology between 1984 and 1987. It was with those students that I explored the meanings of science and, specifically, social science. I am grateful to all the people I have mentioned for pointing out major flaws in the chapter, forcing me to revise, clarify, and elaborate its claims.

1. It is important to emphasize that those who have criticized the use of the "scientific method" to study the social world have assumed and adopted outdated positivist conceptions of science. The irony is that the alternative interpretive approaches to sociology, proposed by humanists with an antiscientific bent, often turn out to be similar to the historical understandings of science as found in, for example, Polanyi (1958), Kuhn (1962), Toulmin (1972), Feyerabend (1975), and Lakatos (1978). In this chapter I follow Lakatos's methodology of research programs not because it best fits Trotsky's approach but because it most satisfactorily explains the growth of scientific knowledge.

2. It is particularly strange, therefore, to find Skocpol vilifying Marxism along with other theories because it "theorize[s] on the basis of a voluntarist image of how revolution happens . . . focus[es] primarily or exclusively upon *intra*national conflicts and processes of modernization . . . analytically collapse[s] state and society or they reduce political and state actions to representations of socioeconomic forces and interests" (Skocpol 1979: 14). Inexplicably, we hear nothing of Trotsky—neither his view of history as a dramatic script in which actors can interpret only their assigned parts, nor his theory of the combined and uneven development of capitalism on a world scale, nor

even his obsessive interest in the autonomy of the state. Indeed, throughout the whole of her book she refers to him twice and then only in passing: in connection with his remark that 1905 was a dress rehearsal for 1917 and when describing the organization of the Red Army (1979: 94, 217). There is no reference to his theory of the Russian Revolution or indeed to his writings on the French Revolution or his prophetic commentaries on the Chinese Revolution.

3. Lakatos (1978: 8–101). Apart from Lakatos's own work, three volumes apply and discuss his ideas: Howson (1976); Cohen, Feyerabend, and Wartofsky (1976); and Radnitzsky and Andersson (1978).

4. Eli Zahar (1978), for example, addresses this problem directly by trying to show that the methodology of scientific research programs represents the best available reconstruction of the intuitive methodology in cases of major scientific advance.

5. Just as this chapter is not concerned with social revolutions per se, it is also not intended as a defense of Marxism. It is a discussion of two methodologies that are not necessarily tied to any particular theoretical framework. Accordingly, I link Trotsky's theories to the methodology of research programs and not to the methodological prescriptions of Marx. The methodology of research programs has also informed reconstructions of "structural functionalism." See, for example, Jeffrey Alexander (1982, 1983, and 1987). These reconstructions do not strictly follow Lakatos as they give little weight to the discovery and corroboration of new facts, and indeed one could say it was a good example of a degenerating research program.

6. Critics have complained that I deal with only a single example of each methodology and therefore I have not demonstrated my claims about the consequences of adopting different methodologies. Undoubtedly, my argument would be more persuasive if other cases were included. Even if space were not a problem, finding suitable cases is not so easy. To isolate the effects of methodology, each case should be, as far as possible, methodologically pure and postulate comparable theories. Such were the reasons that led me to Skocpol and Trotsky. Although these examples are not perfect, better cases might be hard to find.

7. Skocpol (1979: 6). Charles Ragin and David Zaret (1983: 746) claim that Weber's method of genetic explanation, which seeks particular historical trajectories, is "no less evident in work by Bendix and Skocpol." Contrary to her own conception of what she is doing, they claim that her adoption of Mill's methods is *not* in pursuit of generic explanation characteristic of statistical analysis. In what follows I show she does attempt to mimic statistical strategies of comparison, and with the adverse consequences Ragin and Zaret anticipate. Nevertheless, their assessment reflects a real tension in Skocpol's book. I follow Elizabeth Nichols's (1986) identification of the latent genetic, or "conjunctural," analysis behind Skocpol's reduction of all revolutions to peasant revolt and international pressure on the state. Skocpol explains these two factors as emergent from a constellation of forces particular to each revolution, a mode of explanation that is at odds with Mill's canons of induction. Her rejoinder to Nichols (Skocpol 1986) refuses to recognize Weber's distinction, following Rickert, between the generalizing and the particularizing cultural sciences. She misunderstands the critique as accusing her of misapplying Mill's canons, when Nichols was pointing to the coexistence of a different method. She seems so caught up in a linear causality in which every factor must make the same causal contribution to each revolution that she is blind to her own subterranean use of a different notion of causality. Skocpol (1973) treats Barrington Moore's *Social Origins of Dictatorship and Democracy* in a similar way, forcing it into the mold of generic (generalizing) explanation, when much of his analysis seeks genetic (particular) explanations for modernization.

8. While it is true that John Stuart Mill (1888) did advocate, with important qualifications, the method of induction, or what he calls the experimental or chemical method for the natural sciences, he explicitly repudiates its applicability to the social sciences. In the study of society where "the causes of every social phenomenon . . . are infinitely numerous" (1888: 612), one cannot assume that one effect has always the same causes, so that revolutions, for example, may be caused by different factors in different countries. The method of difference is

of even less value, according to Mill. One must find cases in which two societies are alike in every respect except the one that we are trying to isolate as a causal factor. "But the supposition that two such instances can be met with is manifestly absurd" (610). Skocpol's resolute application of the two canons justifies Mill's skepticism. The point is not that Skocpol failed to execute the method of induction properly but rather the method is, as Mill well knew, "completely out of the question" in the social sciences. Skocpol, of course, is quite aware of these flaws—the impossibility of so controlling the variables as to execute the method of difference, that the units being compared are rarely if ever independent and that induction cannot be a substitute for theory (Skocpol 1979: 38–39). Yet she still clings to this as the best approach. While not "without its difficulties and limitations," nevertheless, "provided it is not mechanically applied, it can prompt both theoretical extensions and reformulations, on the one hand, and new ways of looking at concrete historical cases, on the other" (40).

9. Charles Tilly (1984: 105–15) argues that Skocpol pays too much attention to the method of agreement and not enough attention to the method of difference. He suggests looking at variations within those societies that experienced revolutions, both regional differences at the time of its outbreak and why revolution did not occur at earlier periods. Elsewhere, however, Tilly (1976: 159) notes that revolution is a state of a whole society and cannot be explained by comparison of its parts. As to comparing different moments in a society's history, it is notoriously difficult to explain a nonevent. There are, as Mill warns, just too many variables to control for. The problem lies not with Skocpol's failure to use the method of difference but with the method of induction itself, which underestimates the importance of earlier theory and takes the facts as given. Very different is the method of *The Vendee,* where Tilly is sensitive to the social construction and tendentiousness of historical facts as well as to the necessity of proceeding deductively from a theory, in his case a theory of urbanization. When a researcher collects his or her own data with a view to careful comparative analysis, the need to grapple with the illusive, complex,

and uncertain character of "facts" compels a much stronger dependency upon earlier theorizing. Even more important, Tilly seeks to reconstruct theory based on an anomaly—a counterrevolutionary movement in revolutionary France—rather than discover theory inductively.

10. Skocpol (1979:4). She also writes: "Social Revolutions are rapid, basic transformations of a society's state and class structures." One has to ask whether the Chinese Revolution of 1911 fits this definition, given that the transformation is completed only in 1949. Skocpol herself refers to the period 1911 to 1949 as a revolutionary interregnum (1979: 80, 148). How rapid is "rapid"?

11. Here again Mill (1888: 612) himself warns against the method of agreement: "From the mere fact, therefore, of our having been able to eliminate some circumstances, we can by no means infer that this circumstance was not instrumental to the effect in some of the very instances from which we have eliminated it. We can conclude that the effect is sometimes produced without it; but not that, when present, it does not contribute its share." Even in the discussion of the natural sciences Mill (book 3, chap. 10) sensitizes us to the problem of plurality of causes, that the method of agreement assumes "that there is only one assemblage of conditions from which the given effect could result" (1888: 311).

12. Carl Hempel's deductive-nomological model recodifies Humean causality of "constant conjunction" by insisting that the connection between antecedent conditions and outcomes has to be explained by universal "covering laws." Hempel would argue that Skocpol does not distinguish between antecedent conditions and "laws": "A related error occurs in singling out one of several important groups of factors which would have to be stated in the initial conditions, and then claiming that the phenomenon in question is 'determined' by that one group of factors and thus can be explained in terms of it" (Hempel 1965: 239). That his model is in fact rarely carried out in historical analysis Hempel attributes to the complexity of historical laws, while Popper (1957) contrarily argues it is often their triviality that leads to their omissions. Be that as it may, Skocpol seems to share

Hempel's distrust of invoking causal mechanisms as a defining feature of explanation. For a general critique of the shortcomings of such empiricism, see, for example, Richard Miller (1987, pt. 1).

13. In her rejoinder to Sewell's review Skocpol (1985a: 86–87) writes: "Few aspects of *States and Social Revolutions* have been more misunderstood than its call for a 'nonvoluntarist,' 'structuralist' approach to explaining social revolutions. . . . For the point is simply that no single acting group, whether a class or an ideological vanguard, deliberately shapes the complex and multiply determined conflicts that bring about revolutionary crises and outcomes." But which serious scholar argues that the intentional action of a single actor is a sufficient cause for revolution? Here Skocpol criticizes theories no one holds and holds theories no one criticizes. The actual claim she pursues in her book is more interesting. There she denies that the intention of a collective actor to make a revolution is necessary for its outbreak. However, this is not empirically examined, let alone justified, and is linked, I argue, to the character of her causal analysis.

14. Stinchcombe (1983: 12–15, 247–50) makes the same criticism of Skocpol for leaving out the microfoundations of revolutionary process but does not attribute this to her method.

15. Although Mill does not regard facts as problematical, he does recognize their underdetermination of explanation: "Accordingly, most thinkers of any degree of sobriety allow that an hypothesis of this kind is not to be received as probably true because it accounts for all the known phenomena, since this is a condition sometimes fulfilled tolerably well by two conflicting hypotheses; while there are probably many others which are equally possible, but which, for want of anything analogous in our experience, our minds are unfitted to conceive. But it seems to be thought that an hypothesis of the sort in question is entitled to a more favorable reception, if, besides accounting for all the facts previously known, it has led to the anticipation and prediction of others which experience afterwards verified" (Mill 1888: 356).

16. As Karl Popper (1963: 50) has pointed out, there is a latent affinity between induction and dogmatism: "For the dogmatic attitude is

clearly related to the tendency to *verify* our laws and schema by seeking to apply them and to confirm them, even to the point of neglecting refutations, whereas the critical attitude is one of readiness to change them—to test them; to refute them; to *falsify* them, if possible. This suggests that we may identify the critical attitude with the scientific attitude, and the dogmatic attitude with the one which we have described as pseudo-scientific."

17. Subsequently, Skocpol (1985b) did examine the capacity of states, and with it her hostility to research traditions takes a new twist. On the one hand neo-Marxist theories of the state are severed from their Marxist roots, locating them in the academic debates in the United States of the 1960s and 1970s. As Paul Cammack (n.d.) suggests, this is a curious move for one so committed to historical analysis. On the other hand, in the very act of rejecting research programs tout court she launches her own, calling on Weber and Hintze as potential forefathers of the "state centric" perspective. But even here she vacillates between a strong thesis in which state dynamics are the central force in history and a weak thesis that argues simply that the state cannot be left out of account. There continues to be a strong inductivist commitment to confirmation, to purging her theories of counterexamples even at the cost of their explanatory power. Thus, when confronted with anomalies, instead of specifying and reconstructing her strong thesis, she abandons it for her weak thesis, which is trivially true. See Erik Wright (1986).

18. Similar arguments have been made against classical anthropological studies in Clifford and Marcus (1986). Introductory remarks or reflections on fieldwork are separated from the "real" science of anthropology. On further examination those remarks and reflections prove to be constitutive of, not separate from, the main text. Thus Renato Rosaldo shows how the results of Evans-Pritchard's study of the Nuer were influenced by the context of colonial domination and civil war, just as Le Roy Ladurie's account of Montaillou represses the effect of relying on data gathered in an inquisition (Clifford and Marcus 1986: 77–97). Both bracket the domination that makes knowledge possible.

Clifford argues that anthropological texts have multiple "registers"—a manifest voice of science alongside a latent voice in search of an essential, uncontaminated, natural world, what he calls the pastoral mode (98–121). Ethnography is an allegory with ethical or political messages for advanced industrial societies. For example, Derek Freeman's critique of Margaret Mead's controlled experiment in the field makes her account of the Samoans look less like science than a moral and practical lesson for the American people (see chapter 2).

19. Peter Beilharz (1987) has argued that Trotsky, far from deducing the direction of history, imposes a telos on history—the inevitability of socialism and the view that in the final analysis history must be on the side of the working class. Beilharz seeks to discover in Trotsky's early writings the seeds of his later unimaginative defense of Marxism. All that he finds there is Trotsky's use of generative metaphors of birth and death, disease and health, seed and fruit, and the idea of history as theater in which actors can interpret only scripts handed to them. But Trotsky's writings cannot be reduced to metaphor or to his eschatology. How one reaches socialism, with what means and when, is not given but the subject of his investigations, his innovations, his prophecies, as well as his struggles. In projecting back into Trotsky's early writings the most dogmatic formulations in his later writings, Beilharz is committing the same generative sin of which he accuses Trotsky. In so doing he marginalizes Trotsky's important contributions to Marxism.

20. Lakatos (1978: 48). Lakatos himself considered Marxism to be a degenerate research program, a claim he made from within the context of Soviet Marxism. To be sure, this would become a degenerate branch of the Marxist tradition, but the branch must not be mistaken for the whole tree. See Burawoy (1990b).

21. Trotsky (1969: 52). After the revolution of 1917, and particularly after Lenin's death in 1924, Trotsky, like the other Bolsheviks, would seek out parallels with the French Revolution. Unwillingly, Trotsky would come to the conclusion that the bureaucratization of the revolution could be seen as a Soviet Thermidor and that Stalin had become the Soviet Bonaparte. But while Trotsky saw the process of

bureaucratization as similar, he nevertheless regarded the outcomes as well as the causes of the French and Russian revolutions as different. See Trotsky ([1936]1972, chap. 5), Knei-Paz (1978: 392–94), Deutscher (1959: 311–14, 342–47, and 457–64), and Deutscher (1963: 313–18).

22. This is a capsule summary of chapters 1 and 2 of *Results and Prospects* and of the same argument presented in more detail in chapter 1 and appendix 1 of volume 1 of *The History of the Russian Revolution*.

23. Stinchcombe (1978, chap. 2). I do not endorse Stinchcombe's (1978) claim that Trotsky's insights have nothing to do with his Marxism, that good theory comes from inspired interrogation of the facts. "Deep analogies" don't spring tabula rasa, under the influence of genius, from "the facts." Trotsky's commitment to Marxism and his need to revise it led him to delve into the molecular processes of revolution. Fortunately, Stinchcombe's (1978: 65–66) theoretical sense gets the better of his empiricist polemic when he recognizes that Trotsky's account of the Russian Revolution can be understood only in the light of his earlier theory of combined and uneven development. In fact, his empiricist polemic is confined to the opening and concluding chapters and does not obscure his fascinating reconstructions in between. Stinchcombe's comparison of Tocqueville and Trotsky does indeed illuminate the construction of causal processes out of historical events, but it does not demonstrate the irrelevance of the intellectual traditions in which each is embedded. As Charles Tilly (1981, chap. 1) has underlined, historical analysis as immaculate conception is a myth.

24. This is also how John Roemer (1986: 192) sees the project of analytical Marxism: "What Marxists must provide are explanations of *mechanisms,* at the micro-level, for the phenomena they claim come about for teleological reasons." In a similar vein what Jon Elster (1985: 5) finds of lasting importance in Marx is the use of methodological individualism: "[T]he doctrine that all social phenomena—their structure and their change—are in principle explicable in ways that only involve individuals—their properties, their goals, their beliefs and their actions." In drawing on the rational choice models of neoclassical economics, they

move toward a mythological rather than a methodological individualism (Burawoy 1986, 1995). If they are serious about their microfoundations, they would do better to study Trotsky's *History of the Russian Revolution* than Walras.

25. The same can be said of "Trotskyism," itself very much divided by what it inherits from Trotsky. On the one hand C. L. R. James and Raya Dunayevskaya return to Trotsky's early hostility to Bolshevism and his spontaneitist faith in the revolutionary spirit of the working class while characterizing the Soviet Union as state capitalism. On the other hand, Ernest Mandel and Isaac Deutscher embrace a more top-down view of history as well as a more optimistic assessment of the Soviet Union as a degenerate workers' state. See Beilharz (1987, pt. 2).

26. Although "facts" are themselves theoretical constructs of sense data, what Feyerabend (1975) calls natural interpretations, they have greater stability than the theories created to explain them. That is to say, they have an obduracy—if for no other reason than by convention, as in Popper's basic statements—that allows them to act as falsifications of explanatory theories.

CHAPTER FOUR

Acknowledgements: This chapter has benefited from comments at various seminars, including those at the Departments of Sociology at Lancaster University and Newcastle University and the Anthropology of Europe Workshop at the University of Chicago.

1. This section draws on the analysis in Burawoy (1980).

2. This section draws on analysis previously reported in Burawoy (1985).

3. I would also throw the "colonial despotism" of southern Africa into the mix, but it is not essential to the story I tell here.

4. This section draws on research previously reported in part 1 of Burawoy and Lukács (1992).

5. This section draws on research previously reported in part 2 of Burawoy and Lukács (1992).

6. This section is based on research previously reported in Burawoy and Hendley (1992).

7. This section draws on research previously reported in Burawoy and Krotov (1992, 1993) and Burawoy (1996).

8. This section draws on the research previously reported in Burawoy, Lytkina, and Krotov (2000) and Burawoy (2001).

CONCLUSION

1. The Real Utopias Project is Wright's undertaking at the Havens Center at the University of Wisconsin. So far four books have been published, but Fong and Wright (2003) is perhaps the best representative of the project, examining the logic, the limits, and the possibilities of experiments in deepening democracy in different parts of the world. Wright (2006) has elaborated a broad theory that encompasses the broader vision of the real utopias project.

REFERENCES

Abbott, Andrew. 1992. "What Do Cases Do?" In *What Is a Case?* edited by Charles Ragin and Howard Becker, 53–82. Cambridge: Cambridge University Press.

———. 1997. "Of Time and Space: The Contemporary Relevance of the Chicago School." *Social Forces* 75:1149–82.

———. 1999. *Department and Discipline.* Chicago: University of Chicago Press.

———. 2001. *Chaos of Disciplines.* Chicago: University of Chicago Press.

———. 2007. "Against Narrative: A Preface to Lyrical Sociology." *Sociological Theory* 25:67–99.

Adams, Julia, Elisabeth Clemens, and Anne Shola Orloff, eds. 2005. *Remaking Modernity: Politics, History and Sociology.* Durham, NC: Duke University Press.

Alexander, Jeffrey. 1982. *Positivism, Presuppositions, and Current Controversies.* Berkeley: University of California Press.

———. 1983. *The Modern Reconstruction of Classical Thought.* Berkeley: University of California Press.

———. 1987. "The Centrality of the Classics." In *Social Theory Today,* edited by Anthony Giddens and Jonathan Turner, 11–57. London: Basil Blackwell.

Anderson, Elijah. 1990. *Streetwise: Race, Class, and Change in an Urban Community*. Chicago: University of Chicago Press.

Appadurai, Arjun. 1988. "Putting Hierarchy in Its Place." *Cultural Anthropology* 3 (1): 36–49.

Asad, Talal. 1972. "Market Model, Class Structure and Consent: A Reconsideration of Swat Political Organisation." *Man* 7:74–94.

———, ed. 1973. *Anthropology and the Colonial Encounter*. Atlantic Highlands, NJ: Humanities Press.

Bahr, Howard. 1982. "The Perrigo Paper: A Local Influence upon *Middletown in Transition*." *Indiana Magazine of History* 78:1–25.

Bahr, Howard, Theodore Caplow, and Bruce Chadwick. 1983. "Middletown III: Problems of Replication, Longitudinal Measurement, and Triangulation." *Annual Review of Sociology* 9:243–64.

Barth, Fredrik. 1959. *Political Leadership among the Swat Pathans*. London: Athlone.

Bates, Robert. 1971. *Unions, Parties, and Political Development*. New Haven, CT: Yale University Press.

Bauman, Zygmunt. 1987. *Legislators and Interpreters*. Cambridge: Polity.

Becker, Howard. 1958. "Problems of Inference and Proof in Participant Observation." *American Sociological Review* 23:652–60.

———. 1998. *Tricks of the Trade*. Chicago: University of Chicago Press.

Becker, Howard, Blanche Greer, Everett Hughes, and Anselm Strauss. 1961. *Boys in White*. Chicago: University of Chicago Press.

Behar, Ruth. 1993. *Translated Woman*. Boston: Beacon.

Beilharz, Peter. 1987. *Trotsky, Trotskyism and the Transition to Socialism*. London: Croom Helm.

Bhaskar, Roy. 1979. *The Possibility of Naturalism*. Atlantic Highlands, NJ: Humanities Press.

Bischoping, Katherine, and Howard Schuman. 1992. "Pens and Polls in Nicaragua: An Analysis of the 1990 Preelection Surveys." *American Journal of Political Science* 36 (2): 331–50.

Bloch, Marc. 1953. *The Historian's Craft*. New York: Knopf.

Blum, Linda. 1991. *Between Feminism and Labor: The Significance of the Comparable Worth Movement*. Berkeley: University of California Press.

Bock, Philip. 1980. "Tepoztlan Reconsidered." *Journal of Latin American Lore* 6:129–50.

Boelen, Marianne. 1992. "Street Corner Society: Cornerville Revisited." *Journal of Contemporary Ethnography* 21:11–51.

Bourdieu, Pierre. 1977. *Outline of a Theory of Practice*. Cambridge: Cambridge University Press.

———. 1990. *The Logic of Practice*. Stanford, CA: Stanford University Press.

Bourdieu, Pierre, and Loïc Wacquant. 1992. *An Invitation to Reflexive Sociology*. Chicago: University of Chicago Press.

Bourgois, Philippe. 1995. *In Search of Respect*. New York: Cambridge University Press.

Bulmer, Martin. 1984. *The Chicago School of Sociology*. Chicago: University of Chicago Press.

Burawoy, Michael. 1972a. *The Colour of Class on the Copper Mines: From African Advancement to Zambianization*. Manchester, UK: Manchester University Press for Institute for Social Research, University of Zambia.

———. 1972b. "Another Look at the Mineworker." *African Social Research* 14:239–87.

———. 1974. *Constraint and Manipulation in Industrial Conflict—A Comparison of Strikes among Zambian Workers in a Clothing Factory and the Mining Industry*. Zambia: Institute for African Studies.

———. 1979. *Manufacturing Consent*. Chicago: University of Chicago Press.

———. 1980. "The Politics of Production and the Production of Politics: A Comparative Analysis of Piecework Machine Shops in Hungary and the United States." *Political Power and Social Theory* 1:259–97.

———. 1982. "The Written and the Repressed in Gouldner's Industrial Sociology." *Theory and Society* 11:831–51.

————. 1985. *The Politics of Production.* London: Verso.

————. 1986. "Making Nonsense of Marx." *Contemporary Sociology* 15:704–707.

————. 1990a. "Marxism Is Dead: Long Live Marxism!" *Socialist Review* 90 (2): 7–19.

————. 1990b. "Marxism as Science: Historical Challenges and Theoretical Growth." *American Sociological Review* 55:775–93.

————. 1995. "Mythological Individualism." In *Rational Choice Marxism,* edited by Terrell Carver and Paul Thomas, 191–99. London: Macmillan.

————. 1996. "The State and Economic Involution: Russia through a Chinese Lens." *World Development* 24:1105–17.

————. 2001. "Transition without Transformation: Russia's Involutionary Road to Capitalism." *East European Politics and Societies* 15:269–90.

————. 2005. "Antinomian Marxist." In *The Disobedient Generation,* edited by Alan Sica and Stephen Turner, 48–71. Chicago: University of Chicago Press.

Burawoy, Michael, and Kathryn Hendley. 1992. "Between Perestroika and Privatization: Divided Strategies and Political Crisis in a Soviet Enterprise." *Soviet Studies* 44:371–402.

Burawoy, Michael, and Pavel Krotov. 1992. "The Soviet Transition from Socialism to Capitalism: Worker Control and Economic Bargaining in the Wood Industry." *American Sociological Review* 57:16–38.

————. 1993. "The Economic Basis of Russia's Political Crisis." *New Left Review* 198:49–70.

Burawoy, Michael, and János Lukács. 1992. *The Radiant Past.* Chicago: University of Chicago Press.

Burawoy, Michael, and Katherine Verdery, eds. 1999. *Uncertain Transition: Ethnographies of Change in the Post Socialist World.* Lanham, MD: Rowman and Littlefield.

Burawoy, Michael, Joseph A. Blum, Sheba George, Zsuzsa Gille, Teresa Gowan, Lynne Haney, Maren Klawiter, Steven H. Lopez,

Sean Ó Riain, and Millie Thayer. 2000. *Global Ethnography.* Berkeley: University of California Press.

Burawoy, Michael, Alice Burton, Ann Arnett Ferguson, Kathryn J. Fox, Joshua Gamson, Nadine Gartrell, Leslie Hurst, Charles Kurzman, Leslie Salzinger, Josepha Schiffman, and Shiori Ui. 1991. *Ethnography Unbound.* Berkeley: University of California Press.

Burawoy, Michael, Tatyana Lytkina, and Pavel Krotov. 2000. "Involution and Destitution in Capitalist Russia." *Ethnography* 1:43–65.

Burgess, Ernest W. 1927. "Statistics and Case Studies." *Sociology and Social Research* 12 (2):103–20.

Caccamo, Rita. 2000. *Back to Middletown: Three Generations of Sociological Reflection.* Stanford, CA: Stanford University Press.

Cammack, Paul. n.d. "Bringing the State Back In: A Polemic." Unpublished manuscript.

Caplow, Theodore. 1984. "Social Criticism in Middletown: Taking Aim at a Moving Target." *Qualitative Sociology* 7:337–39.

Caplow, Theodore, and Howard Bahr. 1979. "Half a Century of Change in Adolescent Attitudes: Replication of a Middletown Survey by the Lynds." *Public Opinion Quarterly* 43:1–17.

Caplow, Theodore, and Bruce Chadwick. 1979. "Inequality and Life-Styles in Middletown, 1920–1978." *Social Science Quarterly* 60:367–86.

Caplow, Theodore, Howard M. Bahr, Bruce A. Chadwick, Reuben Hill, and Margaret Holmes Williamson. 1982. *Middletown Families: Fifty Years of Change and Continuity.* Minneapolis: University of Minnesota Press.

Carr, Edward. 1961. *What Is History?* New York: Random House.

Caton, Hiram. 1990. *The Samoa Reader: Anthropologists Take Stock.* Lanham, MD: University Press of America.

Chapoulie, Jean-Michel. 1996. "Everett Hughes and the Chicago Tradition." *Sociological Theory* 14:3–29.

Chodorow, Nancy. 1999. *The Power of Feelings: Personal Meaning in Psychoanalysis, Gender, and Culture.* New Haven, CT: Yale University Press.

Cicourel, Aaron. 1964. *Method and Measurement in Sociology.* New York: Free Press.

———. 1967. "Fertility, Family Planning and the Social Organization of Family Life: Some Methodological Issues." *Journal of Social Issues* 23 (4): 57–81.

———. 1982. "Interviews, Surveys, and the Problem of Ecological Validity." *American Sociologist* 17 (1): 11–20.

Clark, Herbert H., and Michael F. Schober. 1992. "Asking Questions and Influencing Answers." In Tanur, *Questions about Questions,* 15–48.

Clifford, James. 1988. *The Predicament of Culture.* Cambridge, MA: Harvard University Press.

Clifford, James, and George E. Marcus, eds. 1986. *Writing Culture: The Poetics and Politics of Ethnography.* Berkeley: University of California Press.

Cohen, Morris, and Ernest Nagel. 1934. *An Introduction to Logic and Scientific Method.* New York: Harcourt and Brace.

Cohen, R. S., P. K. Feyerabend, and M. W. Wartofsky, eds. 1976. *Essays in Memory of Imre Lakatos.* Boston Studies in the Philosophy of Science. Vol. 39. Dordrecht, Germany: D. Reidel.

Colignon, Richard. 1996. *Power Plays: Critical Events in the Institutionalization of the Tennessee Valley Authority.* Albany: State University of New York Press.

Collins, Harry. 1985. *Changing Order: Replication and Induction in Scientific Practice.* London: Sage.

Collins, Harry, and Trevor Pinch. 1993. *The Golem: What You Should Know about Science.* Cambridge: Cambridge University Press.

Colson, Elizabeth. 1971. *The Social Consequences of Resettlement.* Manchester, UK: Manchester University Press.

———. 1989. "Overview." *Annual Review of Anthropology* 18:1–16.

Comaroff, Jean, and John Comaroff. 1991. *Of Revelation and Revolution.* Chicago: University of Chicago Press.

———. 1992. *Ethnography and Historical Imagination.* Boulder, CO: Westview.

Converse, Jean M., and Howard Schuman. 1974. *Conversations at Random*. Ann Arbor, MI: Wiley.

Deegan, Mary Jo. 1988. *Jane Adams and the Men of the Chicago School, 1892–1918*. New Brunswick, NJ: Transaction.

Denzin, Norman, and Yvonna Lincoln, eds. 1994. *Handbook of Qualitative Research*. Thousand Oaks, CA: Sage.

Deutscher, Isaac. 1954. *The Prophet Armed, Trotsky: 1879–1921*. New York: Vintage.

———. 1959. *The Prophet Unarmed, Trotsky: 1921–1929*. New York: Vintage.

———. 1963. *The Prophet Outcast, Trotsky: 1929–1940*. New York: Vintage.

DeVault, Marjorie. 1990. "Talking and Listening from Women's Standpoint: Feminist Strategies for Interviewing and Analysis." *Social Problems* 37 (1): 96–116.

———. 1991. *Feeding the Family: The Social Organization of Caring as Gendered Work*. Chicago: University of Chicago Press.

Drake, St. Clair, and Horace Cayton. 1945. *Black Metropolis: A Study of Negro Life in a Northern City*. New York: Harcourt, Brace.

Du Bois, W. E. B. [1899] 1996. *The Philadelphia Negro*. Reprint. Philadelphia: University of Pennsylvania Press.

Duneier, Mitchell. 1999. *Sidewalk*. New York: Farrar, Straus and Giroux.

Edin, Kathryn, and Laura Lein. 1997. *Making Ends Meet: How Single Mothers Survive Welfare and Low-Wage Work*. New York: Russell Sage.

Elster, John. 1985. *Making Sense of Marx*. Cambridge: Cambridge University Press.

Emigh, Rebecca. 1997. "The Power of Negative Thinking: The Use of Negative Case Methodology in the Development of Sociological Theory." *Theory and Society* 26:649–84.

Epstein, A. L. 1958. *Politics in an Urban African Community*. Manchester, UK: Manchester University Press.

Epstein, Steven. 1996. *Impure Science*. Berkeley: University of California Press.

Escobar, Arturo. 1995. *Encountering Development*. Princeton, NJ: Princeton University Press.

Evans-Pritchard, Edward E. 1940. *The Nuer: A Description of the Modes of Livelihood and Political Institutions of a Nilotic People*. Oxford: Oxford University Press.

———. 1951. *Kinship and Marriage among the Nuer*. Oxford: Clarendon.

———. 1956. *Nuer Religion*. Oxford: Clarendon.

Fanon, Frantz. [1952] 1968a. *Black Skin, White Masks*. London: MacGibbon and Kee.

———. [1961] 1968b. *The Wretched of the Earth*. New York: Grove Weidenfeld.

Fantasia, Rick. 1988. *Cultures of Solidarity*. Berkeley: University of California Press.

Ferguson, James. 1990. *The Anti-Politics Machine: "Development," Depoliticization, and Bureaucratic Power in Lesotho*. Cambridge: Cambridge University Press.

———. 1999. *Expectations of Modernity*. Berkeley: University of California Press.

Fernandez-Kelly, Maria Patricia. 1983. *For We Are Sold, I and My People: Women and Industry in Mexico's Frontier*. Albany: State University of New York Press.

Feyerabend, Paul. 1975. *Against Method*. London: Verso.

Fine, Gary, ed. 1995. *The Second Chicago School? The Development of a Postwar American Sociology*. Chicago: University of Chicago Press.

Firth, Raymond. 1936. *We, the Tikopia*. London: George Allen and Unwin.

———. 1959. *Social Change in Tikopia*. London: George Allen and Unwin.

Fitzpatrick, Ellen. 1990. *Endless Crusade: Women Social Scientists and Progressive Reform*. New York: Oxford.

Fong, Archon, and Erik Wright, eds. 2003. *Deepening Democracy: Institutional Innovations in Empowered Participatory Governance*. London: Verso.

Forsyth, Barbara H., and Judith T. Lessler. 1991. "Cognitive Laboratory Methods: A Taxonomy." In *Measurement Errors in Surveys,* edited by Paul B. Biemer et al., 393–418. New York: Wiley.

Foster, George, Thayer Scudder, Elizabeth Colson, and Robert Kemper, eds. 1979. *Long-Term Field Research in Social Anthropology.* New York: Academic Press.

Franke, Richard, and James Kaul. 1978. "The Hawthorne Experiments: First Statistical Interpretation." *American Sociological Review* 43:623–43.

Fraser, Nancy. 1989. *Unruly Practices.* Minneapolis: University of Minnesota Press.

Frazier, Edward Franklin. 1957. *Black Bourgeoisie.* Glencoe: Free Press.

Freeman, Derek. 1983. *Margaret Mead and Samoa: The Making and Unmaking of an Anthropological Myth.* Cambridge, MA: Harvard University Press.

———. 1999. *The Fateful Hoaxing of Margaret Mead.* Boulder, CO: Westview.

Fujimura, Joan. 1996. *Crafting Science.* Cambridge, MA: Harvard University Press.

Furet, François. 1981. *Interpreting the French Revolution* Cambridge: Cambridge University Press.

Gadamer, Hans. 1975. *Truth and Method.* New York: Crossroad.

Gans, Herbert. 1968. "The Participant Observer as Human Being." In *Institutions and the Person: Papers Presented to Everett C. Hughes,* edited by Howard Becker, Blanche Greer, David Reisman, and Robert Weiss, 300–17. Chicago: Aldine.

———. 1982. *The Urban Villagers.* Updated and expanded ed. New York: Free Press.

Garbett, Kingsley. 1970. "The Analysis of Social Situations." *Man* 5:214–27.

Garfinkel, Harold. 1967. *Studies in Ethnomethodology.* New York: Prentice Hall.

Geertz, Clifford. 1973. *The Interpretation of Cultures.* New York: Basic Books.

————. 1983. *Local Knowledge.* New York: Basic Books.

————. 1995. *After the Fact: Two Countries, Four Decades, One Anthropologist.* Cambridge, MA: Harvard University Press.

Giddens, Anthony. 1984. *The Constitution of Society.* Berkeley: University of California Press.

————. 1992. *The Consequences of Modernity.* Stanford, CA: Stanford University Press.

Gilbert, Nigel, and Michael Mulkay. 1984. *Opening Pandora's Box.* Cambridge: Cambridge University Press.

Glaser, Barney, and Anselm Strauss. 1967. *The Discovery of Grounded Theory.* Chicago: Aldine.

Gluckman, Max. [1940 and 1942] 1958. *Analysis of a Social Situation in Modern Zululand.* Manchester, UK: Manchester University Press for the Rhodes-Livingstone Institute.

————. 1961a. "Ethnographic Data in British Social Anthropology." *Sociological Review* 9:5–17.

————. 1961b. "Anthropological Problems Arising from the African Industrial Revolution." In *Social Change in Modern Africa,* edited by Aidan Southall, 67–82. Oxford: Oxford University Press for International African Institute.

————, ed. 1964. *Closed Systems and Open Minds: The Limits of Naïvety in Social Anthropology.* Chicago: Aldine.

Gordon, Linda. 1992. "Social Insurance and Public Assistance: The Influence of Gender in Welfare Thought in the United States, 1890–1935." *American Historical Review* 97 (1): 19–54.

Gottfried, Heidi, ed. 2001. "From *Manufacturing Consent* to Global Ethnography: A Retrospective Examination." *Contemporary Sociology* 30:435–58.

Gough, Kathleen. 1971. "Nuer Kinship: A Reexamination." In *The Translation of Culture: Essays to E. E. Evans-Pritchard,* edited by T.O. Beidelman, 79–121. London: Tavistock.

Gouldner, Alvin. 1954. *Patterns of Industrial Bureaucracy.* New York: Free Press.

————. 1970. *The Coming Crisis of Sociology.* New York: Basic Books.

————. 1973. "Sociologist as Partisan." In *For Sociology: Renewal and Critique in Sociology Today,* 27–68. London: Allen Lane.

Gramsci, Antonio. 1971. *Selections from the Prison Notebooks.* New York: International Publishers.

Grinker, Richard. 1994. *Houses in the Rain Forest.* Berkeley: University of California Press.

————. 2000. *In the Arms of Africa: The Life of Colin M. Turnbull.* New York: St. Martin's.

Gupta, Akhil, and James Ferguson. 1992. "Beyond 'Culture': Space, Identity, and the Politics of Difference." *Cultural Anthropology* 7 (1): 6–23.

Habermas, Jürgen. 1984. *Reason and the Rationalization of Society.* Vol. 1, *The Theory of Communicative Action.* Boston: Beacon.

————. 1987. *Lifeworld and System: A Critique of Functionalist Reason.* Vol. 2, *The Theory of Communicative Action.* Boston: Beacon.

Haney, Lynne. 1996. "Homeboys, Babies, Men in Suits: The State and the Reproduction of Male Domination." *American Sociological Review* 61:759–78.

————. 2002. *Inventing the Needy: Gender and the Politics of Welfare in Hungary.* Berkeley: University of California Press.

Hannerz, Ulf. 1996. *Transnational Connections.* New York: Routledge.

Haraszti, Miklós. 1977. *A Worker in Worker's State.* Harmondsworth, UK: Penguin.

————. 1987. *The Velvet Prison: Artists under State Socialism.* New York: Basic Books.

Haraway, Donna. 1991. *Simians, Cyborgs, and Women.* New York: Routledge.

Harding, Sandra. 1986. "The Instability of Analytical Categories of Feminist Theory." *Signs* 11 (4): 645–64.

————. 1990. "Feminism, Science, and the Anti-Enlightenment Critiques." In *Feminism/Postmodernism,* edited by Linda Nicholson, 83–106. New York: Routledge.

Heimans, Frank. 1988. *Margaret Mead and Samoa.* New York: Brighton Video.

Hempel, Carl. 1965. *Aspects of Scientific Explanation.* New York: Free Press.

Hobsbawm, Eric. 1994. *Age of Extremes: The Short Twentieth Century, 1914–1991.* London: Michael Joseph.

Hochschild, Arlene, with Anne Machung. 1989. *The Second Shift.* New York: Avon.

Hollingshead, August de Belmont. 1975. *Elmtown's Youth and Elmtown Revisited.* New York: Wiley.

Holmes, Lowell D. 1987. *Quest for the Real Samoa.* South Hadley, MA: Bergin and Garvey.

Hondagneu-Sotelo, Pierrette. 1994. *Gendered Transitions: Mexican Experiences of Immigration.* Berkeley: University of California Press.

Horowitz, Ruth. 1983. *Honor and the American Dream.* New Brunswick, NJ: Rutgers University Press.

Howson, Colin, ed. 1976. *Method and Appraisal in the Physical Sciences.* Cambridge: Cambridge University Press.

Hughes, Everett. 1958. *Men and Their Work.* Glencoe, IL: Free Press.

———. 1971. *The Sociological Eye.* Chicago: Aldine-Atherton.

Hunter, Floyd. 1953. *Community Power Structure.* Chapel Hill: University of North Carolina Press.

———. 1980. *Community Power Succession: Atlanta's Policy Makers Revisited.* Chapel Hill: University of North Carolina Press.

Hutchinson, Sharon. 1996. *Nuer Dilemmas: Coping with Money, War, and the State.* Berkeley: University of California Press.

Hyman, Herbert et al. 1954. *Interviewing in Social Research.* Chicago: University of Chicago Press.

Jacobs, Jane. 1961. *The Death and Life of Great American Cities.* New York: Random House.

Jankowski, Martin Sanchez. 1991. *Islands in the Street: Gangs and American Urban Society.* Berkeley: University of California Press.

Johnston, Paul. 1994. *Success While Others Fail: Social Movement Unionism in the Public Workplace.* Ithaca, NY: ILR Press.

Kanter, Rosabeth. 1977. *Men and Women of the Corporation.* New York: Basic Books.

Katz, Jack. 1983. "A Theory of Qualitative Methodology: The Social System of Analytical Fieldwork." In *Contemporary Field Research,* edited by Robert Emerson, 127–48. Prospect Heights, IL: Waveland.

Keller, Evelyn Fox. 1983. *A Feeling for the Organism.* New York: Freeman.

———. 1985. *Reflections on Gender and Science.* New Haven, CT: Yale University Press.

Kligman, Gail. 1998. *The Politics of Duplicity: Controlling Reproduction in Ceausescu's Romania.* Berkeley: University of California Press.

Knei-Paz, Baruch. 1978. *The Social and Political Thought of Leon Trotsky.* Oxford: Oxford University Press.

Knorr-Cetina, Karin D. 1981. "Introduction: The Micro-sociological Challenge of Macro-sociology: Towards a Reconstruction of Social Theory and Methodology." In *Advances in Social Theory and Methodology,* edited by Karin Knorr-Cetina and Aaron Cicourel, 1–48. Boston: Routledge and Kegan Paul.

Konrád, György, and Iván Szelényi. 1979. *The Intellectuals on the Road to Class Power.* New York: Harcourt Brace Jovanovich.

Kornai, János. 1971. *Anti-Equilibrium.* Amsterdam: North Holland Publishing.

———. 1980. *The Economics of Shortage.* 2 vols. Amsterdam: North Holland Publishing.

Kuhn, Thomas. 1962. *The Structure of Scientific Revolutions.* Chicago: University of Chicago Press.

Lakatos, Imre. 1976. *Proofs and Refutations.* Cambridge: Cambridge University Press.

———. 1978. *The Methodology of Scientific Research Programmes.* Cambridge: Cambridge University Press.

Lamphere, Louise. 1979. "The Long-Term Study among the Navajo." In Foster et al., *Long-Term Field Research in Social Anthropology,* 19–44.

Lamphere, Louise, Patricia Zavella, and Felipe Gonzales, with Peter B. Evans. 1993. *Sunbelt Working Mothers: Reconciling Family and Factory.* Ithaca, NY: Cornell University Press.

Lampland, Martha. 1995. *The Object of Labor: Commodification in Socialist Hungary.* Chicago: University of Chicago Press.

Latour, Bruno. 1988. *The Pasteurization of France.* Cambridge, MA: Harvard University Press.

Latour, Bruno, and Steve Woolgar. 1979. *Laboratory Life.* Beverly Hills, CA: Sage.

Laudan, Larry. 1977. *Progress and Its Problems.* Berkeley: University of California Press.

Lazarus, Neil. 1993. "Disavowing Decolonization: Fanon, Nationalism, and the Problematic of Representation in Current Theories of Colonial Discourse." *Research in African Literatures* 24 (4): 69–98.

Leach, Edmund. 1954. *Political Systems of Highland Burma.* Boston: Beacon.

Levine, Rhonda. 2001. *Class, Networks, and Identity.* Lanham, MD: Rowman and Littlefield.

Levi-Strauss, Claude. 1969. *The Elementary Structures of Kinship.* Boston: Beacon.

Lewis, Oscar. 1951. *Life in a Mexican Village: Tepoztlan Restudied.* Urbana: University of Illinois Press.

Liebow, Elliot. 1967. *Tally's Corner: A Study of Negro Streetcorner Men.* Boston: Little, Brown.

Lopez, Steve. 2003. *Re-Organizing the Rust Belt: An Inside Study of the Contemporary Labor Movement.* Berkeley: University of California Press.

Lupton, Tom. 1963. *On the Shop Floor: Two Studies of Workshop Organization and Output.* New York: Pergamon.

Lynd, Robert S. 1939. *Knowledge for What? The Place of Social Science in American Culture.* Princeton, NJ: Princeton University Press.

Lynd, Robert S., and Helen Merrell Lynd. 1929. *Middletown: A Study in Modern American Culture.* New York: Harcourt, Brace and World.

———. 1937. *Middletown in Transition: A Study in Cultural Conflicts.* New York: Harcourt, Brace and World.

Macdonald, Judith. 2000. "The Tikopia and 'What Raymond Said.'" In *Ethnographic Artifacts: Challenges to a Reflexive Anthropology,* edited by S. Jaarsma and M. Rohatynskyj, 107–23. Honolulu: University of Hawaii Press.

MacLeod, Jay. 1987. *Ain't No Makin' It: Leveled Aspirations in a Low-Income Neighborhood.* Boulder, CO: Westview.

Magubane, Bernard. 1974. Review of *The Colour of Class on the Copper Mines. American Journal of Sociology* 80 (2): 596–98.

Malinowski, Bronislaw. 1922. *Argonauts of the Western Pacific.* London: Routledge.

Marcus, George. 1995. "Ethnography in/of the World System: The Emergence of Multi-Sited Ethnography." *Annual Review of Anthropology* 24:95–117.

Marx, Karl. [1852] 1963. *The Eighteenth Brumaire of Louis Bonaparte.* New York: International Publishers.

———. [1859] 1970. *A Contribution to the Critique of Political Economy.* New York: International Publishers.

Mayer, Adrian. 1989. "Anthropological Memories." *Man* (new series) 24:203–18.

Mead, Margaret. 1928. *Coming of Age in Samoa.* New York: Morrow.

Merton, Robert. 1957. "Priorities in Scientific Discovery: A Chapter in the Sociology of Science." *American Sociological Review* 22:635–59.

———. 1980. "Letter from Robert Merton to Howard Bahr." Lynn Perrigo Papers, Archives and Special Collections Department, Ball State University, Muncie, IN.

Merton, Robert, Marjorie Fiske, and Patricia Kendall. 1956. *The Focused Interview.* Glencoe, IL: Free Press.

Michels, Robert. [1910] 1962. *Political Parties: A Sociological Study of the Oligarchical Tendencies of Modern Democracy.* New York: Free Press.

Milkman, Ruth. 1987. *Gender at Work.* Urbana and Chicago: University of Illinois Press.

Mill, John Stuart. 1888. *A System of Logic.* 8th ed. New York: Harper.

Miller, Richard. 1987. *Fact and Method:* Princeton, NJ: Princeton University Press.

Mills, C. Wright. 1959. *The Sociological Imagination.* New York: Oxford University Press.

Mintz, Sidney. 1985. *Sweetness and Power: The Place of Sugar in Modern History.* New York: Viking.

Mishler, Elliot G. 1986. *Research Interviewing: Context and Narrative.* Cambridge, MA: Harvard University Press.

Mitchell, Clyde. 1956. *The Kalela Dance.* Manchester, UK: Manchester University Press for Rhodes-Livingstone Institute.

———. 1983. "Case and Situation Analysis." *Sociological Review* 31:187–211.

Mitchell, Tim. 1988. *Colonizing Egypt.* Cambridge: Cambridge University Press.

Moore, Henrietta, and Megan Vaughan. 1994. *Cutting Down Trees: Gender, Nutrition, and Agricultural Change in the Northern Province of Zambia, 1890–1990.* Portsmouth, NH: Heinemann.

Morawska, Ewa. 1997. "A Historical Ethnography in the Making." *Historical Methods* 30:58–70.

Nash, June. 2001. *Mayan Visions: The Quest for Autonomy in an Age of Globalization.* New York: Routledge.

Nichols, Elizabeth. 1986. "Skocpol on Revolution: Comparative Analysis vs. Historical Conjecture." *Comparative Social Research* 9:163–86.

Nugent, David. 1982. "Closed Systems and Contradiction: The Kachin in and out of History." *Man* 17:508–27.

Oakley, Ann. 1981. "Interviewing Women: A Contradiction in Terms." In *Doing Feminist Research,* edited by Helen Roberts, 30–61. London: Routledge and Kegan Paul.

Orans, Martin. 1996. *Not Even Wrong.* Novato, CA: Chandler and Sharp.

Orlandella, Angelo Ralph. 1992. "Boelen May Know Holland, Boelen May Know Barzini, but Boelen 'Doesn't Know Diddle about the North End!'" *Journal of Contemporary Ethnography* 21:69–79.

Pattillo-McCoy, Mary. 1999. *Black Picket Fences: Privilege and Peril among the Black Middle Classes.* Chicago: University of Chicago Press.

Phelps, Erin, Frank Furstenberg, and Anne Colby, eds. 2002. *Looking at Lives: American Longitudinal Studies of the Twentieth Century.* New York: Russell Sage Foundation.

Polanyi, Karl. 1944. *The Great Transformation: The Political and Economic Origins of Our Time.* New York: Rinehart.

Polanyi, Michael. 1958. *Personal Knowledge: Towards a Post-Critical Philosophy.* Chicago: University of Chicago Press.

Popper, Karl. 1957. *The Poverty of Historicism.* London: Routledge and Kegan Paul.

———. 1959. *The Logic of Scientific Discovery.* London: Hutchinson.

———. 1963. *Conjectures and Refutations.* London: Routledge and Kegan Paul.

Putnam, Hilary. 1981. "The 'Corroboration' of Theories." In *Scientific Revolutions,* edited by Ian Hacking, 60–79. New York: Oxford University Press.

Rabinow, Paul. 1977. *Reflections on Fieldwork in Morocco.* Berkeley: University of California Press.

Radnitzsky, Gerard, and Gunnar Andersson, eds. 1978. *Progress and Rationality in Science.* Boston Studies in the Philosophy of Science. Vol. 58. Dordrecht, Germany: D. Reidel.

Ragin, Charles. 1987. *The Comparative Method.* Berkeley: University of California Press.

Ragin, Charles, and David Zaret. 1983. "Theory and Method in Comparative Research: Two Strategies," *Social Forces* 61:731–54.

Ray, Raka. 1998. *Fields of Protest: A Comparison of Women's Movements in Two Indian Cities.* Minneapolis: University of Minnesota Press.

Redfield, Robert. 1930. *Tepoztlan: A Mexican Village.* Chicago: University of Chicago Press.

———. 1950. *A Village That Chose Progress: Chan Kom Revisited.* Chicago: University of Chicago Press.

———. 1960. *Little Community, and Peasant Society and Culture.* Chicago: University of Chicago Press.

Richards, Audrey. 1939. *Land, Labour and Diet in Northern Rhodesia: An Economic Study of the Bemba Tribe.* London: Oxford University Press.

Roemer, John, ed. 1986. *Analytical Marxism.* Cambridge: Cambridge University Press.

Rorty, Richard. 1979. *Philosophy and the Mirror of Nature*. Princeton, NJ: Princeton University Press.

Roy, Donald. 1952a. "Quota Restriction and Goldbricking in a Machine Shop." *American Journal of Sociology* 57 (5): 427–42.

———. 1952b. "Restriction of Output in a Piecework Machine Shop." Ph.D. diss., Department of Sociology, University of Chicago, Chicago.

———. 1953. "Work Satisfaction and Social Reward in Quota Achievement: An Analysis of Piecework Incentive." *American Sociological Review* 18:507–14.

———. 1954. "Efficiency and the 'Fix': Informal Intergroup Relations in a Piece-Work Machine Shop." *American Journal of Sociology* 60 (3): 255–66.

———. 1980. "Review of Michael Burawoy, *Manufacturing Consent*." *Berkeley Journal of Sociology* 24:329–39.

Salzinger, Leslie. 2003. *Genders under Production*. Berkeley: University of California Press.

Sanders, Lynn. 1995. "What Is Whiteness?" American Politics Workshop, University of Chicago.

Schaeffer, Nora Cate. 1991. "Conversation with a Purpose—Or Conversation? Interaction in the Standardized Interview." In *Measurement Errors in Surveys*, edited by Paul P. Biemer et al., 367–91. New York: Wiley.

Scheper-Hughes, Nancy. 1992. *Death without Weeping*. Berkeley: University of California Press.

———. 2001. *Saints, Scholars, Schizophrenics*. Berkeley: University of California Press.

Schorske, Carl. 1955. *German Social Democracy, 1905–1917: The Development of a Great Schism*. Cambridge, MA: Harvard University Press.

Schuman, Howard, and Stanley Presser. 1981. *Questions and Answers in Attitude Surveys*. New York: Academic Press.

Scudder, Thayer, and Elizabeth Colson. 1979. "Long-Term Research in Gwembe Valley, Zambia." In Foster et al., *Long-Term Field Research in Social Anthropology*, 227–54.

Selznick, Philip. 1949. *TVA and the Grass Roots.* Berkeley: University of California Press.

Sennett, Richard. 1998. *The Corrosion of Character.* New York: Norton.

Sennett, Richard, and Jonathan Cobb. 1972. *The Hidden Injuries of Class.* New York: Knopf.

Sewell, William. 1985. "Ideologies and Social Revolutions: Reflections on the French Case." *Journal of Modern History* 57 (3): 81–84.

———. 1991. "A Theory of Structure: Duality, Agency and Transformation." *American Journal of Sociology* 98 (1): 1–29.

Shore, Bradd. 1983. "Paradox Regained: Freeman's Margaret Mead and Samoa." *American Anthropologist* 83:935–44.

Sieber, Sam. 1973. "The Integration of Fieldwork and Survey Methods." *American Journal of Sociology* 78 (6): 1335–59.

Simons, H. J., and R. E. Simons. 1969. *Class and Colour in South Africa, 1850–1950.* Harmondsworth, UK: Penguin.

Skocpol, Theda. 1973. "A Critical Review of Barrington Moore's *Social Origins of Dictatorship and Democracy.*" *Politics and Society* 4 (1): 1–34.

———. 1979. *States and Social Revolutions.* Cambridge: Cambridge University Press.

———. 1982. "Rentier State and Shi'a Islam in the Iranian Revolution." *Theory and Society* 11:265–83.

———, ed. 1984. *Vision and Method in Historical Sociology.* Cambridge: Cambridge University Press.

———. 1985a. "Cultural Idioms and Political Ideologies in the Revolutionary Reconstruction of State Power: A Rejoinder to Sewell." *Journal of Modern History* 57 (3): 86–87.

———. 1985b. "Bringing the State Back In: Strategies of Analysis in Current Research." In *Bringing the State Back In,* edited by Peter Evans, Dietrich Rueschemeyer, and Theda Skocpol, 3–37. Cambridge: Cambridge University Press.

———. 1986. "Analyzing Causal Configurations in History: A Rejoinder to Nichols." *Comparative Social Research* 9:187–94.

———. 1988. "An 'Uppity Generation' and the Revitalization of Macroscopic Sociology: Reflections at Midcareer by a Woman from the 1960s." In *Sociological Lives,* edited by Matilda Riley, 145–62. Newbury Park, CA: Sage.

Skocpol, Theda, and Margaret Somers. 1980. "The Uses of Comparative History in Macrosocial Inquiry." *Comparative Studies in Society and History* 22 (2): 174–197.

Smith, Dorothy. 1987. *The Everyday World as Problematic: A Feminist Sociology.* Boston: Northeastern University Press.

———. 2007. *Institutional Ethnography: A Sociology for People.* Lanham, MD: Rowman and Littlefield.

Smith, Mark. 1984. "From Middletown to Middletown III: A Critical Review." *Qualitative Sociology* 74:327–36.

———. 1994. "Robert Lynd and Knowledge for What?" In *Social Science in the Crucible,* 12–58. Durham, NC: Duke University Press.

Smith, Vicki. 1990. *Managing in the Corporate Interest.* Berkeley: University of California Press.

Sniderman, Paul, and Thomas Piazza. 1993. *The Scar of Race.* Cambridge: Harvard University Press.

Somers, Margaret, and Gloria Gibson. 1994. "Reclaiming the Epistemological 'Other': Narrative and the Social Construction of Identity." In *Social Theory and the Politics of Identity,* edited by Craig Calhoun, 37–99. Oxford: Blackwell.

Stacey, Judith. 1990. *Brave New Families.* New York: Basic Books.

Stinchcombe, Arthur. 1978. *Theoretical Methods in Social History.* New York: Academic Press.

———. 1980. "Erving Goffman as a Scientist." Unpublished lecture, Northwestern University, Evanston, IL.

———. 1983. *Economic Sociology.* New York: Academic Press.

Stoler, Ann. 1995. *Race and the Education of Desire.* Durham, NC: Duke University Press.

Strauss, Anselm. 1987. *Qualitative Analysis for Social Scientists.* New York: Cambridge University Press.

Suchman, Lucy, and Brigitte Jordan. 1990. "Interactional Troubles in Face-to-Face Survey Interviews." *Journal of the American Statistical Association* 85 (409): 232–41.

Susser, Ida. 1982. *Norman Street: Poverty and Politics in an Urban Neighborhood*. New York: Oxford University Press.

Susser, Ida, and Thomas Patterson, eds. 2001. *Cultural Diversity in the United States*. New York: Blackwell.

Tanur, Judith, ed. 1992. *Questions about Questions*. New York: Russell Sage Foundation.

Thernstrom, Stephan. 1964. *Poverty and Progress: Social Mobility in a Nineteenth-Century City*. Cambridge, MA: Harvard University Press.

Thomas, Robert. 1985. *Citizenship, Gender and Work*. Berkeley: University of California Press.

Thomas, William I., and Florian Znaniecki. 1918–20. *The Polish Peasant in Europe and America*. 2 vols. Boston: Badger.

Tilly, Charles. 1976. *The Vendee*. Cambridge, MA: Harvard University Press.

———. 1981. *As Sociology Meets History*. New York: Academic Press.

———. 1984. *Big Structures, Large Processes, Huge Comparisons*. New York: Russell Sage.

Toulmin, Stephen. 1972. *Human Understanding*. Princeton, NJ: Princeton University Press.

Touraine, Alain. 1983. *Solidarity: Poland 1980–81*. New York: Cambridge University Press.

———. 1988. *The Return of the Actor*. Minneapolis: University of Minnesota Press.

Trotsky, Leon. [1933] 1977. *The History of the Russian Revolution*. London: Pluto.

———. [1929, 1906] 1969. *The Permanent Revolution* and *Results and Prospects*. New York: Pathfinder.

———. [1936] 1972. *The Revolution Betrayed*. New York: Pathfinder.

Van Maanen, John. 1988. *Tales of the Field: On Writing Ethnography*. Chicago: University of Chicago Press.

Van Velsen, Jaap. 1960. "Labour Migration as a Positive Factor in the Continuity of Tonga Tribal Society." *Economic Development and Cultural Change* 8:265–78.

———. 1964. *The Politics of Kinship*. Manchester, UK: Manchester University Press for the Rhodes-Livingstone Institute.

———. 1967. "The Extended Case Method and Situational Analysis." In *The Craft of Urban Anthropology,* edited by A. I. Epstein, 29–53. London: Tavistock.

Vaughan, Diane. 1996. *The Challenger Launch Decision: Risky Technology, Culture, and Deviance at NASA.* Chicago: University of Chicago Press.

———. 2006. "NASA Revisited: Theory, Analogy, and Public Sociology." *American Journal of Sociology* 112 (2): 353–93.

Venkatesh, Sudhir. 2000. *American Project: The Rise and Fall of a Modern Ghetto.* Cambridge, MA: Harvard University Press.

Verdery, Katherine. 2003. *The Vanishing Hectare: Property and Value in Postsocialist Transylvania.* Ithaca, NY: Cornell University Press.

Vincent, Joan. 1990. *Anthropology and Politics.* Tucson: University of Arizona Press.

Vogt, Evon. 1979. "The Harvard Chiapas Project: 1957–1975." In Foster et al., *Long-Term Field Research in Social Anthropology,* 279–302.

Warner, W. Lloyd, and J. O. Low. 1947. *The Social System of the Modern Factory.* New Haven, CT: Yale University Press.

Weiner, Annette. 1976. *Women of Value, Men of Renown.* Austin: University of Texas Press.

———. 1983. "Ethnographic Determinism: Samoa and the Margaret Mead Controversy." *American Anthropologist* 85:909–19.

Whitehead, Alfred North. 1925. *Science and the Modern World.* New York: Macmillan.

Whyte, William Foot. 1943. *Street Corner Society.* Chicago: University of Chicago Press.

———. 1955. *Street Corner Society.* 2d ed. Chicago: University of Chicago Press.

———. 1992. "In Defense of *Street Corner Society.*" *Journal of Contemporary Ethnography* 21:52–68.

Williamson, David. 1996. *Heretic: Based on the Life of Derek Freeman.* Melbourne, Australia: Penguin.

Willis, Paul. 1977. *Learning to Labour.* Westmead, UK: Saxon House.

Winch, Peter. 1958. *The Idea of Social Science and Its Relation to Philosophy.* London: Routledge and Kegan Paul.

Wirth, Louis. 1928. *The Ghetto.* Chicago: University Press.

Wolf, Eric. 1982. *Europe and the People without History.* Berkeley: University of California Press.

Wolf, Margery. 1992. *A Thrice-Told Tale: Feminism, Postmodernism, and Ethnographic Responsibility.* Stanford, CA: Stanford University Press.

Woodruff, David. 1999. *Money Unmade: Barter and the Fate of Russian Capitalism.* Ithaca, NY: Cornell University Press.

Wright, Erik Olin. 1986. "States and Classes in Recent Radical Theory." Unpublished manuscript, presented in a panel at the American Sociological Association.

———. 2006. "Compass Points." *New Left Review* 41:93–124.

Zahar, Eli. 1978. "'Crucial' Experiments: A Case Study," In Radnitzsky and Andersson, *Progress and Rationality in Science,* 71–98.

INDEX

Text & Display: Granjon
Compositor: International Typesetting and Composition
Indexer: Andrew Christenson
Printer & Binder: Maple-Vail Book